The Forms of Russian

THE FORMS OF RUSSIAN

CHARLES E. GRIBBLE

Bloomington, Indiana, 2014

SLAVICA

ISBN 978-0-89357-448-2

Technical Editor: Christian Flynn

Library of Congress Control Number: 2014950516

Slavica Publishers   [Tel.] 1-812-856-4186
Indiana University   [Toll-free] 1-877-SLAVICA
1430 N. Willis Drive   [Fax] 1-812-856-4187
Bloomington, IN 47404-2146   [Email] slavica@indiana.edu
USA   [www] http://www.slavica.com/

To the cherished memory of

Roman Jakobson

(1896–1982)

and

Alexander Lipson

(1928–1980)

Contents

Acknowledgments

I dedicate this work to the memory of Roman Jakobson, my teacher, whose ideas form the core of the book, and to the memory of Alexander Lipson, friend and teacher, who saw the significance and extensions and applications of Jakobson's ideas in a way that the rest of us did not, and who gladly shared his understanding with us. These two have had immeasurable influence in determining the course of North American Slavistics, both scholarly and pedagogical, over the past sixty years.

This book has had a long and complicated genesis. I first gave a course on the structure of the Russian language at Brandeis University in 1964. In the next forty-five years I gave the course many times, at Brandeis, Indiana University, the University of Virginia, and at Ohio State. I would probably have tried to write a textbook for the course much earlier, had it not been for the availability of Maurice Levin's *Russian Declension and Conjugation*, which covers much of the same material. After using Levin's book as a textbook many times, I found that there were enough differences in our approach—and in our description of Russian—that it seemed worthwhile to try writing my own book, based upon what I had done in teaching the course. The foundations of both of our books lie squarely in the work of Jakobson and Lipson. I am greatly indebted to Levin, who was an outstanding resource during my first year of teaching Russian as a graduate student, and who once again showed the way with his ground-breaking book on the structure of Russian.

Charles Townsend has offered me never-ending assistance, ideas, and friendship for more than fifty years. His influence is felt throughout this book; my debt to him is immeasurable. Other valuable input has come from David Birnbaum, Wayles Browne, Catherine V. Chvany, Robert Rothstein, and Ernest Scatton. Professor Birnbaum taught a course using an almost final version of this book. He shared his comments and those of the students with me, which was very helpful. Finishing this book has been possible only because of the crucial support given to me by my wife, Lyubomira, who has made my life better for more than thirty years.

Errors are of course my responsibility. Suggestions and corrections will be gratefully accepted. Please send them to Slavica Publishers at slavica@indiana.edu or mail them to us at:

ATTN: Charles Gribble
C/O Slavica Publishers
1430 N Willis Drive
Bloomington, IN 47404

Introduction:
Orthography, and Pronunciation

1.0. Introduction

Have you ever wondered if there wasn't an easier way to learn the genitive plural of Russian nouns than through the seventeen rules the typical textbook gives? Have you ever tried to figure out just how many stress patterns the Russian noun (or adjective, or verb) has, or whether derived imperfective verbs (e.g. переписа́ть/перепи́сывать, замкну́ть/ замыка́ть, задержа́ть/ заде́рживать) are predictable? Have you ever envied the 12-year-old Russian who seems to know all kinds of things that you don't? If so, this book is for you. If you want to go on memorizing multiple forms and stresses for everything, then just close the book quietly and put it back on the shelf.

You know things about English that you probably weren't aware that you know. For example, if I make the statement "This book is unbinkable," you can rephrase it to say "This book is incapable of being binked, it cannot be binked," even though you don't know what *bink* means. You know to look the word up in a dictionary under the letter "b" rather than "u." You also know that *bink* is a verb, rather than a noun, since only verbs, not nouns, go into the "un-X-able" construction (e.g., unsummarizable, unsinkable, unanodizable, but not *unsummaryable,[1] *unanodizationable). You can also be fairly certain that the past participle is *binked*, rather than *bunk. Why? Because although you could take either *drink/sink* or *link/wink* as models, with participles *drunk/sunk* or *linked/ winked*, you are aware that almost any previously unknown English verb that you meet is likely to follow the *-ed* model of participle formation. You use your knowledge of English to "understand" a poem like Lewis Carroll's "Jabberwocky":

---

[1] The asterisk means that the form does not occur.

'Twas brillig, and the slithy toves
Did gyre and gimble in the wabe:
All mimsy were the borogoves,
And the mome raths outgrabe

"Beware the Jabberwock, my son!
The jaws that bite, the claws that catch!
Beware the Jubjub bird, and shun
The frumious Bandersnatch."

He took his vorpal sword in hand:
Long time the manxome foe he sought —
So rested he by the Tumtum tree,
And stood awhile in thought.

And, as in uffish thought he stood,
The Jabberwock, with eyes of flame,
Came whiffling through the tulgey wood,
And burbled as it came!

One, two! One, two! And through and through
The vorpal blade went snicker-snack!
He left it dead, and with its head
He went galumphing back.

"And hast thou slain the Jabberwock?
Come to my arms, my beamish boy!
O frabjous day! Callooh! Callay!"
He chortled in his joy.

'Twas brillig, and the slithy toves
Did gyre and gimble in the wabe:
All mimsy were the borogoves,
And the mome raths outgrabe.

Russians use the same sort of knowledge about Russian to help them. They know that непобедимый, неуловимый, неразделимый mean "that which one cannot победить, уловить, разделить." Most words constructed in this way are not in the dictionary, just as the corresponding English ones are not. As with the English words, only the base verb is given.

Just as English speakers "understand" "Jabberwocky," Russian speakers also understand things they have never seen before. The (allegedly) humorous Soviet magazine Крокодил had a regular section titled "Нарочно не придумаешь," which featured barbarities committed against the Russian language by bureaucrats, semi-literates, and others. In most cases, a good feeling for the system of the Russian language was needed to understand why the item was funny. Some examples follow:

Твистунов на мороз! (sign in a Siberian clubhouse) '(Throw) people addicted to dancing the Twist out in the cold!' The English word *Twist* (denoting a vigorous and potentially erotic dance which was anathema to puritanical official Soviet morality) is joined to the Russian suffix -ун, denoting a person who does something a great deal or to excess (говорун 'chatterbox, person who talks too much'; свистун 'person given to loud and frequent whistling').

Коллектив бани борется в августе месяце за 16 тысяч человекопомывок 'The collective (workers' group, staff) of the public bath is struggling to achieve 16,000 person-washings in the month of August'. The humor comes from the invented word человекопомывка, which looks like such real compound words as трудодень 'day's labor (on a collective farm)'.

Ему отказали в свидетельстве об изобретении, когда при рассмотрении выяснилось, что его *навозоразбрасыватель* не что иное, как лошадь 'He was denied a patent on his invention when on examination it turned out that his "manure spreader" was nothing more than a horse'. The long word навозоразбрасыватель sounds very technological and innovative.

The great Russian linguist Lev Shcherba used to quote the phrase "Глокая куздра штеко будланула бокра." Even though none of his listeners knew what the words meant, they knew that some kind (глокая—adjective) of куздра had in some way (штеко—adverb) done something (будланула—probably quickly, energetically, and only once) to a something (бокор or бокр, if an animate masc. noun) or somethings (бокро, if neuter pl.) They could make this analysis because they knew the *structure* of Russian intuitively (although probably not explicitly), just as you know the structure of English and could thus interpret "Jabberwocky."

We can use knowledge of a language's structure to state many facts about a word, especially in context. For example, if a sentence talks about using the переворачивающимися parts of a machine, we can extract the meaning and stress without having to consult the dictionary, thereby saving time and effort.

First we segment the form as best we can: пере|ворач|ива|ющ|ими|ся is a reasonable beginning. Пере- is a prefix with several meanings. Two of the most common are 'again, re-' and 'across'. From the other end, we can pick off -ся as the "reflexive particle," -ими as the instrumental plural ending of adjectives, including participles, then -ющ as the suffix of the present active participle, and finally -ива as the suffix of derived imperfective verbs (обсадить/обсаживать, остановить/останавливать, спросить / спрашивать). This suffix never bears the stress, but the syllable before it always does. We are left with -ворач-, which bears the same relationship to вороти- as саж- does to сади-, станавл- does to станови-, and праш- does to проси-. The root ворот- means 'turn', or to be Latin-fancy, 'volv-'. The whole word then means 're-volv-ing', with the -ся showing habitual or constant meaning (cf. собака кусается "It's a biting dog, it habitually bites").

Structure exists on a number of levels: phonetic, phonemic, morphological, lexical, syntactic, etc.[2] In this book we will talk mainly about morphology (forms) and phonology (sounds).

The book has two main goals: the first is to give a concrete description of selected aspects of the structure of the language so that working with Russian becomes easier. You will see that you really only need three *ordered* rules to explain the genitive plural, not seventeen or however many your textbook gave (and you certainly don't need to memorize every genitive plural, as some textbooks make you do!). The second goal is to explain how we establish a systematic description of Russian and what the issues are. A consideration of issues and ideas will be an important theme of the book, but it will be on the basis of factual information designed to help your Russian, or, if you are a native speaker of Russian, to help you be better prepared to explain Russian grammar to your American students.

This book does not assume any previous contact with linguistics. It does assume some knowledge of Russian. Some people will find one year of college Russian sufficient background; others will need two or even three years to feel fully comfortable. It should be possible to cover the material in this book fairly thoroughly in one semester.

---

[2] We will find out what each of these terms covers.

In this book I have tried to describe the language of a careful, educated speaker of Russian. The information given is largely **normative**; that is, it reflects the views of the "authorities" on what **should be** said and written, rather than what sometimes **is** actually said and written. In general, foreign learners of a language should try to use the same language used by careful native speakers and writers (i.e., what **should be** used), avoiding overly colloquial or slang elements. Imagine the reaction if a Russian President greeted an American President and a British Prime Minister with "Heyyah guys, wuzzup? Let's hunker down and get our rear ends in gear for some tough palaver."

The three main authorities upon whom I have relied are the Academy Grammar (*Русская грамматика* = *Грамматика 1980*), Zaliznyak's *Грамматический словарь*, and the *Орфоэпический словарь*. For details and suggestions for further reading, please see the annotated bibliography at the end of this book.

This book is designed to explain to you the system that holds the Russian language together. It treats the patterns of declension and conjugation, but does not try to give every detail and every exception in the way that a detailed reference grammar would. I have tried not to obscure the лес with the individual деревья. My book focuses on giving you a grasp of how the language works—its fundamental patterns. In the process of doing so, it will also introduce you to many basic concepts of modern linguistics, but the linguistics is introduced only so far as it helps to elucidate the language. The goal of the book is to improve your Russian, not to teach linguistics.

Several of the exercises contain imaginary words or little-known real words. An imaginary word is no different from a real word that you don't know. These words fully conform to the structure of Russian in every way. Their purpose is to provide exercise material which forces you to apply the information in this book, rather than relying upon just what you happen to have already learned elsewhere. In particular, they put native speakers and heritage speakers of Russian on an equal footing with English-speaking learners, since everybody has to work from the rules. Consider the word bink on the first page of this chapter: its forms and their use do not depend upon whether the word is real or made-up. Also compare burble and chortle in "Jabberwocky." Are they both "real"

English words, attested at least in Middle English, or are they "made-up" words?[3]

The Russian material is presented in Cyrillic, except in those instances where transcription is essential for clarity. This is done to make a stronger connection between what you see in this book and the Russian that you read everywhere. It should make assimilation and application of the material easier for those language learners (a strong majority, in my experience) who have a visual memory. Using unnecessary transcription disconnects material from "real" Russian and hinders learning.

1.0.2. "Orthography" is the more precise name for what we often call "spelling" in English. "Orthography" is from two Greek roots and means 'right/correct writing'. The orthography of a language is the set of rules governing how the language is written. Examples of these rules are the use of capital letters, punctuation, rules for letter combinations (e.g., *и* but not *ы* in Russian after the letters *к, г, х*). In Russian you will find not only an орфографи́ческий слова́рь, which tells you how to *write* things correctly, but also an орфоэпи́ческий слова́рь. The orthoepic dictionary tells you how to *pronounce* things correctly (e.g., place of stress, hard or soft consonant before the letter *e* in words borrowed from foreign languages). In this first chapter you will meet six Russian "spelling rules." Some, such as Spelling Rule 2, are really "pronunciation rules," but in order to simplify things, we will call all the rules in this chapter "spelling rules."

1.1. Spelling Rule 1

The first Russian "spelling rule" that we will consider involves *ы*, which becomes *и* after *к, г*, and *х* (and of course the consonant becomes "soft"). Стол 'table' has the plural столы́, but учени́к 'pupil' has ученики́, круг 'circle' has круги́, and грех 'sin' has грехи́. In word formation we see раб 'slave' with feminine рабы́ня, but бог 'god' with боги́ня.

    Spelling Rule 1 thus says that *ы* → *и* after *к, г*, and *х*.

---

[3] *Burble* occurs in Middle English, but Lewis Carroll made *chortle*, first published in 1872, by combining *chuckle* and *snort*.

1.2. Spelling Rule 2

A rule of the Russian sound system says that all consonants automatically become "soft" when the vowel /e/[4] is added: we see nom. sg. стол 'table' with a "hard" last consonant, but на столе́ 'on the table' with a "soft"
last consonant. Compare бе́лый 'white' with беле́ть 'show or appear
white', as in Lermontov's famous poem "Беле́ет па́рус одино́кий" 'A
Lonely Sail Shows/Appears White'.

Spelling Rule 2 thus states that a consonant will always be soft in
front of the letter *e* unless that consonant is always hard (there are three
such: *ж*, *ш*, and *ц*; see Section 1.3.2 below).

1.3. Palatalization (Hard and Soft Consonants)

Since we will be talking about pronunciation, we need to have a more accurate way of denoting sounds than the ordinary Russian orthographical
system provides. One way would be to use Cyrillic with modifications.
In that case we could write a hard consonant with the usual letter, and a
soft consonant with a little superscript soft sign next to it: стол but на
стол^ье́. This is done in some Russian publications.

It causes two major problems. The first is that it looks confusingly
similar to spellings like в статье́ 'in the article', although the two spellings stand for quite different things (more about the sequence consonant
letter plus ь or ъ plus vowel letter in section 1.5, later in this chapter).

The second problem is that putting a small soft sign *after* the consonant letter might give the impression that the sequence of two *letters*
stands for a sequence of two *sounds*. Nothing could be further from the
truth. A Russian soft consonant is a single sound (although it usually has
two places of simultaneous articulation in the mouth).

A second way to denote sounds is to **transcribe** (i.e., rewrite) them
into Latin characters. Although in general we will use Cyrillic as much
as possible in this book, the use of Latin transcription will help us to see
some things better. As mentioned above, a soft consonant normally has
two places of articulation. One is the same as for the hard consonant, and
the second is the back of the roof of the mouth, or the hard palate. This
is why soft consonants are called **palatalized**: a palatal articulation is
added to the basic one. We can denote this double articulation by using
a double symbol. For convenience, we will use a hook under or over the

---

[4] The slashes on either side show that this is a structural unit of the language called a
"phoneme." Phonemes will be discussed later in this chapter.

letter, so a soft л is denoted with /ļ/, a soft m with /m̦/, and a soft г with /g̦/. The hook represents the second articulation, so the sign /ţ/ shows that the sound has a dental articulation (tip of the tongue behind the teeth) and a *simultaneous* palatal one (middle of the tongue against the hard palate). When we compare стол and (на) столе́ in transcription, we see easily that стол consists of four sounds (/stol/) and столе́ consists of five sounds (/staļé/—unstressed o → a!), not six (i.e., not */stalyé/).[5]

Transcription uses mostly English letters, but since we want to have one sound always represented by one letter (rather than a pair of letters), we will introduce a few letters used in other languages: č for ч, š for ш, ž for ж, c for ц, x for x, šč for щ, and j for й.[6]

1.3.1. As you know, Russian vowel letters are divided into five "hard" vowel letters (а, э, ы, о, у) and five "soft" vowel letters (я, е, и, ё, ю). Of course, it's not really the letters which are "hard" or "soft"—it's the consonants which are "hard" or "soft," and the vowel letters are the indicators.

When the soft vowel letters, such as ю and я, come after a consonant, they stand for "soft consonant plus vowel," so we write "soft consonant letter plus vowel" in transcription: писа́теля, писа́телю give /p̦isáţeļa/, /p̦isáţeļu/. When the soft vowel letters are initial or follow a vowel letter (or the hard or soft sign, as in статья́, объе́хать, which will be discussed later), they represent the consonant /j/ plus vowel: зна́ю, зна́я, ю́жная, я́сная, represent /znáju/, /znája/, /júžnaja/, /jásnaja/.

When no vowel follows a soft consonant, Russian writes a consonant letter followed by the soft sign: писа́тель denotes /p̦isáţeļ/.

1.3.2. If instead of писа́тель /p̦isáţeļ/ we transcribe учи́тель, it can be written /učíţeļ/, with no hook under /č/, although /č/ is a "soft" consonant. There are six consonants which are "unpaired." Three of the six are always soft: /č/ (written ч), /šč/ (written щ and, sometimes, other ways, and often pronounced as a long soft ș̌ș̌), and /j/ (written й or as a "soft vowel letter" [е, ё, и, ю, я] when not immediately following a consonant

---

[5] An asterisk before a word or form means that the item does not occur; it is either unattested or contrary to the rules of the language. We might thus write the forms *drinked, *thunk, *mans, *louses, *hice, *oxes, *axen with an asterisk in English.

[6] The symbols č, š, ž, c, and j are used for these same sounds in Croatian, Czech, Slovak, and Slovenian, all of which are Slavic languages, like Russian. German uses j for й.

letter—see below). Three of the six are always hard: /ž/ (written *ж*), /š/ (written *ш*), and /c/ (written *ц*). Since the three soft unpaired consonants are always, and automatically, soft, there is no need to write a hook under them.

These six are known as the **unpaired** consonants, because most Russian consonants come in pairs: one hard, one soft. These six occur either only hard or only soft. The "paired" consonants are the others: /p ~ p̨ (or p̧), b ~ b̨, m ~ m̨, f ~ f̨, v ~ v̨, t ~ t̨, d ~ d̨, n ~ n̨, s ~ s̨, z ~ z̨, r ~ r̨, l ~ l̨, k ~ k̨, g ~ g̨, x ~ x̨/.

The six "unpaired" consonants just mentioned create a number of special problems and rules in spelling and pronunciation. These will be discussed later in this chapter.

1.3.3. There is one fundamental exception to the rule that consonants soften before an ending or suffix beginning with /e/ in Russian. As noted above, the three consonants *ж*, *ш*, *ц* are always hard in Russian, no matter what. For this reason в ноже́, в карандаше́, в конце́ all have a hard consonant at the end of the stem, in spite of the sound /e/ following: /vnažé/, /fkarandašé/, /fkancé/, with hard /ž/, /š/, /c/.

1.3.4. You may ask why, if *ж* and *ш* are always hard, and *ч* and *щ* are always soft, one sometimes sees a soft sign written after them in certain words and forms. One might assert that a soft sign after hard consonants is "incorrect," and a soft sign after consonants which are always soft is superfluous.

If we analyze the instances of such usage, it turns out that they fall into five categories: 1. nom. sg. of fem. third declension nouns: ночь 'night', рожь 'rye', мышь 'mouse', вещь 'thing'; 2. imperative forms of verbs: плачь(те) 'cry', прячь(те) 'hide', режь(те) 'cut'; 3. second person singular present tense forms: идёшь 'you go', зна́ешь 'you know', хо́дишь 'you go'; 4. infinitives in -чь: печь 'bake', стричь 'shear, cut'; 5. some adverbial forms: прочь 'away, off', на́стежь 'wide open'.

In these instances the soft sign tells something about the word other than its pronunciation. In case 1, it says that the noun is feminine, not masculine, so плач 'lament' and ключ 'key' are masculine, whereas ночь 'night' is feminine. Similarly, нож 'knife' is masculine, and рожь 'rye' is feminine. In case 2, the soft sign differentiates the imperative плачь 'cry!' from the masc. noun плач 'lament'. In cases 3, 4, and 5 there are no *minimal pairs* (two items differentiated only by a single thing, as плач and плачь are differentiated by the soft sign) in spelling, but the soft sign still serves for identification. It is often said that the soft sign in these five categories serves a "grammatical" function, but this is not strictly accurate. Although the five instances each belong to a specific grammatical category, the soft sign does not define the category. One must recognize the word in groups 1, 2, 4, and 5 to know the grammatical category (the vowels e, ё, and и before the -шь make group 3 immediately clear).

1.3.5. There is another spelling rule connected with the unpaired consonants *ш, ж, ч,* and *щ,* and it too is arbitrary. Since *ш* and *ж* are always hard and *ч* and *щ* are always soft, one would expect the letters *а, э, ы, о,* or *y* after *ш* and *ж,* and *я, е, и, ё,* or *ю* after *ч* and *щ.* In fact, we get *а, е, и, о/ё,* or *y* after all four of them. For *о, ё,* and *e,* see 1.7.3.

   Spelling Rule 3 thus says that after *ш, ж, ч,* and *щ* the letters *а, е, и, о,* and *y* and under certain circumstances, *ё,* are to be written. The sounds /š/ and /ž/ are phonetically hard, as we have seen above, so after them one pronounces [i]. Жить and шить are thus pronounced [žɨt] and [šɨt], in spite of the spelling.

   Spelling Rule 4 is that in *endings* after the letter *ц* we use *а, е, ы, о/e,* or *y.* For *о, (ё),* and *e,* see 1.7.3. In the *root* of words, however, we normally write *ци-*; a few words use *цы-* instead. You can check the dictionary for a list.

1.4. Spelling Vowels and Consonants

The Russian orthography is very efficient for the consonants, but not so efficient for the vowels. As we have seen above, each Cyrillic consonant letter usually stands for two consonants—a "hard" (or non-palatalized) one and a "soft" (or palatalized) one. The only exceptions to this are the six unpaired consonants. There are fifteen paired consonants (*п б м ф в т д н с з л р к г х*) and six unpaired (*ш ж ц ч щ й*),[7] for a total of 36 consonant phonemes. By contrast, there are only five vowel phonemes (/a e i o u/), each written with two letters (*а/я, э/е, ы/и, о/ё, у/ю*). Russian thus represents 41 units with 33 letters: 21 consonant letters, 10 vowel letters, and the hard and soft signs (more about these soon). If each phoneme were to have its own letter, we would need 41 letters (36 consonant let-

___

[7] I am leaving aside the complicated question of whether *щ* should be treated as a single consonant or as a combination of *ш* and *ч.* There are arguments for both views.

ters and 5 vowel letters). The way the Russian spelling system represents the consonant units came about more by accident than by planning, but it works.

1.4.1. As you know, words in Russian are differentiated by whether they have a hard or soft consonant: стал 'became; started to stand' :: сталь 'steel'; мат 'checkmate; cursing' :: мать 'mother' :: мят 'rumpled' (past passive participle) :: мять 'to rumple'; вол 'ox' :: вёл 'led'. In transcription these can be given as /stal/, /staļ/, /mat/, /maţ/, /m̦at/, /m̦aţ/, /vol/, /ɣol/.

1.4.2. At this point let us return to the concept of a *phoneme*. A phoneme may be defined briefly as a unit of sound that can differentiate words or forms in a given language. The easiest way to determine the *phonemic* status of a sound is to try finding minimal pairs like those given above.[8]

Experiment: Try to find the phonemes of English. Start with the consonants, which are easier in some ways. Not all phonemes can be determined with the minimal pair method; for example, you will not find any minimal pairs in English for /h/ ~ /ŋ/ (as in sing), although they are different phonemes.

The number of vowel phonemes present in English depends upon your analysis and is too far afield to examine in detail here. One analysis that you can work with has the following: /i/ as in *beat*, /ɨ/ as in *bit*, /e/ as in *bait*, /ɛ/ as in *bet*, /æ/ as in *bat*, /a/ as in the first vowel of *body* in American English (= the vowel in *father*), /ɔ/ as in *bawl, bawdy*, /o/ as in *bowl, boat*, /ʊ/ as in *foot*, /u/ as in *boot*, /ə/ as in *bud*. Since the "long" English vowels are phonetically diphthongs (combinations of two vowels or a vowel and a glide (/j/ or /w/), another view analyzes some of the vowels as diphthongs, yielding fewer simple vowel phonemes: /iy i ey e æ a o ow u uw ə/.

As you experiment with the vowels and consonants of English, you will probably find some variants that don't differentiate words, but which you can hear if you try. For example, a vowel is longer in English before a final *voiced* consonant (such as /b, v, d, z, g/): *bad* has a longer vowel than *bat*, *bed* has a longer vowel than *bet*, etc.[9]

---

[8] We write *phonemes* with slashes: /b/ /p/ /b̦/ /p̦/ /biț/ /b̦iț/; *phonetic transcriptions* are enclosed in brackets: Russian [byț], English [pʰin].

[9] If the colon after a vowel letter stands for a *long* vowel (cf. Latin *rosa* 'rose' ~ *rosā* 'with a rose, by means of a rose' = [rosa] vs. [rosa:]), then half of a colon (a raised dot)

Among the consonants you will find three varieties of /p/, /t/, and /k/. The first occurs in initial position before a stressed vowel. The /p/ in *pin* is **aspirated**; that is, it has a puff of breath after the consonant. If you put your hand in front of your face, you can feel the puff of breath. You can also say the word near a candle and see the flame waver. Many English and German speakers carry this aspiration over into Russian, and it is part of their "foreign accent."

If the initial consonant has an /s/ in front of it, there is no aspiration. Put your hand in front of your mouth and compare *pin* and *spin*, *tick* and *stick*, *kin* and *skin*. Another variety of /p/, /t/, and /k/ occurs in final position if the consonant is not fully released. The three kinds of /p/ /t/ /k/ do not differentiate words in English, although aspirated and non-aspirated consonants do differentiate words in many languages of the world, including Chinese, most of the languages of India, and many in the Caucasus, to name only a few.

The aspirated [pʰ tʰ kʰ] in English occur only before a stressed vowel when not preceded by /s/. The non-aspirated variants occur after /s/ or when the following vowel is not stressed, thus *top* is realized as [tʰap], *stop* as [stap], and *totter* as [tʰátər]. The unreleased version of /p t k/ occurs only in final position, where its occurrence is optional and depends upon a number of factors, including speed of speech, what, if anything, follows, etc.

1.4.3. This variation in English is of two types: **conditioned** and **free**. *Conditioned* means that there is some determining factor, such as the presence or absence of /s/ or stress. *Free* means that either variant may occur and that there is no absolute determining factor.

The three variants of the same unit are called **allophones** of the same phoneme. The prefix *allo-* means 'different, variant'. The suffix *-eme* means 'having significance'. These concepts may be extended to other areas of language. If a phoneme is the smallest significant (differentiating) unit of sound, then a **morpheme** is the smallest significant unit of form, and variations in a morpheme are **allomorphs**. Thus, in English, the plural morpheme has three basic allomorphs: /z/ (*bee/bees; dog/dogs*), /s/ (*cat/cats*), and /əz/ (*pass/passes; church/churches*), plus some less common ones (oxen, children, mice, deer, etc.). The basic al-

---

can be used for the automatic half-long vowel before a voiced consonant in English: *bet* [bɛt] ~ *bed* [bɛ·d]. Cf. the short ~ long distinction in German *kann* 'he/she/it can' [kan] vs. *Kahn* 'small boat' [kaːn].

lomorphs have a conditioned (predictable) distribution: /z/ after a vowel or a voiced consonant, /s/ after a voiceless consonant, and /əz/ after a hissing or hushing consonant. The other allomorphs of the plural (e.g., *-en*, Ø /, æ → ε as in *ox ~ oxen, deer ~ deer, man ~ men*) are predictable only by listing the words which use them.

The conditioned allophones and allomorphs are in ***complementary distribution***, which means that where one occurs, the other(s) do not. Question for thought: what is the relationship between Clark Kent and Superman? (See 1.9.1 for the answer.)

1.4.4. Now we can apply the concept of the phoneme to some questions of Russian. As I listed the vowel and consonant phonemes in 1.4, you probably were particularly curious about the status of *ы* and *u* , since they sound so different. If they are to be considered allophones of the same phoneme, then we must be able to state what phonetic properties they have in common and what the distribution of each allophone is. Both tasks are relatively easy. Phonetically they are both ***high*** vowels (made with the tongue raised close to the roof of the mouth, leaving a small opening) and ***unrounded*** vowels (made with no rounding of the lips, unlike *y*, which is a high rounded vowel, and *o*, which is a ***mid rounded*** vowel (made with the tongue raised part-way up).

They also alternate in predictable ways: *ы* appears after a hard consonant, *u* after a soft consonant: стол 'table', nom. pl. столы́; конь 'steed', nom. pl. ко́ни. Only *u* appears initially, but an initial *u* becomes *ы* after a prefix ending with a hard consonant: игра́ть 'play', perfective сыгра́ть, изве́стный 'well-known, famous', безызве́стный 'unknown'.

The vowel letters *u* and *ы* are different from all the other vowel letters in two ways. First, *ы* is the only vowel letter that never occurs initially. Second, *u* is the only one of the soft vowel letters that does not have /j/ pronounced when it is initial: я́ма 'pit' /jáma/, юг 'south' /juk/, ёж 'hedgehog' /još/, ешь! 'eat!' /ješ/, but игра́ть 'play' /igráṭ/, и́ва 'willow' /íva/.

1.4.5. Questions are also often raised about the status of the *velars к, г, x*, since their hard or soft status is chiefly determined by the following vowel: they are hard before *a, o,* and *y* and soft before *e* and *u* (they usually don't occur before *я, э, ы, ё, ю*). As the old saying goes, the devil is in the details. The velars *do* sometimes occur soft before /a/, /o/, and

/u/ and hard before /i/. Most of the instances involve foreign place and personal names, but not all.

There are even a few minimal pairs: садко́м (instr. sg. < садо́к 'place to keep live creatures') ~ соткём (first p. pl. < сотка́ть 'weave') (where the devoicing of *д* before /k/ gives /t/ and reduction of unstressed *o* in the verb gives /a/, so the contrast is /satkóm/ ~ /satk̦óm/). There is also берега́ (pl. < бе́рег 'shore, bank') ~ берегя́ (colloquial and not standard, but widespread, present gerund < бере́чь 'guard, watch'). Another example is the word кюри́ 'curie (unit of radioactivity; derived from the name Кюри́ [Mme. Maria Curie, Polish/French Nobel Prize winner]) ~ кури́! (imperative from кури́ть 'smoke'). Like all paired Russian consonants, *к, г,* and *x* indeed do not normally occur hard before /e/.

We thus see that while *к, г,* and *x* operate a bit differently than the other paired consonants, they are indeed paired and occur both hard and soft before the same vowels where other paired consonants occur. There is only one significant restriction on the occurrence of /k̦, g, x̦/ as opposed to the other twelve paired consonants: they do not occur in final position. Forms like *лягь! 'lie down!' (imperative) are thus impossible.

1.5. The "Signs of Separation": ъ and ь

Pushkin wrote a bit of doggerel which will never compete with *Евгений Онегин*, but is of interest to us. When asked to report on a case of crop failure, he stated: "Саранча́ лете́ла, лете́ла—и се́ла. Сиде́ла, сиде́ла, всё съе́ла, и вновь улете́ла" "The locust flew, flew, and landed. It sat, sat, ate everything, and flew off again." There is a word play on се́ла versus съе́ла. How is се́ла different from съе́ла? The phonemic transcription of се́ла is straighforward: /şéla/. How do we transcribe съе́ла?

1.5.1. As mentioned above, in 1.3.1, the soft vowel letters, such as *ю* and *я*, stand for soft consonant plus vowel when *immediately* following a consonant letter: лю́бим /l̦úb̦im/ 'we love', сидя́т /şid̦át/ 'they sit'. We can now make a more precise formulation of the rule: when the soft vowel letters do *not* immediately follow a consonant letter (that is, when they are in initial position, after a vowel letter, *or after the hard or soft sign*), they stand for the consonant /j/ plus a vowel. Thus, as in 1.3.1, зна́ю, зна́я, я́сная, ю́жная give /znáju/, /znája/, /jásnaja/, /júžnaja/.

The forms of the word статья́ 'article' give us examples of each soft vowel letter after a soft sign: статья́, статьи́, статье́ статью́, статьёй.

Since the soft vowel letters do not immediately follow a consonant letter, they stand for /j/ plus vowel. Since the soft sign follows a consonant letter (as it always must), it stands for softness of the preceding consonant. We thus have a soft consonant followed by the consonant /j/ followed by a vowel: статья́ /statjá/, статьи́ /statjí/, статье́ /statjé/, статью́ /statjú/, статьёй /statjój/.

Note that /j/ is just as much a consonant as any other Russian consonant, and the cluster /tj/ in статья́ /statjá/ 'article' and тре́тья /tŗétja/ 'third' is just as real a cluster as /tr/ in ве́тра /vḛtra/ 'wind' (gen. sg.), тре́тья /tŗétja/ 'third', тру /tru/ 'I rub', or тро́нуть /trónuţ/ 'touch'.

Because the soft sign seems to "separate" the soft consonant from the /j/, the hard and soft signs are sometimes called "signs of separation." This is not a very accurate name, since the hard and soft signs don't really separate the other consonant from the /j/. They merely show that the consonant is hard or soft (just as the soft sign does in other positions: мать, си́льный), and the soft vowel letter not immediately after a consonant letter shows that /j/ plus vowel is present, just as it does in other positions (initial or after a vowel letter). By the information just given, you can tell that съе́ла represents /sjéla/, so we have a contrast of /şéla/ vs. /sjéla/. Although many Russians still pronounce a hard consonant before /j/ when ъ is written, the pronunciation with a soft consonant is more common: /şjéla/. This applies to other similar cases, such as отъе́хать /atjéxaţ/ or /atjéxaţ/ 'go away by conveyance', объём /abjóm/ or /aḅjóm/ 'capacity', объясни́ть /abjasņiţ/ or /aḅjasņiţ/ 'explain, clarify' etc. The exact details about hardness or softness of the consonant can be found in the standard works on Russian pronunciation (see the bibliography).

1.6. The Spelling of /j/ and Some Other Special Cases

1.6.1. Most Russian consonants are normally represented by one letter: /p/ and /p̦/ by *п*, /b/ and /ḅ/ by *б*, /m/ and /m̦/ by *м*, /f/ and /f̦/ by *ф*, /v/ and /ɣ/ by *в*, /t/ and /ţ/ by *т*, /d/ and /ḏ/ by *д*, /n/ and /ņ/ by *н*, /s/ and /ş/ by *с*, /z/ and /ẓ/ by *з*, /r/ and /ŗ/ by *р*, /l/ and /ļ/ by *л*, /k/ and /ķ/ by *к*, /g/ and /g̦/ by *г*, /x/ and /x̣/ by *х*, /š/ by *ш*, /ž/ by *ж*, /c/ by *ц*, and /č/ by *ч*. This does not include those cases where assimilation takes place: с + шить 'sew together' is pronounced /ššiţ/, с + де́лать 'do' is pronounced /zḏélaţ/, and the final *б* in слаб 'weak' assimilates to the voicelessness (silence) following the end of a word: /slap/.

Two consonants require special comment. The first is щ. If the pronunciation is /šč/, then we may regard this as a special case where two consonants, each of which has its own single letter, have a special combined letter when they occur together and in a specific order (if the order is /čš/, then the ordinary letters are used: лу́чший 'better').

The second is /j/. There are two ways of spelling it. The letter й is used after a vowel letter when anything other than a vowel follows (i.e., a consonant or the end of a word): да́йте! /dájt̯e/ 'give!', нейтра́льный /n̯ejtrál̯nij/ 'neutral', дай! /daj/ 'give!', пей! /p̯ej/ 'drink!', зда́ний /zdáin̯j/ 'buildings', мой! /moj/ 'wash!', пой! /pój/ 'sing!') атаку́й! /atakúj/ 'attack'.

The soft vowel letters я, ю, ё, е, and и are used when a vowel follows the /j/ (i.e., in word initial position (яма /jáma/ 'pit', юг /juk/ 'south'), in the middle of a word after a vowel letter (моя́ /majá/ 'my', мою́ /majú/ 'my', мо́ю /móju/ 'I wash'), and in the middle of a word after a consonant (written with the hard or soft sign: пью /p̯ju/ 'I drink', шью /šju/ 'I sew').

The letter й is also used before another vowel letter in a few words borrowed from foreign languages: майо́р /majór/ 'major', Нью Йорк /ṇju jork/ 'New York'. These are minor exceptions to the general orthographical rules.

1.6.2. We thus see that the phoneme /j/ is exceptional in Russian by having two regular methods of representation. This often causes confusion in learners, since /j/, like all consonants, sometimes appears before a consonant or at the end of a word, and other times before a vowel. Let us consider what happens when we add the gen. sg. ending /a/ to three nouns:

Set	Nom. sg.			Gen. sg.	
1	/stul/	стул	'chair'	/stúla/	сту́ла
2	/gost̯/	гость	'guest'	/góst̯a/	го́стя
3	/boj/	бой	'battle'	/bója/	бо́я

The first set is very simple: one sound equals one letter. The second set has five letters and four sounds in the nominative, but five letters and five sounds in the genitive. The third set has three letters in both the nominative and the genitive, but four sounds in the genitive as opposed to three in the nominative. In the word бой/боя we see /j/ spelled two different ways.

The two methods of spelling soft consonants (either followed by the soft sign or by a soft vowel letter) and the two methods of spelling /j/ frequently turn up in making the genitive plural of feminine and neuter nouns. The rule for the genitive plural says: if the word has a vowel ending in the nom. sg., chop off that ending for the gen. pl.: рукá 'hand' → рук, лицó 'face; person' → лиц. In this first set of two words the procedure is very transparent, either in Cyrillic or in transcription: /ruká/ → /ruk/, /ḷicó/ → /ḷic/. It is less so in Cyrillic in бáня 'bath' → бань, but transcription makes it quite clear: /báṇa/ → /baṇ/. Finally, we have as a third set those cases where /j/ is the final consonant of the stem: струя́ → струй 'stream' (/strujá/ → /struj/), ли́ния → ли́ний 'line' (/ḷíṇija/ → /ḷíṇij/). In sets two and three the underlying simplicity of the rule is hidden by the Cyrillic spelling.

1.6.3. The phoneme /j/ varies in its pronunciation, depending upon speaker and position in the word. In final position it normally gets a fair amount of friction, more than a final English /y/. If possible, compare a native Russian speaker's pronunciation of бой with a native English speaker's pronunciation of *boy*. For most Russians, the /j/ will have much more friction. Also compare Russian /j/ in есть 'is' with /y/ in English *yes*. The Russian consonant again has more friction.

1.6.4. As pointed out above (1.4.4), the letter *и* in initial position is not pronounced with /j/ preceding the vowel, so the combination /ji/ occurs initially only as the result of vowel reduction: ежá /jižá/ gen. sg. ← ёж / još/ 'hedgehog'; егó /jivó/ gen. sg. ← он 'he'. The consonant /j/ occurs initially in combination with the other vowel phonemes, and is denoted by the other 'soft' vowel letters, as listed in 1.4.4.[10]

Within a word /j/ occurs before any vowel, at least in theory: мою́, моё, моя́, моéй, мои́ /majú, majó, majá, majéj, mají/. In actual fact, the /j/ is often pronounced weakly before front vowels (in Russian the *front vowels* are /e/ and /i/—the constriction of the air passage by the tongue is in the front part of the mouth), and it often disappears completely, especially before /i/ in rapid speech. The actual pronunciation thus varies

---

[10] Avanesov (1968: 92) notes that in the past in some people's pronunciation, initial /ji/ spelled by *и* occurred only in the words их, им, ими 'them (gen.-prep., dat., instr.) and in the possessive их 'their.' Why? The answer is in 1.9.2 at the end of this chapter.

from [maʲéj] and [maʲí] to [maéj/ and [maí]. We have to put the /j/ in the **underlying form**, since the stem is clearly /maj-/ (or better, /moj-/). We will discuss the concept of underlying forms, which are written between { and } (called **braces**) in 1.8.

1.7. The Spelling of Underlying {o}

1.7.1. Russian orthography is quite consistent about spelling an underlying {o} after hard paired consonants. Regardless of its phonetic realization under different conditions of stress placement, it is always spelled with the letter *o*: стороны 'sides', многосторонний 'many-sided, versatile', сторона 'side'. These three forms are realized as [stórənɨ], [mnəgəstʌrónnij],[11] [stərʌná], with the allophone [ə] occuring after the stress ([stórənɨ]) or more than one syllable before the stress ([stərʌná]), the allophone [ʌ] occurring immediately before the stressed syllable ([mnəgəstʌrónnij], [stərʌná]), and the allophone [o] occurring under stress ([stórənɨ], [mnəgəstʌrónnij]). (The vowel [ʌ] is a shorter and higher version of [a]; [ə] is a mid-high central vowel, like the *a* in English *sofa* or the *u* in *putt* or the *o* in *love*). Both [ʌ] and [ə] are allophones of /a/ and /o/.

1.7.2. Russian orthography treats underlying {o} after soft paired consonants quite differently. The letter for {o} after soft consonants is *ё*, but as you know, this letter is not used in ordinary texts. It is used only in dictionaries, grammars, and books for children and foreigners (and occasionally to eliminate possible ambiguity: вот всё! ~ вот все! "Here's everything!" ~ "Here's all/everybody").

When the letter *ё* is used, it is only under stress: вёл 'he led', вела, вело, вели 'she/it/they led'. Although underlying {o}, just like underlying {a} and {e}, is reduced to [i][12] after a soft consonant when not stressed, the letters for {a} and {e} don't change, but the letter for {o} does: пять 'five', gen. пяти; семь 'seven', gen. семи; грабёж 'robbery', gen. грабежа. These are pronounced [pat̢] [pit̢í] [sem̢] [s̢im̢í] [grab̢óš] [grəb̢iža].

Logically, one should always write an underlying {o} after a soft consonant with the letter *ё*, with the understanding that if the stress does

---

[11] With assimilation for softness of the /n/ to the following /n̢/.

[12] Except in some noun and adjective endings, where it goes to [ə]; see 1.8.4 and 4.1.6.3 for more information.

not fall on that syllable, then the vowel is reduced, as are {a} and {e}. For historical reasons, Russian does not do so, and the student is forced to regard each unstressed *e* with suspicion: is a *ë* lurking there, to manifest itself under stress? Why should the plural of река́ 'river' be ре́ки, but the plural of сестра́ 'sister' be сёстры? Why should the form секли́ 'they chopped' have a masc. sg. сек, but the form пекли́ 'they baked' have a masc. sg. пёк? Note that the situation is confusing even for educated Russians: since all other verbs in this group (see Chapter 8) have *ë* (он тёк, пёк, влёк, -рёк, лёг, берёг, стерёг) during the past half-century the preferred form has become он сёк instead of он сёк.

1.7.3. Underlying {o} after the unpaired consonants (š, ž, c, č, šč, j) requires more spelling rules. Underlying {jo} is simple: if it is stressed, write the letter *ë*; if not, write *e*. For example, nom. sg. ёж 'hedgehog', gen. sg. ежа́; nom. sg. masc. мой 'my', dat. sg. masc. моему́ (< {moj} + {omu}) nom. sg. neut. моё (< {moj} + {o}). The rules for the other five consonants are not so simple.

    Spelling Rule 5 applies to endings and fill vowels in nouns and adjectives: if {o} is stressed after *ш, ж, ц, ч,* or *щ,* spell {o} with the letter *o,* if not stressed, spell it with the letter *e.* The adjective большо́й 'big' and the comparative бо́льший 'bigger' provide some very nice examples: gen. sg. m. большо́го 'big', бо́льшего 'bigger', prep. sg. m. большо́м 'big', бо́льшем 'bigger'. Consider also борщ 'borshch (soup)', instr. sg. борщо́м, това́рищ 'comrade', instr. sg. това́рищем, отец 'father', instr. sg. отцо́м, не́мец 'German', instr. sg. не́мцем, gen. pl. отцо́в and не́мцев.

    Spelling Rule 6: in endings and fill vowels of verbs, an underlying {o} after unpaired consonant is always spelled with the letters *ë* or *e,* never *o*: печём 'we bake' (< печь), стрижём 'we shear, cut' (< стричь), бережём 'we guard, save'(< бере́чь), мо́жем 'we can, are able' (< мочь), жжём 'we burn, ignite' (< жечь). Note also the *ë* as a fill vowel within verb forms: прочёл 'he read' (< прочесть, stem прочт-), ожёг 'he burned' (< ожёчь, stem ожг-).

    There are no verbs with *ц* before the ending, but in a few forms it appears before a suffix and the vowel {o} of the suffix is spelled *o* if stressed and *e* if unstressed: перетанцо́вывать 'dance something again', perfective перетанцева́ть.

    In the **root** of nouns, adjectives, and verbs the vowel letter *o* is used if the {o} always remains /o/ and under stress: ожо́г 'burn', чо́порный 'prim, stuck-up', чо́каться 'clink glasses', but in чёрт 'devil' (pl. че́рти), шёпот 'whisper' (verb inf. шепта́ть, third sg. ше́пчет), пчёлы 'bees' (sg. пчела́), the *ё* is used because of the change of vowel or place of stress.

1.8. Underlying Forms

In the text above we have several times dealt, implicitly or explicitly, with the notion of underlying forms (where a "form" means an element of the language, whether a sound, a root, an ending, a word, or some other part of the language). Underlying forms usually undergo the action of one or more processes to produce the actual forms of the language, or the *surface forms*.

An ***underlying*** sound or form is given in ***braces***: {storoná}, {stóroni}, {mnogostorónņij}, while phonetic realizations are in ***brackets***: [stərʌná], [stórənɨ], [mnəgəstʌrónņij],[13] and ***phonemic transcriptions*** in slashes: /staraná/, /stórani/, /mnagastarónņij/.

A phonetic transcription will attempt to show as many details as is practical and will thus be useful in pronunciation practice for beginners in the language. Intermediate and advanced students will usually know the rules of pronunciation well enough that they can best use a phonemic transcription, which shows different basic sounds, but ignores allophonic differences. A phonetic transcription of э́тот го́род, э́ти города́, в э́том огоро́де would show [étət górət éţi gərʌdá vétəm ʌgʌródi], while a phonemic one would show /état górat éţi garadá vétam agaródi/.

An underlying form is given in ***morphophonemic transcription***. Morphophonemic transcription tries, in general, to keep the same phonemic representation for each morpheme, with the various predictable rules being applied to produce the final (= surface) form. Thus, the units listed above, э́тот го́род, э́ти города́, в э́том огоро́де would have a morphophonemic representation as {état górod éţi gorodá vétom ogoróde}, with vowel reduction rules taking care of the realization of the unstressed instances of {o} as [ʌ] or [ə] and unstressed {e} as [i]. The softening of {de} to [ḍe] is taken care of by the rule in 1.2 about consonants before {e} in the same word. We need this last stipulation to deal with {v étom}, which keeps the hard [v], and does not soften to [γetom]. Finally the devoicing of final {d} in [górət] is accomplished by a rule evoking automatic devoicing in final position.

---

[13] Or [mnògəstʌrónņij], /mnògastarónņij/. The question of secondary stress is too complicated to treat here. See the works in the bibliography.

Note that while the surface form is always derivable from the under-lying form, the reverse is often not true: the first two vowels in [gərʌdá] do not tell us whether the underlying form is {garadá}, {goradá}, {ga-rodá}, or {gorodá}, just as the final [t] in [górət] gives no clue as to whether the underlying consonant is {t} or {d} (cf. [nʌrót] from наро́д, на род, на рот).

You will learn to derive underlying forms as the course progresses.

1.8.1. The (partial) rule for forming the genitive plural given in 1.6.2 is a good example of the advantages of starting with underlying forms. We take underlying forms ({ruká, ḷicó, bán̦a, strujá, ḷin̦ija}) and apply a rule which says, "if the nominative singular has an ending, remove it to form the genitive plural." As a result of this process we easily and transpar-ently obtain the forms /ruk, ḷic, bán̦, struj, ḷin̦ij/, which can be converted back into Cyrillic рук, лиц, бань, струй, ли́ний.

1.8.2. Further good examples of underlying forms and the application of rules are furnished by forms of the words холо́дный 'cold' (underlying form for the time being: {xolodnij}), and по́лоз 'runner' (underlying form: {poloz}, both with stress specifications which we will leave aside for now).

Three rules are applied. By Rule one, an unstressed {o} after a hard consonant is reduced to [ʌ] in the syllable immediately before the stressed syllable: холо́дный 'cold' [xʌlódnij]. By Rule two, if the unstressed {o} begins the word, it goes to [ʌ] regardless of the position of the stress: обмыва́ть 'wash' [ʌbmɨvát]. By Rule three, unstressed {o} goes to [ə] in all syllables which either follow the stressed syllable or come more than one syllable before the stressed syllable: хо́лодно (neut. short form) [xólədnə}, погаси́ть 'cancel' [pəgʌṣít], холодна́ (fem. short form) [xəlʌdná], хорошо́ (neut. short form) [xərʌšó].

Note that these rules must be applied *in order*, that is, they are **ordered rules**. If Rule three were to be applied before Rule two, we would get *[əbmivát] instead of the correct [ʌbmivát]. We will frequently need to order our rules for the description of Russian. The principle of ordering is something like an automatic coin sorter: the first hole has to be small, so that only dimes can pass through. The next hole lets through pennies, and the next nickels, and the next quarters, and so on. If one starts with the biggest hole, for half-dollars, everything will go through the first hole and no sorting will occur. The *order* of the sort is vital.

1.8.3. In order to get the phonetic realization of {póloz}, we need to add one rule: voiced consonants become voiceless in final position. Thus we apply rule three from 1.8.2 above and the devoicing rule to turn {póloz} into [pólǝs]. In this case the order of application does not matter. Question for thought: when, in general, is the order of application of rules likely to be irrelevant? (See 1.9.3 for an answer.)

1.8.4. The rules for reduction of unstressed {a, e, o} after a soft or unpaired consonant are quite simple if the vowel is not in an ending. Except in endings, all three unstressed vowels go to [i], regardless of where they are in relation to the stressed syllable. Thus in 1.7.2 we had вёл 'he led', вела́, вело́, вели́ 'she/it /they led' (underlying {γól} {γolá} {γoló} {γoḷí}), realized as [γól] [γilá] [γiló] [γiḷí] and пять 'five', gen. пяти́ (underlying {paṭí}), семь 'seven', gen. семи́ (underlying {şeṃí}), грабёж 'robbery', gen. грабежа́ (underlying {graḇožá}). These are realized in pronunciation as [paṭ] [pịṭí] [şeṃ] [şiṃí] [grʌḇóš] [grǝḇižá]. The verb пережева́ть 'masticate' (underlying {peṛežováṭ}) gives [piṛiživáṭ], with *i* after the hard *ž*, and similarly жара́ 'heat' gives [žirá].

If the underlying vowel in an ending is {e}, it will be realized as [i]: стол 'table' стул 'chair' жена́ 'wife' ме́ра 'measure' село́ 'village' по́ле 'field', have a loc. sg. на столе́ (the /e/ under stress proves that the underlying vowel is indeed {e}, not {o}) на сту́ле на жене́ на ме́ре на селе́ на по́ле, realized as [nǝstʌḷé] [nʌstúḷi] [nǝžiṇé] [nʌḷéṛi] [nǝşiḷé] [nʌpóḷi].

If the underlying vowel in an ending is {a} or {o}, it will in general be realized as [ǝ]: nom. sg. неде́ля 'week' ли́ния 'line' но́вая 'new' third pl. ви́дят 'see' pres. gerund зна́я 'know' nom. sg. враньё 'nonsense зда́ние 'building' по́ле 'field' но́вое 'new', realized as [ṇiḍéḷǝ] [líṇijǝ] [nóvǝjǝ] [ɣíḍǝt] [znájǝ] [vrʌṇjó] [zdáṇijǝ] [póḷǝ] [nóvǝjǝ].

The two forms of по́ле, nom./acc. and prep., which are spelled the same, have two different underlying vowels and for most Russians, two different pronunciations. The written sentence они́ е́дут в по́ле has two realizations: [aṇí jédut fpóḷǝ] 'they ride into the field' (acc. sg.) and [aṇí jédut fpóḷi] 'they ride (while) in the field' (prep. sg.).

There are a number of complications, such as having underlying {o} after a soft consonant or unpaired consonant when it is not the last sound in an ending (e.g., gen. sg. masc. большо́го, си́него, and хоро́шего according to Spelling Rule 4 in 1.7.3). In this case the {o} may be realized as either [ǝ] or [i], with [i]/[ɨ] being the more common pronunciation in contemporary Russian: [bʌḷšóvǝ], [şíṇivǝ] or [şíṇǝvǝ], [xʌróšivǝ] or [xʌróšəvə], with [ʂiɳivə] and [xʌróšɨvə] being decidedly more frequent. For details, consult the standard books on Russian pronunciation (see the bibliography).

1.9. Additional Information

1.9.1. Clark Kent and Superman are **allohomes** of the same **homeme** (unit of personhood). The allohomes are in complementary distribution. Where one occurs, the other does not.

1.9.2. *Answer to the question in footnote 10:* Russians generally seem to perceive words as consisting of zero, one, or more prefixes plus a root plus zero, one, or more suffixes, plus an ending (and occasionally a particle, such as пройдёмте-ка 'let's both/all pass/go through, if you please'). While the absence of a prefix and/or the absence of a suffix are both common, and the absence of an ending (as opposed to a zero ending [see in Chapter 2]) is not unknown, the only word apparently without a root in modern Russian is вы́нуть 'take out', with a prefix вы-and a suffix/ending -ну-ть. If их, им, и́ми are to be pronounced [ix] [im] [íɱi] instead of [jix] [jim] [jíɱi], then they seem to consist only of an ending with no stem/root. Apparently to avoid this, many Russians of previous generations used the [jix] [jim] [jíɱi] pronunciations, but as far as I can tell from questioning, almost nobody uses the [j-] pronunciations any longer.

1.9.3. Answer to 1.8.3: when the rules apply to different situations. In the case of {gorod}, the vowel reduction rules apply to unstressed vowels, and the devoicing rule applies to consonants in final position, so they apply to different areas and their order of application with respect to each other doesn't matter.

1.9.4. *Transliteration* differs from transcription in both its uses and its nature. Transliteration normally is used to turn the units of one writing system (such as Cyrillic, Greek, or Devanagari) into the units of another writing system (such as Latin, although the reverse is equally valid).

The transliteration system which you are probably most familiar with is that of the Library of Congress (LC), used by most libraries in the USA. It comes in two versions, with and without **diacritics** (the little flyspecks over, under, and between characters, such as: ˇ ´ ` _ ° ‾ ⌢ in č, š, ž, ё, á, à, a̲, å, ā, ă, ą, i͡a, t͡s). In the electronic catalogs of today, the transliteration is normally without the diacritics: ia, ts.

Transliteration does not try to show anything about the structure or pronunciation of the words; it is merely a symbol-to-symbol conversion. Thus, [stórənɨ] (стóроны) 'sides', [starón] (сторóн), and [stərʌná] (сторонá) 'side' all have the same first six letters in transliteration: *storony, storon, storona*. In transcription моего will be shown as phonetic [məjivó] or phonemic /majivó/, whereas in transliteration it will be *moego*.

Table 1-1. Chart of LC Transliteration without Diacritics

а	б	в	г	д	е	ё	ж	з	и	й	к	л	м	н	о	п	р	с	т	у	ф
a	b	v	g	d	e	e	zh	z	i	i	k	l	m	n	o	p	r	s	t	u	f

х	ц	ч	ш	щ	ъ	ы	ь	э	ю	я
kh	ts	ch	sh	shch	"	y	'	e	iu	ia

Appendix
Phonetic Transcription Sample

В. В. Иванов: Историческая фонолóгия рýсского языкá, М. 1968,
[istʌɽíčiskəjə   fənʌlóǵijə rúskəvə jizɨká]

От áвтора
[ʌtáftərə]

В настоящей   кнúге дéлается   по существý пéрвая
[vnəstʌjáščəj (or: -ščij) kɲíǵi ḏéləjica[14] pəsuščistvú p̚érvəjə]

попытка дáть óчерк истори́ческой фонолóгии рýсского языкá.
[pʌpɨtkə daṭ óčirk istʌɽíčiskəj   fənʌlóǵi(j)ɪ rúskəvə jizɨká]

Несмотря на тó, что наýка об истóрии фонологи́ческой
[ɲismʌtɽá nʌtó štə nʌúkə ʌbɨstóɽi(j)i fənəlʌǵíčiskəj]

систéмы разли́чных языкóв имéет   бóлее
[ṣisṭémɨ rʌzl̠íčnɨx   jizɨkóf iṃé(j)it bóḽijə]

---

[14] Remember that the infinitive and 3rd person sg. and pl. present tense forms of reflexive verbs are always pronounced [cə], as if they were written *-ца*, and *ц* is *always* hard.

чем   тридцатилéтнюю дáвность, до сих пóр почтú
[čem/čim tɾicəţiḷétɲuju   dávnəşţ   dəşixpór   pʌčţí]

не существýет исслéдований, в котóрых со всéй возмóжной
[ɲisuščistvú(j)it iṣḷédəvəɲij   fkʌtórɨx   sʌfşej   vʌzmóžnəj]

полнотóй раскрывáлись   бы фонологúческие отношéния
[pəlnʌtój rəskrɨváḷiş (or: ʐ) bɨ   fənəlʌǵíčisķi(j)i   ʌtnʌšéɲijə]

и изменéние э́тих отношéний в истóрии рýсского языкá.
[iizɱiɲéɲijə éţix ʌtnʌšéɲij   vɨstóɾi(j)i   rúskəvə   jizɨká]

Поэ́тому сво́ю основнýю задáчу áвтор вúдит в тóм, чтобы
[pʌétəmu svʌjú ʌsnʌvnúju zʌdáču aftər   vídit   ftom   štəbɨ]

показáть, как склáдывались и развивáлись фонологúческие
[pəkʌzáţ kʌk skládɨvəḷiş   irəzɣiváḷiş   fənəlʌǵíčisķi(j)i]

Exercises

I. Give definitions or brief answers to the following:

1. What would you expect to find in an orthoepic dictionary of English? In an orthographic dictionary?
2. Is "hard" and "soft" vowel letter a good term?
3. What is "ordering of rules"? Give an example.
4. Complementary distribution
5. What does an asterisk in front of a form mean?
6. Soft vowel letter
7. Conditioned and free variation.
8. Palatalized consonant
9. Transliteration versus transcription
10. Orthoepic
11. Allograph
12. What's wrong with using modified Cyrillic for transcription?
13. What's good and bad about using the Latin alphabet for transcription?
14. How many ways can you differentiate consonants in Russian (e.g., palatalization or lack of it)?
15. Discuss the phonemic status of the soft velars in Russian.

16. Is the Russian orthographical system phonetic, phonemic, morpho-phonemic, or something else?
17. Rules for writing /o/ after the six unpaired consonants
18. Why do we use a hook under the letter to transcribe palatalized consonants, instead of putting a superscript "y" or an apostrophe after the consonant (i.e., why ļ instead of lʸ or l')?
19. The pronunciation /jix/, /jim/, /jíɱi/ for the third person pronoun.
20. What is the function of the soft sign in the words несёшь, печь, and мышь?
21. Consonants by their point of articulation (labial, labio-dental, dental, alveolar, palatal, velar)
22. Vowels by their articulation characteristics (e.g., high, front, rounded, etc.): [а, э, и, о, ы, ъ, ʌ, у]

II. Transcribe in narrow phonetic transcription (differentiating ə from ʌ from a, ɨ from i); good luck with deciphering the meanings!

1. Говору́нов ма́ло. Из-за одного́ обновля́ющегося молокосо́са э́ти культу́рные де́ятели продолжа́ют ре́дко проявля́ть интере́с к теорети́ческим вопро́сам прямолине́йного языкозна́ния.
2. Ежи́ интересу́ют меня́, осо́бенно э́тот большу́щий ёж на сверка́ющей реке́.
3. По всей вероя́тности щу́ка клю́нет под мосто́м.
4. Он постоя́нно беспоко́ится бессмы́сленными перевора́чивающимися дета́лями на вновь изобрета́емых водоворо́тах.
5. Веду́щие ча́сти Организа́ции объединённых вреди́телей нахо́дятся в ожесточённейшей борьбе́ с неиссяка́емой ды́ней и с жи́ром.
6. Без щита́, но с вы́игрышем мы переезжа́ем на обновля́ющуюся кварти́ру с балко́ном.
7. Не ежь чересчу́р. Щёки твои́ ещё полны́ бле́щущими ло́жками.
8. Не подлежи́т сомне́нию, что усто́йчивость спосо́бствует.
9. Вся́кое притяжа́тельное употребле́ние вытесня́ющихся значе́ний препя́тствует с катего́рией обозначе́ния предме́тов, дава́емых любо́вью.
10. Вме́сте мы переезжа́ем на но́вое по́ле пе́ред щито́м э́тих не́мцев.
11. Обомле́вшие камыши́ плюю́т на жела́вших их ви́деть.
12. В пятьдеся́тый раз он беспоко́ил бра́тьев струёй горя́чей воды́.

2

Noun Declension

2.0. Introduction

The forms of Russian are inextricably connected with questions of stress. One need only consider such pairs as го́рода ~ города́ 'city', сло́ва ~ слова́ 'word', письма́ ~ пи́сьма 'letter', горы́ ~ го́ры 'mountain', where in each case the genitive singular is distinguished from the nominative plural solely by the place of the stress (differing vowel reduction is a consequence of the place of the stress). This chapter will discuss the basic facts of noun declension. Chapter 3 will consider stress patterns systematically.

2.0.1. Traditionally six cases, plus the "second genitive" ("partitive") and "second prepositional" ("locative") are distinguished in Russian, although no noun has six different forms in the basic six cases of either the singular or the plural. Question for thought as you work through this chapter: what are the maximum and minimum numbers of different forms shown by Russian nouns in the singular and in the plural? Compare nouns to adjectives, pronouns, and numerals when you study Chapters 4, 5, and 6.

2.0.2. Russian has three basic patterns of noun declension. Nouns ending in {-а} (жена́, неде́ля, ю́ноша, дя́дя, пья́ница) are usually called the *first* declension in Russian-language grammars, but the *second* in English-language grammars; masc. nouns in a consonant (стол, конь) and neuter nouns in {-о} сло́во, мо́ре, зда́ние) are called the *first* declension in English-language grammars and the *second* in Russian grammars. Both traditions agree in naming nouns like кость and ночь the *third* declension. We will follow the English-language tradition in this book, making стол first declension and жена́ second.

2.0.3. As you know, Russian has a number of variants in the endings of the written forms of nouns. Examples would be nom. sg. стол but конь, gen. sg. стола́ but коня́, dat. sg. столу́ but коню́, instr. sg. столо́м but конём, nom. pl. столы́ but ко́ни. Nouns ending in a velar consonant (*к, г, х*) or an unpaired consonant (*ж, ш, ц, ч, щ, й*) show their own differences: nom. sg. зал, каранда́ш, парк, but nom. pl. за́лы, карандаши́, па́рки, where зал and каранда́ш both end in a hard consonant but spell the plural ending differently, and парк also ends in a hard consonant but softens it in the plural.

The question is to what extent are different and unpredictable endings involved. Some grammars set up each of these types as a separate declension and tell you to memorize them. If we go back to 1.6.2 in the previous chapter, we see that many of the differences are due to spelling rules, and not to different endings.

Nom. Sg.			**Gen. Sg.**		
/stul/	стул	'chair'	/stúla/	сту́ла
/gosţ/	гость	'guest'	/gósţa/	го́стя
/boj/	бой	'battle'	/bója/	бо́я

There is obviously a single ending, {a}, for the gen. sg. in all three nouns, and it is only the Cyrillic spelling that obscures this fact. If you will look at the last paragraph in that same section, and at 1.8.1, you will see that a similar situation applies to the formation of the gen. pl.

рука́ 'hand'	→	рук	/ruká/	→	/ruk/
лицо́ 'face; person'	→	лиц	/ļicó/	→	/ļic/
ба́ня 'bath'	→	бань	/báņa/	→	/baņ/
струя́ 'stream'	→	струй	/strujá/	→	/struj/
ли́ния 'line'	→	ли́ний	/ļíņija/	→	/ļíņij/

If we work with the concept of *underlying forms*, introduced in 1.8, and the six Spelling Rules, we find that a single underlying form is all we need to describe most case endings. In first declension nouns only in the nom. pl. and gen. pl. do we commonly find real competing endings: {i} vs. {a} in the nom. and {ov} vs. {ej} in the gen. (see below).

2.1. The Non-Feminine (First) Declension

This declension contains masculine and neuter nouns. The endings for the masculine and neuter are the same except in the nominative and accusative. Neuters do not have the alternative -*y* endings in the genitive and prepositional.

2.1.1. Nouns of the first declension have the endings shown in Table 2-1. The -Ø ending is called the "zero ending." Russian nouns, in principle, have an ending for each case in both the singular and the plural. When there is no actual phonetic realization of the ending, we may call it a "zero ending." A case form with a zero ending is distinguished from all other case forms in exactly the same way as a tailless dog or sheep is distinguished from other dogs or sheep: by the absence of something expected.

Table 2-1. First Declension Basic Noun Endings

	Masc. Sg.	Neut. Sg.	Masc. Pl.	Neut. Pl.
Nom.	-Ø	-о	-ы/-á	-а
Acc.	= nom. or gen.	= nom.	= nom. or gen.	= nom. or gen.
Gen.	-а		-ов/-ей	-Ø
Dat.	-у		-ам	
Instr.	-ом		-ами	
Prep.	-е		-ах	
2nd Gen.	-у			
2nd Prep.	-ý			

2.1.2. The usual spelling rules apply to these endings, so -*ы* after *к г х* becomes -*и*. For examples, see 1.1 in Chapter 1. The spelling of {о} after soft paired consonants will be *ё* or *е* (see 1.7.2 in Chapter 1). The spelling of {о} after unpaired consonants is discussed in 1.7.3 in Chapter 1.

There is one spelling detail that is not covered by the spelling rules given in Chapter 1. When the stem ends in -*ий* ({-ij-}), the **prep. sg.** ending {-е} is spelled -*и* (of course, since the {е} is unstressed, the pronunciation would be [i] with either spelling): гéний 'genius' здáние 'building', prep. о гéнии, о здáнии. This same rule operates with the nouns of the second declension in the prep. and dative sg.: лúния 'line' о лúнии, по лúнии (see 2.3.2 below). Note that this spelling rule does *not* apply to the nominative sg. neut., where the underlying vowel is {o}: зда́ние {zdáņijo}.

2.1.3. The rule about making genitive plurals by removing a final vowel (discussed in section 1.6.2 of Chapter 1) is part of a larger, more general set of ordered rules:

Genitive Plural Rule 1: if a noun has an ending in the nom. sg., remove it to make the gen. pl.: e.g. nom. sg. сло́во gen. pl. слов 'word', зда́ние gen. pl. зда́ний 'building', река́ gen. pl. рек 'river', ба́ня gen. pl. бань 'bath', ли́ния gen. pl. ли́ний 'line'.

Genitive Plural Rule 2: if there is no ending in the nom. sg. (i.e., if the ending is -Ø), then add one in the genitive plural.

Genitive Plural Rule 2a: if the final consonant of the stem is a soft paired consonant or a "husher" (*ж, ш, ч, щ*), add the ending *-ей* to form the gen. pl.: конь 'steed' ~ коне́й, жи́тель 'inhabitant' ~ жи́телей, нож 'knife' ~ ноже́й.

Genitive Plural Rule 2b: if the final consonant of the stem is a hard paired consonant or *ц* or *й*, add the ending *-ов* to form the gen. pl.: стол 'table' ~ столо́в, оте́ц 'father' ~ отцо́в, край 'edge' ~ краёв {krajov}, не́мец ~ не́мцев, музе́й ~ музе́ев.

Note that these three rules apply to all Russian nouns, regardless of gender: жена́ ~ жён, ба́ня ~ бань, ли́ния ~ линий, кость ~ косте́й, ночь ~ ноче́й, путь ~ путей. When the zero ending appears either in the nom. sg. or the gen. pl., a *fill vowel* may be used. For a discussion of fill vowels, see 2.3.5.

Rules 2a and 2b are not ordered, since they apply to different situations. Where V stands for any vowel, C for any consonant, C^h for any hard paired consonant, and C^s for any soft paired consonant:

Table 2-2. Genitive Plural Endings

Nom. Sg. in:	Gen. Pl. Ending:		
	-Ø	-ов	-ей
-C+V	✓		
-C^h+ Ø	✓	✓	
-C^s+ Ø			✓
-ж/ш/ч/щ+ Ø			✓
-ц/й+ Ø		✓	

2.2. Notes on Individual Cases and Endings

2.2.1. Many scholars count the second genitive and second prepositional as full-fledged cases, giving Russian a total of eight. Others object, since the second genitive occurs only with a limited number of masculine nouns, all of which belong to only one type of declension (e.g., са́хару, сне́гу, мёду, ча́ю, шокола́ду, табаку́, и́з дому, со́ смеху, ни ра́зу), and the second prepositional (or locative [loc.]) occurs only with a limited number of nouns belonging to two types of declension (first and third). It is used only after the prepositions в and на. It shows a form in /ú/ (на берегу́, в бою́, на краю́, в лесу́, в снегу́), or /í/ (в ночи́, на мели́, в крови́, на печи́). The loc. is not used when the phrase has a figurative meaning: Он разбира́ется в ле́се, он зна́ет толк в ле́се "He's an expert on/is well informed about forests"; Она́ играет в "Вишнёвом са́де" "She is performing in 'The Cherry Orchard'." Когда́ он вошёл в дом, он был весь в сне́ге "when he entered the house, he was covered with snow."

Are these phenomena to be regarded as separate case forms? The fact that the second gen. and the loc. have meanings and forms which are distinct from the regular gen. and the prepositional seems to argue in favor of constituting them as such. The opposing argument would note that not all nouns can form them. A situation where a distinctive case-form is not formed by all nouns is however not at all unusual. Examples could be given from the instrumental in Old English, both the locative and the vocative in Latin, the ablative in Sanskrit, the vocative in those Slavic languages that have it (most of them—Russian is not typical), and many others. We must then say that Russian has eight cases, but that two of them are not distinguished in the majority of Russian nouns.

2.2.2. We will not go further into the usage and meaning of the second gen. and loc., since those questions belong to syntax and other fields, while this book is about the *forms* of Russian. Let me note only that the term "partitive" is not completely satisfactory, since some uses of the second gen. do not fit the concept of "partitive," although the basic meaning found in ча́шка ча́ю or таре́лка су́пу is clearly partitive.

2.2.3. The second gen. is formed from a rather substantial number of masc. nouns. The exact number is hard to determine, since authoritative reference books differ significantly in their lists. *Грамматика*

1980 (§1179–81) lists nearly 450 of what it calls the "... наиболее употребительные слова" which have this ending.

If we look for common features among the words, we find that the list includes both native words and a large number of borrowed words. Most, but not all, of the words end in a hard paired consonant or /j/, but there are several in a soft resonant: (ль, нь, рь). Almost all of the soft stems are originally borrowings: имби́рь/рю́, карто́фель/лю, ка́фель/лю, кисе́ль/лю́, минда́ль/лю́, митка́ль/лю́, нашаты́рь/рю́, реве́нь/ню́, хме́ль/лю, шта́пель/лю, ште́бень/бню, янта́рь/рю́, ячме́нь/ню́. There are six stems ending in an unpaired consonant other than {j}: пе́рец/рцу́, пу́нш/шу́, си́тец/тцу́, сма́лец/льцу́, у́держ/у, фа́рш/у.

Most of the words with a second gen. are stem stressed, but a few do have end stress: имби́рь/рю́, кипято́к/тку́, кисе́ль/лю́, коня́к/ку́, минда́ль/лю́, митка́ль/лю́, нашаты́рь/рю́, песо́к/ску́, реве́нь/ню́, таба́к/ку́, янта́рь/рю́, ячме́нь/ню́, plus some diminutives such as медо́к/дку́, ледо́к/дку́, чаёк/чайку́.

2.2.4. The second prepositional, or *locative,* occurs in the first and third declensions with a much smaller number of nouns, the overwhelming majority of which are monosyllabic and native Russian words. The first declension *locative* case ending -ý is always stressed. Masc. nouns of the 1st declension which have the locative form normally end in a hard paired consonant or /j/, and most belong to the stress pattern that has stem stress in the singular and end stress in the plural (нос, но́са, на носу́, носы́, носо́в; бой, бо́я, в бою́, бои́, боёв; бе́рег; бе́рега, на берегу́, берега́, берего́в). Normally the second gen. and loc. do not occur in the same noun.

The two exceptions to the rule about final consonants are плац and хмель: на плацу́ 'on the parade-ground/drill-ground', на хмелю́ 'on the hops', во хмелю́ 'tipsy, drunk'. There are about a dozen non-monosyllabic nouns which take this ending, such as на берегу́ 'on the bank', на ветру́ (← ве́тер) 'on the wind'. Half of these nouns are historically monosyllabic stems (e.g., бе́рег comes from an earlier **berg-*; cf. German *Berg* 'mountain'). The word ве́тер has a monosyllabic stem in all forms except the nom. sg. and historically even the nom. stem was monosyllabic. One polysyllabic foreign borrowing has acquired this ending in modern times: в аэропорту́ 'at the airport' (probably because of в порту́ 'in port').

For a detailed listing of nouns which form a second prepositional/ locative, see *Грамматика 1980* (§1182–83).

2.2.5. The nominative plural in -á (e.g., глазá, домá, бокá, городá, учителя́, докторá, лесá, лугá) is used by a significant number of masculine nouns. For a detailed listing of nouns which form a plural in -á, see *Грамматика 1980* (§1202, 1203, 1204, 1243, 1245).

This group of nouns is expanding, and more forms with -á are accepted as standard as time goes on. An example is тракторá 'tractors' (with трáкторы equally acceptable), on the model of/*by analogy to* other foreign words in -тор, such as инспéктор 'inspector', and дóктор 'doctor', which have long had a plural in -á. Many more nouns are used with this ending in substandard speech, e.g., офицéр ~ офицерá 'officer'.

2.2.6. A relatively small number of neuter nouns have the endings -*ов* and -*ей* in the genitive plural: очкó 'point; pip' ~ очкóв, óблако 'cloud' ~ облакóв, мóре 'sea' ~ морéй, пóле 'field' ~ полéй. It is interesting that almost every beginning Russian textbook uses either мóре or пóле as the model for a neuter soft stem, even though the genitive plural forms are irregular from the standpoint of the system of declension in Russian. The reason for choosing one of these two is simple: these two nouns are the *only* neuter nouns whose stem ends in a soft paired consonant (there is a third, гóре 'woe', but it does not have plural forms from this stem). The regular neuter gen. pl. in -Ø is seen in numerous nouns which end in unpaired consonant plus {o}: здáние 'building' ~ здáний, жилúще 'abode' ~ жилúщ. Choosing a model which is irregular and represented by only two words, instead of regular and represented by many words, is bad pedagogy and bad scholarship.

2.2.7. A significant number of masculine nouns have the -Ø ending in the gen. pl. Examples are солдáт, раз, глаз, грамм. One interesting case is nom. sg. вóлос, gen. pl. волóс, where the two forms have different stresses. For a detailed listing of masculine nouns which have a zero ending in the gen. pl. , see *Грамматика 1980* (§1207).

Nouns of nationality with the suffix -*ин* lose the -*ин* in the plural, as noted below, have -*e* in the nom. pl., and have -Ø in the gen. pl.: англичáнин ~ англичáне ~ англичáн ~ англичáнам. For a detailed treatment of nouns with the suffix -*ин*, see *Грамматика 1980* (§1213).

Two special cases to note are господи́н, господа́ (pl. in -*á*), госпо́д, господа́м; граждани́н, гра́ждане (stress shifts from suffix to first syllable of stem), гра́ждан, гра́жданам.

2.2.8. Some nouns have stem changes between the sg. and the pl., e.g. бра́тья 'brothers', коло́сья 'ears of grain' (← ко́лос), дере́вья 'trees' (← де́рево) which show softening plus an inserted suffix {j} before an unstressed {a} ending: (/brátja/, /kalóṣja/). Some changes seem to be confined to as few as two or three words (e.g., сосе́д ~ сосе́ди 'neighbor', чёрт ~ че́рти 'devil', коле́но ~ коле́ни 'knee', which show softening plus /i/ as the ending).

Changes between sg. and pl. usually involve lengthening the stem in the plural (e.g. брат ~ бра́тья, перо́ ~ пе́рья, муж ~ мужья́, сын ~ сыновья́), with an inserted {-j-} or {-ovj-}, but in at least one set of words a suffix *(-ин)* is removed in the plural (e.g., англича́нин ~ англича́не 'Englishman', which shows loss of the suffix *-ин*).[1] Sometimes one suffix is replaced by another: телёнок 'calf' ~ теля́та.

The gen. pl. of those nouns which have stressed {-já}, spelled *-ья́*, is {-ejØ} with fill vowel {e} before {j}, spelled *-е́й:* мужья́ ~ муже́й, сыновья́ ~ сынове́й. If the ending is unstressed {-ja}, spelled *-ья*, then the gen. pl. takes the ending {-ov}, spelled *-ьев*, also unstressed: бра́тья ~ бра́тьев, дере́вья ~дере́вьев, сту́лья ~ сту́льев, коло́сья ~ коло́сьев.

For a detailed treatment of nouns with pl. stems which differ from the sg. stems, see *Грамматика 1980* (§1208–14).

2.3. The Non-Neuter Declension

The *second* declension, with a nom. sg. in {-a}, contains mostly feminine nouns, such as жена́ 'wife', река́ 'river', ла́мпа 'lamp', неде́ля 'week', but it also has a few masculines, such as слуга́ 'servant', ю́ноша 'youth', дя́дя 'uncle', and many diminutives of personal names, such as Ко́ля (← Никола́й), Са́ша (← Алекса́ндр, Алекса́ндра), and some *epicene* (*common gender*) nouns, such as пья́ница 'drunkard', сирота́ 'orphan'. This last category normally has a pejorative meaning and can have either feminine or masculine modifiers, depending upon what or who is referenced. Thus, вот го́рькая пья́ница 'there's a confirmed drunkard'

---

[1] This *-ин-* suffix is known as a *singulative* suffix; cf. the same *-ин-* in и́нок 'a monk who lives alone, a hermit monk', and in the old word for 'unicorn' иноро́г (modern единоро́г).

(female referent), but вот го́рький пья́ница (same meaning, but male referent).

2.3.1. The basic endings for the second declension are shown in Table 2-3.

Table 2-3. Second Declension Basic Noun Endings

	Sing.	**Pl.**
Nom.	-а	-ы
Acc.	-у	= nom. or gen.
Gen.	-ы	-Ø
Dat.	-е	-ам
Instr.	-ой/ -ою	-ами
Prep.	-е	-ах

2.3.2. The same rule about *-e* going to *-u* after a stem ending in *-uй* that we saw in 2.1.2 applies here to both the prep. and the dative: ли́ния 'line', dat. & prep. ли́нии, вокализа́ция 'vocalization', dat. & prep. вокализа́ции.

2.3.3. The choice of the endings *-ой* and *-ою* in the instr. sg. depends upon a number of factors, including rhythm, degree of formality, and others. In general, *-ою* is restricted to poetry, the written language and formal varieties of speech, and even there it is the less common of the two forms. The second syllable of *-ою* is never stressed.

2.3.4. Of the second declension nouns whose stem ends in a soft paired consonant or a "husher" before {a}, there is a significant number that should have a gen. pl. in -Ø according to the rules, but in fact have *-ей*. Examples are тётей ← тётя 'aunt', ноздре́й ← ноздря́ 'nostril', дя́дей ← дя́дя 'uncle', ю́ношей ← ю́ноша 'lad, youth'. These simply have to be learned.

2.3.5. Fill vowels. In nouns the -Ø ending occurs in the nom. sg. of first declension masculines, in the gen. pl of first declension neuters and second declension feminines, and in the nom. sg. of third declension feminines (see 2.4.1). In many words the -Ø ending is preceded by a consonant cluster. In most cases these clusters will be broken up by a "fill" or "mobile" vowel. The clusters {st}, {zd}, and {stv} are normally left alone: мост 'bridge' (nom. sg.), звёзд (gen. pl. ← звезда́ 'star'), веще́ств (gen. pl. ← вещество́ 'substance'). Clusters consisting of a nasal consonant ({m} or {n}) plus a stop consonant made in the same position in the mouth are also usually left: ламп 'lamps' (gen. pl.), бомб 'bombs' (gen. pl.), бунт 'revolt', фонд 'fund; stock; archive', банк 'bank', ранг 'rank'. In borrowed words the clusters -*mp* and -*др* are also left alone: gen. sg. ве́тра 'wind', теа́тра 'theater', Алекса́ндра 'Alexander' give nom. sg. ве́тер, теа́тр, Алекса́ндр. There are several instances in which a fill vowel is either lacking when expected (бе́здна 'abyss', gen. pl. бездн) or present when not expected ((до́лгий 'long', masc. short form до́лог; see Chapter 4 [Adjectives] for more examples.)

The fill vowels are (Cyrillic) *o*, *e*, *ë*, and, rarely, *u*. Which one to use is determined by another set of ordered rules.

Fill Vowel Rule 1: *after к г х insert o*: окно́ 'window', gen. pl. о́кон,[2] ку́кла 'doll, puppet', gen. pl. ку́кол, ко́готь 'claw' (nom. sg. ← ко́гтя), ку́хня 'kitchen', gen. pl. ку́хонь, у́гол 'corner' (nom. sg. ← угла́ [nom. sg. stress irregular])

Fill Vowel Rule 2: *before hard р л м н insert ë*: сестра́ 'sister', gen. pl. сестёр, котёл 'cauldron, kettle (nom. sg. ← котла́). Although there are quite a few examples for *р* and *л*, there seems to be only one set of words with stressed *ë* before *м*.[3] The good examples for *н* come from adjective short forms: умён ← у́мный 'intelligent, clever', силён ← си́льный 'strong'. Since *р л м* and *н* all belong to a class of consonants called **resonants**, and since three of them produce an unambiguous *ë*, it seems theoretically justified to make a unified rule, rather than leaving *м* unmentioned.

Fill Vowel Rule 3: *before* a soft paired consonant or the unpaired consonants *ц* ({c}) and *й* ({j}), use *e*: земля́ 'land', gen. pl. земе́ль, дере́вня 'village', gen. pl. дереве́нь, се́рдце 'heart', gen. pl. серде́ц, статья́ 'article', gen. pl. стате́й ({staṭjá} → {staṭj} → {staṭej}, with {e}

---

[2] The double stress means that both о́кон and око́н occur as stresses for this word. See the discussion in Chapter 3.

[3] These are all from the root йм-/ьм- 'take; have, get': заём ~ за́йма 'loan', наём ~ на́йма 'rent'. There are a few other words with final hard *м* preceded by a consonant in the gen. pl., but the dictionaries do not explicitly give the forms. More numerous are words with consonant clusters which are not expected to take a fill vowel and do not: катакли́зм 'cataclysm', холм 'hill', фе́рма 'farm', по́йма 'flood', gen. pl. пойм.

inserted into the final cluster). For the spelling of {j}, review 1.5 and 1.6 in Chapter 1.

Fill Vowel Rule 4: *before* any other consonant, use *o*. In fact, what is left is primarily *к:* лóдка 'boat', gen. pl. лóдок, конёк 'horse (dim.), hobby-horse', gen. sg. конькá, сынóк 'son (dim.)', gen. sg. сынкá, чаёк 'tea (dim.)', gen. sg. чайкá, рожóк 'small horn', gen. sg. рожкá, дéвушка 'girl', gen. pl. дéвушек (unstressed -шок → -шек by Spelling Rule 5).

Fill Vowel Rule 5: a few nouns with an unstressed fill vowel {e} before {j} spell the inserted {e} with *и*. This is purely a spelling convention, like the use of *и* for *e* in the prep. sg. of nouns with a stem in *-ий-*, see 2.1.2 above. Thus, гóстья 'female guest', gen. pl. гóстий, повéрье 'superstition', gen. pl. повéрий. The same is true of a group of pronominals whose stem ends in {Cj}, e.g., трéтий, трéтья, лúсий, лúсья; see 5.11.

2.3.5.1. In a few words we have a fill vowel *o* where *ё* or *e* would be expected by the rules given above: e.g., сон 'sleep, dream', gen. sg. снá; любóвь 'love', gen. sg. любвú; in adjectives we have the short form зол from злой 'malicious, evil'. In пёс 'dog', gen. sg. пса, we have *ё* where *o* would be expected.

There are a few nouns with a mobile vowel, always {o}, before the "hushers" *ж ш ч* and *щ*: рожь 'rye', gen. sg. ржи; ложь 'lie', gen. sg. лжи; вошь 'louse', gen. sg. вши.

2.3.5.2. The rules given above *must* be applied in order. Applying Rules Two and Three before One would give the incorrect forms *óкен (← *óкён),*кýкел (← *кýкёл), *кóгеть, *кýкень, *ýгел (← *ýгёл).

2.3.5.3. Remember that according to 1.7.3, the relatively few instances of inserted {o} in verbs are spelled *ё*, e.g., он зажёг, онá зажглá 'ignited', stem за-жг+; он прочёл, онá прочлá 'read', stem про-чт+. In infinitives, *e* is inserted before the soft consonant: зажéчь, прочéсть. See also Chapters 7 and 8.

2.4. The Third Declension

This declension is often incorrectly called the "feminine declension." In fact, nouns of all three genders belong to it, although well over 95% are feminines ending in a soft consonant or husher (e.g., кость 'bone', бровь 'eyebrow', печа́ль 'grief', но́вость 'news' ночь 'night', мышь 'mouse', рожь 'rye', вещь 'thing'). In accordance with 1.3.4, those ending in a husher are written with a soft sign on the end to indicate their gender and declension type.

One masculine noun, путь 'way, path', belongs to this declension (see 2.4.4 below), and ten neuters (e.g., вре́мя 'time') belong to it in the singular only (see 2.4.5 below). The basic endings for the third declension are shown in Table 2-4:

Table 2-4. Third Declension Basic Noun Endings

	Sing.	**Pl.**
Nom.	-Ø	-и
Acc.	-Ø	= nom./gen.
Gen.	-и	-ей
Dat.	-и	-ам
Instr.	-ью	-ами
Prep.	-и	-ах
2nd Prep.	-и́	

2.4.1. In this declension the nom. and acc. sg. always have the same ending: кость, дочь, путь, время.

2.4.2. The instr. sg. ending -ью is never stressed; any stress which should fall on this ending is retracted onto the previous syllable: любо́вь 'love', gen. sg. любви́, but instr. sg. любо́вью, вошь 'louse', gen. sg. вши, but instr. sg. во́шью, глушь 'the sticks, Podunk', gen. dat. prep. sg. глуши́ but instr. sg. глу́шью. The ending -ью can be stressed only in numerals (с пятью́ това́рищами, which is one of the many things that differentiate numerals from nouns (see Chapter 6). There are a few nouns with the instr. pl. ending -ьми́. For дочерьми́, лошадьми́, and людьми́ it is the only orthoepic form. Details in *Грамматика 1980* (§1198).

2.4.3. The second prepositional, or locative, ending in stressed -и́, as with the -у́ of the first declension, is used only with the prepositions в and на, is always stressed on the ending, and occurs only with monosyllabic nouns. Examples are: в ночи́ 'in the night', в грязи́ 'in mud', в связи́ 'in connection, in contact', в крови́ 'in blood', на Руси́ 'in Rus'/Russia'. For a complete list, see *Грамматика 1980* (§1188).

2.4.4. The sole masculine noun belonging to this declension is путь 'way, path'. It differs from the feminines by having an instr. sg. ending -ём: путём. The ending -ём is also used for the ten neuters which belong to this declension (see 2.4.6 below). The endings of путь are all stressed: gen. sg., dat. sg., prep. sg. пути́, pl. пути́, путе́й, путя́м, путя́ми, путя́х.

2.4.5. There are ten neuter nouns (e.g., вре́мя 'time') which belong to the third declension in the singular only; in the plural, they look like ordinary hard stem neuter nouns of the first declension. Since they are non-feminine, they have the (unstressed) ending -ём in the instr. sg. (like путь; see 2.4.4 above). In the singular they all have stress on the first syllable of the stem: nom./acc. вре́мя, gen./dat./prep. вре́мени, instr. вре́менем. Note that in spite of the spelling with -я, the nom./acc. sg. ends in underlying {o}, like other neuters: {vŗémo}; other case forms all lengthen the stem to {vŗémoņ+} (with soft {ņ}) in the singular and {vŗémon+} (with hard {n}) in the plural.

The plural is a hard stem and is end-stressed for nine of the ten nouns: nom./acc. времена́, gen. времён, dat. времена́м, instr. времена́ми, prep. времена́х, but зна́мя 'banner', pl. знамёна. For details, see *Грамматика 1980* (§1190).

2.5. Declension Type and Gender

We have seen that there is no declension which is gender-specific: the first has masculine and neuter nouns; the second has feminine and masculine (and epicene) nouns; the third has nouns of all three genders. Similarly there is almost no ending which is gender-specific. To take some examples: the zero ending in the nom. sg. is used by masc. nouns of the first declension and fem. nouns of the third. In the genitive plural the zero ending is used by nouns of all three genders. The -a ending of the nom. sg. is used by masc. and fem. and epicene nouns of the second declension. The -a ending of the nom. pl. is used by masc. and neuter nouns of the first declension.

Even the less common ways of forming the plural are usually shared by nouns of more than one gender in the singular. A good example is the formation of the plural with an inserted stem addition {j} plus an ending {a} of the nom. pl. This is shared by masc. and neut. nouns: брат ~ бра́тья 'brother', де́рево ~ дере́вья 'tree'.

The instr. sg. in *-ью* of the third declension comes closest to being gender-specific, in that it is used only with feminine nouns, but in numerals it goes with nouns of all three genders: с шестью жёнами, с шестью мужьями, с шестью словами.

2.5.1. Since, with the exception of *-ью*, an ending does not specify the gender of the noun to which it is attached, we must determine the gender of a noun by some other method. This is generally done by considering the forms of words in agreement with the noun. Such words can be adjectives, pronouns, or the past tense of verbs: Эта новая женщина пришла, этот новый мужчина пришёл, это новое вещество пришло (по почте).

In the singular gender is established easily, but in the plural no such method is to be found: Эти новые женщины/мужчины /вещества пришли. Indeed, no amount of trying will find a method. Pronouns, adjectives, and the past tense of verbs all have but a single form for the plural in each case. Nouns themselves have no gender-specific case endings in the plural. The nominative in *-ы* is used for masc., fem., and some neut. The gen. in *-Ø* is used by nouns of all three genders; the gen. in *-ов* is used by masc. and neut.; the gen. in *-ей* is used by all three genders (коней, ночей, морей). The use of the gen. case form for the acc. case of animate nouns, limited in the sg. to masc. nouns, extends to all nouns in the pl.: я вижу коней, жён, чудовищ, подозрительных лиц и животных 'I see steeds, wives, monsters, suspicious persons, and animals'.

2.5.2. After considering the situation thoroughly, we can only conclude that Russian does not distinguish gender in the plural. One can talk about the plural of neuter nouns, as I did above in Table 2-1, but this means "the plural form of nouns which are of neuter gender in the singular." Indeed, we can summarize and restate the rules for forming the plural to cover the nouns of all three declensions and genders (Tables 2-1, 2-3, and 2-4):

Nom. pl. Nouns which end in {-Ø} or {-a}, as well as some in {-o} in the nom. sg., have the ending {-i} in the pl. (столы, жёны, дяди, пьяницы, кости, ночи, пути, очки 'points; eye-glasses', горлышки 'necks of bottles'). Most nouns with {-o} in the sg. have {-a} in the plural (слова, сёла 'villages'), as well as some with {-Ø} in the sg.: (города, бра́тья). The {-a} may be stressed (слова́, города́) or unstressed (сёла, бра́тья).

Gen. pl. See the rules given in 2.1.3. Note again that they apply to all nouns, regardless of gender. Note also that both the zero ending and the {-ej} endings are used by nouns belonging to all three genders in the sg., and that the {-ov} ending is used by nouns belonging to both the masc. and the neut. genders in the sg.

Acc. pl. equals nom. pl. or gen. pl. (gen. for animate nouns of all three genders in the sg., as explained in the last paragraph of 2.5.1).

Dat., instr., prep. pl. The endings are {-am}, {-aми}, {-ax} for almost all Russian nouns except the half-dozen instr. in {-ми}.

2.6. Indeclinable Nouns

Nouns which do not fit into the morphological and phonological patterns of Russian do not decline. This includes, among others, nouns ending in a hard consonant which refer to females (мада́м 'madam, lady'), and nouns ending in a vowel not occuring in Russian nouns in the singular (ле́ди 'lady', кенгуру́ 'kangaroo', такси́ 'taxicab', меню́ 'menu', шимпанзе́ 'chimpanzee').[4]

There are also borrowed nouns in stressed and unstressed -o (метро́ 'subway', эмба́рго 'embargo') and in stressed -a (буржуа́ 'burgeois') which do not decline.

Indeclinable nouns referring to female persons are feminine (мада́м, ле́ди); those referring to animals of any sex or male persons are masculine (маэ́стро 'maestro', кенгуру́, шимпанзе́), and all others are neuter (такси́, меню́).

Exercises

I. Give, either orally or in writing, all case forms, both sg. and pl., for the following nouns. The note [F] means that stress is fixed on the same syllable for all forms [Fe] means "fixed on the endings"; the note [S] means that the stress shifts to the other syllable between singular and plural: ме́сто ~ места́, вино́ ~ ви́на. The ё in an unstressed syllable (e.g., жена́) means that when stressed, the resulting vowel will be ё, not e.

---

[4] Native Russian nouns may have an underlying {-o} ending, spelled -e, but not an underlying {-e}. The treatment of шимпанзе́ is one proof that all native Russian neuter nouns have the underlying {-o} rather than {-e}.

1. кни́га [F] 'book'
2. чу́вство [F] 'feeling'
3. неде́ля 'week' [F]
4. черта́ [F] 'line'
5. моро́з [F] 'frost'
6. враг [Fe] 'enemy'
7. ме́сто [S] 'place'
8. мель [F] (f.) 'shallows'
9. вино́ [S] 'wine'
10. жёна́ [S] 'wife'
11. звёзда́ [S] 'star'
12. сёло́ [S] 'village
13. струя́ [S] 'stream'
14. ло́жка [F] 'spoon'
15. воробе́й[Fe](mobile vowel) 'sparrow'
16. княжна́ [F] 'princess'
17. у́лей, у́лья [F] 'bee-hive'

II. Now here are some imaginary nouns to practice on. Give gen. sg., nom. pl., gen. pl. and dat. pl., plus any other form requested, for the following nouns:

1. дли́га [F]
2. волг [Fe]
3. сдинья́ [S](instr. & prep. sg.)
4. бло́жка [F]
5. мой [S]
6. звруя́ [S] (instr. sg., prep. sg.)
7. стрия́ [F] instr. sg.
8. по́лья instr. sg. [F]
9. гры́нч instr. sg. [F]
10. осл+Ø [Fe] (nom. sg. has fill vowel)
11. желя́ [F]
12. бринья́ [F] instr. sg.
13. ворг [SR]
14. флочь [SR]

3

Noun Stress

This chapter is a systematic survey of the stress patterns of the Russian noun.

3.1. Stress in Russian

Russian stress (in general, not just for nouns) first subdivides into *fixed* and *shifting*. Fixed stress means that the stress falls in the same place in all forms of the word. Examples are дед 'grandfather', ры́ло 'snout', ла́мпа 'lamp', левша́ 'left-handed person' ("epicene" or "common" gender, irreg gen. pl.).

Table 3-1. Forms of Four Nouns, with Stress

Nom. Sg.	дед	ры́ло	ла́мпа	левша́
Acc. Sg.	= gen.	= nom.	ла́мпу	левшу́
Gen. Sg.	де́да	ры́ла	ла́мпы	левши́
Dat. Sg.	де́ду	ры́лу	ла́мпе	левше́
Instr. Sg.	де́дом	ры́лом	ла́мпой	левшо́й
Prep. Sg.	де́де	ры́ле	ла́мпе	левше́
Nom. Pl.	де́ды	ры́ла	ла́мпы	левши́
Acc. Pl.	= gen.	= nom.	= nom.	= gen.
Gen. Pl.	де́дов	рыл	ламп	левше́й
Dat. Pl.	де́дам	ры́лам	ла́мпам	левша́м
Instr. Pl.	де́дами	ры́лами	ла́мпами	левша́ми
Prep. Pl.	де́дах	ры́лах	ла́мпах	левша́х

The four nouns given all have stress fixed on the same syllable throughout the paradigm. Now consider the following nouns, which are characterized by some textbooks as having shifting stress: стол 'table', карандáш 'pencil', раб 'male slave', рабá 'female slave'.

Table 3-2. Four Nouns with Stem Stress in One Form

Nom. Sg.	стол	карандáш	раб	рабá
Acc. Sg.	= nom.	= nom.	= gen.	рабý
Gen. Sg.	столá	карандашá	рабá	рабы́
Dat. Sg.	столý	карандашý	рабý	рабé
Instr. Sg.	столóм	карандашóм	рабóм	рабóй
Prep. Sg.	столé	карандашé	рабé	рабé
Nom. Pl.	столы́	карандаши́	рабы́	рабы́
Acc. Pl.	= nom.	= nom.	= gen.	= gen.
Gen. Pl.	столóв	карандашéй	рабóв	раб
Dat. Pl.	столáм	карандашáм	рабáм	рабáм
Instr. Pl.	столáми	карандашáми	рабáми	рабáми
Prep. Pl.	столáх	карандашáх	рабáх	рабáх

The reasoning usually given for calling this "shifting" stress is that the stress "shifts" from the stem in the nom. sg. (стол, карандáш, раб) to the endings in the other cases (столá, карандашá, рабá, etc.) or from the endings in nom. sg., gen. sg., etc. (рабá, рабы́) to the stem in the gen. pl. (раб).

In which circumstances does the alleged shift occur? Only in those cases when there is no possible choice of the place of the stress, since one cannot stress something that is not there (the -Ø ending, in this case). Each of the four words puts the stress on any ending present, and by default puts the stress on the last syllable before the ending when the ending has no phonetic realization that could bear a stress. In order to speak of a shift, we must have at least two possible places of stress, as in страны́ 'country' (gen. sg.) ~ стрáны (nom. pl.).

You may have noted that the nom. sg. forms стол and раб and the gen. pl. form раб do not have a stress written on them. This is because the placement of the stress is automatic, on the only syllable of the word. In the case of карандáш, we need to have the stress mark written to tell us which of the three syllables bears the stress. If we were to write the nom. sg. as карандашǾ, then we could say that end stress is automatically retracted from the zero ending and has to be on the last realized syllable of the word.

When stress is fixed on the endings of a noun which has a zero ending in the nom. sg. (the citation form), we will denote this by the letters *Fe* in brackets; if it is fixed on the syllable which is stressed in the nom. (whether stem or ending), this will be shown by a simple *F* in brackets. The eight nouns considered so far would thus have stress marked as: дед [F], рыло [F], лампа [F], левша [F], стол [Fe], карандаш [Fe], раб [Fe], раба [F].[1]

3.2. Shifting Stress

We may say that stress *shifts* in declension and conjugation when a choice of syllables is available and it is on one syllable (e.g., the first) in some forms and on another syllable (e.g., the last) in other forms.

The contrast, or shift, may be either 1) between stem and endings, or 2) between different syllables of the stem. The only two nominal endings with more than one syllable are the instr. sg. in *-ою* and the instr. pl. in *-ами*. Neither of these endings permits stress on the last syllable, so shift between syllables of an ending is not possible. In the case of the half-dozen nouns with *-ьми* in the instr. pl., the stress falls on the only syllable of the ending.

Table 3-3. Examples of Stress Shift from Stem to Ending

Nom. Sg.	Gen. Sg.	Nom. Pl.	Gen. Pl.	Dat. Pl.
го́род	го́рода	города́	городо́в	города́м
час	ча́са	часы́	часо́в	часа́м
сло́во	сло́ва	слова́	слов	слова́м
вре́мя	вре́мени	времена́	времён	времена́м

There are no feminine nouns (of either the second or the third declension) with this stress pattern.

---

[1] Exercise: try to pronounce the zero ending of стол ,каранда́ш, and раб.

Table 3-4. Examples of Stress Shift from Ending to Stem

Nom. Sg.	Gen. Sg.	Nom. Pl.	Gen. Pl.	Dat. Pl.
лицо́	лица́	ли́ца	лиц	ли́цам
страна́	страны́	стра́ны	стран	стра́нам
колбаса́	колбасы́	колба́сы	колба́с	колба́сам
волокно́	волокна́	воло́кна	воло́кон	воло́кнам

There are no more than 14 masculine nouns of the first declension with this type of stress.[2]

3.2.1. The last two words in the table, колбаса́ 'sausage', and волокно́ 'fiber, filament' introduce a new complication, since the stem has more than one syllable and we need to know which syllable the stress shifts to.

When stress shifts from the stem to the ending, it by definition must skip over intervening syllables (if any) of the stem to reach the ending, as in го́род, nom. pl. города́, ко́локол 'bell', nom. pl. колокола́, но́вость 'news', dat. pl. новостя́м, вре́мя 'time', nom. pl. времена́.

When the stress moves back from the ending to the stem, it may either move one syllable, as in колбаса́ 'sausage', nom. pl. колба́сы, or it may move all the way back to the beginning, as in тягота́ 'burden, care', nom. pl. тя́готы, and сторона́ 'side', nom. pl. сто́роны. The ultimate example of this type of move is сковорода́ 'frying pan', nom. pl. ско́вороды.

3.2.2. In most words with only one syllable in the stem, we cannot determine whether the stress moves back only one syllable or moves back to the initial syllable, since the syllable before the endings and the initial syllable are the same: лицо́ ~ ли́ца, страна́ ~ стра́ны. In some words, however, a fill vowel is inserted in the gen. pl., and then we can differentiate: сосна́ 'pine', nom. pl. со́сны, gen. pl. со́сен, with stress in the plural on the first syllable, but сестра́ 'sister', nom. pl. сёстры, gen. pl. сестёр with stress on the syllable before the endings. In every form of the plural except the gen., the syllable before the ending is also the first syllable: со́сны, со́снам, со́снами, со́снах, but со́сен has

---

[2] Fedjanina 1982: 71 lists the fourteen, but the only example which does not require at least special considerations seems to be каза́к gen. sg. казака́, pl. каза́ки 'Cossack'. Many of the remaining words use a different stem in the plural, and Avanesov 1989 regards the others as not having a singular.

two syllables in the stem and thus can differentiate; сёстры, сёстрам, сёстрами, сёстрах but сестёр with two syllables can also differentiate. We can see easily that сосен is stressed on the initial syllable but сестёр is stressed on the syllable before the ending (-Ø in both cases).

A similar pair is given by числó 'number', gen. pl. чúсел with stress on the initial syllable, but земля́ 'land', gen. pl. земéль with stress on the syllable before the ending. In each case where the stress is on the syllable before the ending, this means that the stress has moved back one syllable from the ending, rather than all the way to the beginning.

3.2.2.1. We have just discussed another important concept: stress on the syllable before the endings. This applies to колбáсы and сестёр, but it also applies to заём 'loan', gen. sg. зáйма. This word does not shift stress—it is always stressed on the syllable before the endings.

3.2.3. The question of stress in the gen. pl. shows how important it is to apply the rules in proper order: first the fill vowel is inserted, then the determination of stress is made. If the stress were placed before the fill vowel is inserted, we would wind up with initial stress in all such cases. Consider сестрá: after we remove the final vowel, giving gen. pl. сестр, if we first place the stress on the ё, then insert the fill vowel, we get incorrect *сёстер. Similarly with земля́: after the final vowel is removed, leaving зéмль, if the stress is placed on the initial and only vowel, before inserting the fill vowel, we get incorrect *зéмель.

The double gen. pl. stress of окнó (óкон and окóн; see Chapter 2, section 2.2.5), is a result of uncertainty about which accent class окнó belongs to: nouns with initial stress in the plural or nouns with stress on the syllable before the endings.

3.2.4. The principle that stress may move either only one syllable or "skip" (move all the way to the other end of the word) applies not only when moving from the ending to the stem, but also when moving from the first syllable (or, in plurals in -á, from a middle syllable) toward the end of the word. Thus the plurals гóрод ~ городá, дирéктор ~ директорá, кóлокол ~ колоколá, зéркало ~ зеркалá 'mirror' shift all the way to the end, but кóлос 'ear of grain' ~ колóсья, óзеро 'lake' ~ озёра, дéрево 'tree' ~ дерéвья have a shift of only one syllable forward.

3.2.5. Nouns which have shifting stress will be marked with [S], unless it is a masc. noun with a nom. pl. in -á, in which case [á] will be used, since this notation simultaneously gives us the nom. pl. ending and shows the place of the accent throughout the plural (example: го́род [á] shows us that the pl. forms are nom. города́, gen. городо́в, acc. города́, dat. города́м, instr. города́ми, prep. города́х).

Since shift between beginning and end of the word or end and beginning is by far the most common pattern, nouns having this pattern will be marked with [S] only. Those where the movement is only one syllable will be marked with [S1]. We thus have страна́, nom. pl. стра́ны with a citation form страна́ [S], зе́ркало, nom. pl. зеркала́ with a citation form зе́ркало [S] and so forth. The nouns о́зеро, nom. pl. озёра, колбаса́, nom. pl. колба́сы, and волокно́ , nom. pl. воло́кна are marked with [S1]: о́зеро [S1], колбаса́ [S1] and волокно́ [S1],

As we will see when discussing verbs, the same principles of stress movement apply there, although the options are more limited. In the past tense, the only movement is between beginning and end (на́чал 'begin', начала́, на́чало; пе́режил 'live through, experience', пережила́, пе́режило), and in the present tense shifting one syllable back from the ending is the only type that occurs (бормота́ть 'mutter', бормочу́, бормо́чешь).

3.3. Patterns of Stress Movement

Stress movement in Russian *nouns* is used to make two basic distinctions: the place of stress may 1) distinguish sg. from pl., or it may 2) distinguish the *direct* cases (nom. and acc.) from the *oblique* cases (gen., dat., instr., prep.), or both types may occur in the same word. Examples of type 1 are: го́род ~ города́, сло́во ~ слова́, лицо́ ~ ли́ца, страна́ ~ стра́ны (citation forms го́род [á], сло́во [S], лицо́ [S], страна́ [S]).

Since Russian does not have a separate form for the acc. pl. (of any gender; see 2.4.1 and 2.4.2), there cannot be a stress distinction in the acc. pl. form. Similarly, because there is no separate form for the acc. sg. in any nouns of the first declension or the third declension, there also cannot be a stress distinction in the form of the acc. sg. in the first or third declensions.

In all three genders, the nom. sg. does not distinguish itself from the gen., dat., instr., and prep. by place of stress (for a discussion of the surface difference in end-stressed nouns with a zero ending, see 3.1 above). This means that in the sg. only the acc. of fem. nouns in -*á* may have a different place of stress (e.g. рука́ ~ ру́ку), since all other nouns have

acc. sg. equal to either nom. sg. or gen. sg.. In the pl. only the nom. may
have a place of stress different from the other cases (e.g. ру́ки ~ рука́м).

This difference of stress in acc. sg. and/or nom. pl. is always by *retraction*, and it is always the "skipping" type (all the way back to the first
syllable of the stem, if there is more than one stem syllable). Examples of
the acc. sg. are: гора́ 'mountain' ~ го́ру, сторона́ 'side' ~ сто́рону, and,
at the extreme, our friend сковорода́, which has a somewhat old-fashioned acc. sg. stress ско́вороду. In the nom. pl. we find the same words
with retraction: го́ры, сто́роны, ско́вороды (the only possible stress).

In general, words which have retraction in the acc. sg. have it in
the nom. pl., but the reverse is not true: a number of words which have
retraction in the nom. pl. do not have it in the acc. sg. Examples are:
слеза́ 'tear', acc. слезу́, nom. pl. слёзы, gen. pl. слёз, dat. pl. слеза́м,
and masc. конь 'steed', gen. sg. коня́, nom. pl. ко́ни, gen. pl. коне́й, dat.
pl. коня́м. In both слеза́ and конь every form except the nom. pl. is end
stressed (if, of course, there is an ending to stress; see 3.1 above).

3.3.1. Nouns which have *retraction* in both the acc. sg. and the nom.
pl. will be marked with *R* (retraction in acc. and nom.) in brackets: [R].
Those with retraction in the nom. pl. only will be marked with [Rn]. The
nouns гора́ and сторона́ will thus be marked гора́ [R] and сторона́ [R],
whereas слеза́ and конь will be слёза́ [Rn] and конь [Rn]. Since retraction is a pulling back from an ending, only nouns with end stress on all
other forms of the sg. can have acc. retraction, and only nouns with end
stress on all other forms of the pl. can have nom. retraction. Retraction
may also be combined with shifting stress: вода́ [SR] means stress re-
tracts in the acc. sg. and shifts back in the pl.

Table 3-5. Stress Retraction

Stem	гора́ [R]	конь [Rn]	слеза́ [Rn]	вода́ [SR]
Nom. Sg.	гора́	конь	слеза́	вода́
Acc. Sg.	го́ру	коня́	слезу́	во́ду
Gen. Sg.	горы́	коня́	слезы́	воды́
Dat. Sg.	горе́	коню́	слезе́	воде́
Nom. Pl.	го́ры	ко́ни	слёзы	во́ды
Gen. Pl.	гор	коне́й	слёз	во́д
Dat. Pl.	гора́м	коня́м	слеза́м	во́дам

Remember that when the oblique cases of the plural are end stressed, this includes the gen.: сторона́ [R], sg. сторона́, сто́рону, стороны́, стороне́, стороно́й, стороне́, pl. сто́роны, сто́роны, *сторо́н*, сторона́м, сторона́ми, сторона́х.

3.3.2. There is a common pattern of stress in Russian where the stress is on the first syllable of the stem in all forms of the sg. and in the nom. pl., with all other forms of the plural having final stress. This pattern is called Eplobl. (pronounced "éppleobble") by some books, meaning "end stress on the oblique case forms of the plural."

Here we encounter a significant issue of description: do we add one more designation of stress pattern to our list, or can this pattern be accounted for by using the types we already have? If we regard it as shifting stress with retraction in the nom., we accurately describe the facts and avoid complicating our list. In general, the best description is the one which accounts for all the observed facts in the simplest possible way.

Nouns of this pattern ([SRn]) occur with masc. nouns of the first declension (e.g., зуб 'tooth', волк 'wolf') and fem. nouns of the third declension (e.g. кость 'bone', но́вость 'news, new information').

Table 3-6 Nouns with the [SRn] Pattern

Stem	зуб [SRn]	волк [SRn]	кость [SRn]	но́вость [SRn]
Nom. Sg.	зуб	волк	кость	но́вость
Acc. Sg.	зуб	во́лка	кость	но́вость
Gen. Sg.	зу́ба	во́лка	ко́сти	но́вости
Dat. Sg.	зу́бу	во́лку	ко́сти	но́вости
Nom. Pl.	зу́бы	во́лки	ко́сти	но́вости
Gen. Pl.	зубо́в	волко́в	косте́й	новосте́й
Dat. Pl.	зуба́м	волка́м	костя́м	новостя́м

3.3.3. To summarize, there are two basic types of Russian noun stress: *fixed* ([F], with the notation [Fe] not representing a different type of fixed stress, but being used for clarity where the nom. sg. is ambiguous) and *shifting* ([S]), with the shift possible either from stem to ending or ending to stem. Shifting has a less common subtype in which the shift is only by one syllable ([S1]); in this case the shift may be from one syllable of the stem to the next syllable of the stem (toward the end of the word) or from the ending back toward the beginning of the word, to the last syllable of the stem before the endings.

A type of shift specific to individual forms is *retraction*, which can take place in the acc. sg. and nom. pl. of fem. nouns in -*á* (marked [R]), or in the nom. pl. of nouns of all three genders and declensions (marked [Rn]).

Examples of the various types are 1) fixed: дед [F], стол [Fe], статья́ [F], кни́га [F]; 2) shifting: дар [S], шаг [S], бой [S], час [S], ус [S], сло́во [S], го́род [á], страна́ [S], лицо́ [S]; 3) shifting by one syllable: ко́лос [S1ья], колбаса́ [S1]; 4) retracting: конь [FeRn], сторона́ [R], губа́ [SR], вода́ [SR], но́вость [SRn], зуб [SRn], волк [SRn], вор [SRn], ло́коть [SRn].

3.4. Predicting Stress Patterns

In the preceding pages of this chapter we have discussed the patterns of fixed and shifting stress. Let us now take up the question of to what extent you can narrow down the possible stress patterns for a given word. It is very useful to have less possibilities to worry about, and of course it is particularly reassuring to know that stress does not shift in a word.

We will start from the dictionary form of nouns, that is to say, the nominative singular.

3.4.1. Nouns which are stressed on any syllable other than the first or last will never shift stress: неде́ля, боло́то, маши́на, cannot and will not change the place of the stress. There is one important exception to this rule: a number of masculine nouns with the plural in -*á* do shift: профе́ссор ~ профессора́, учи́тель ~ учителя́.

3.4.2. Nouns ending in -*a* in the nominative singular never shift if the -*a* is not stressed. Thus, кни́га, неде́ля, and ла́мпа cannot shift, whereas рука́, сестра́, жена́, and земля́ can and do shift in various ways; черта́ and статья́ can shift, but do not.

3.4.3. Two-syllable nouns ending in -*o* or -*e* may and frequently do shift stress: сло́во, де́ло, село́, окно́, кольцо́, мо́ре. Words of three syllables or more usually do not shift, although a few do: зе́ркало ~ зеркала́.

3.4.4. Masculine nouns ending in a consonant do not shift stress unless the stress in the nominative singular is on the first or only syllable; thus, бал, бой, волк, зуб, го́род, бе́рег, can and do shift; дед, у́лей can but do not shift; and горо́х, моро́з, слова́рь [Fe] cannot shift.

3.4.5. Feminine nouns of the third declension have either fixed stress on a syllable of the stem or have stress shift to the endings in the plural, with retraction in the nominative plural. Most nouns in this group have fixed stress if there is more than one syllable in the stem: мель ~ ме́ли, ме́лей, ра́дость ~ ра́дости, ра́достей, but ночь ~ но́чи, ноче́й, кость ~ ко́сти, косте́й, но́вость ~ но́вости, новосте́й.[3]

Exercises

I. First, give, either orally or in writing, all case forms, both sg. and pl., for the following nouns. Second, look up some of the nouns in several dictionaries, both Russian-English and Russian-Russian, to see how the stress patterns are noted. The *ё* in an unstressed syllable means that when stressed, the resulting vowel will be *ё*, not *e* (жёны).

1. кни́га [F] 'book'
2. чу́вство [F] 'feeling'
3. неде́ля [F] 'week'
4. долг [S] 'debt'
5. го́род [á] 'city'
6. де́ло [S] 'deed; business'
7. ме́сто [S] 'place'
8. число́ [S] 'number'
9. вино́ [S] 'wine'
10. жёна́ [S] 'wife'
11. звёзда́ [S] 'star'
12. сёло́ [S] 'village
13. сёстра́ [S1] 'sister'
14. волк [SRn] 'wolf'
15. ночь [SRn] 'night'
16. дверь [SRn] 'door'
17. слёза́ [Rn] 'tear'
18. блоха́ [Rn] 'flea'

---

[3] There is a small group of nouns which decline as members of the third declension but have the stress on the endings of the gen., dat., and prep. of the sg. Most don't have plural forms. The various sources disagree considerably about which words belong to this group, and whether the group exists at all. Probable members of this group include глушь 'backwoods, Podunk', грудь 'chest', любо́вь 'love', ось 'axle', and the place names Обь, Омь, Пермь, Русь, Тверь. Also frequently mentioned are вошь 'louse',. ложь 'lie', and рожь 'rye', but in reality. all three words have no contrast possible in any form, since dropping the fill vowel *o* when there is a non-zero ending makes monosyllables of all forms except the instr. sg. and pl., and the ending -*ью* is non-stressable (see 3.2) and the second syllable of -*ами* is also nonstressable. Вошь has the forms вши in the gen., dat., and prep. sg., and nom. pl.: вшей, вшам, вшах in the gen., dat., and prep. pl., and во́шью, вша́ми in the instr., sg. and pl.

19. водá [SR] 'water'
20. душá [SR] 'soul'
21. головá [R] 'head'
22. горá [R] 'mountain'
23. ногá [R] 'foot'
24. рекá [R] 'river'
25. стенá [R] 'wall'
26. щёкá [R] 'cheek'
27. колбасá [S1] 'sausage'
28. красотá [S1] 'beauty'
29. кольцó [S1] 'ring'
30. таврó [Rn or S, g. pl. тавр] 'brand/blaze on an animal'
31. враг [Fe] 'enemy'
32. бровь [SRn] 'brow' (f)
33. гвоздь [FeRn] 'nail' (m)
34. чертá [F] 'line'
35. мост [S and E] 'bridge'
36. окнó [S] 'window'
37. окнó [S1] 'window
38. земля́ [S1R] 'land, earth'

39. овцá [S1] 'ewe'
40. свинья́ '[S1] 'swine, pig'
41. тюрьмá [S] 'prison'
42. лóжка [F] 'spoon'
43. воробéй [Fe] 'sparrow' (mobile vowel)
44. мель [F] 'shallows' (f)
45. стёклó [S] 'glass'
46. бой [S] 'battle'
47. струя́ [S] 'stream'
48. скобá [Rn] 'clamp'
49. плеть [SRn] 'lash' (f)
50. сéно [S] 'hay'
51. кнут [Fe] 'whip'
52. пéкарь [á] 'baker'
53. пéрстень [SRn] 'ring'
54. четá [F] 'pair, couple'
55. ольхá [S] 'alder'
56. княжнá [F] 'princess'
57. ýлей, ýлья [F] 'bee-hive'

II. Here are some imaginary nouns to practice on. Give gen. sg., nom. pl., gen. pl. and dat. pl., plus any other form requested, for the following nouns:

1. слúга [F]
2. чéльство [F]
3. дедéня [F] (instr. sg.)
4. болг [S]
5. пóгод [á]
6. ривлó [S1]
7. свёздó [S]
8. вёздрá [S] acc. sg.
9. золк [S]
10. рочь [SRn]
11. плезá [Rn] acc. sg.
12. годá [SR] acc. sg.
13. долтарá [S1] acc. sg.

14. торьцó [S1]
15. свость [FeRn] (m) (instr. sg.)
16. стинья́ [S](instr. & prep. sg.)
17. дяльмó [S]
18. клóжка [F]
19. своболéй [Fe] (mobile vowel) (prep. sg.)
20. лой [S]
21. збруя́ [S] (instr.&prep sg.)
22. пéнзель+Ø [á] instr. sg.
23. щукá [R] acc. sg.

24. стрия́ [F] instr. sg.
25. гла́тмо [S]
26. то́лья [F] instr. sg.
27. ры́нч+Ø [SRn]
28. шосе́й [F] instr. sg. (gen. sg. is шося́)
29. лавро́ [S1]
30. осл+Ø [Fe] nom. sg. (has fill vowel)
31. дорозда́ [FR] acc. sg.
32. шеля́ [F]
33. ко́лоз [á]
34. читло́ [S]
35. дестра́ [S]
36. лочь [SRn]
37. нольцо́ [S1]
38. черта́ [F]
39. щемля́ [S]
40. окцо́ [S]
41. тринья́ [F] instr. sg.

42. шольцо́ [F]
43. ли́па [F]
44. гра́вство [F]
45. зеля́ [S]
46. вдолк [Fe]
47. зело́ [F]
48. висло́ [S]
49. местра́ [S] acc. sg.
50. ворк [SRn]
51. длочь [SRn]
52. сверь [SRn] instr. sg. (m)
53. жлеза́ [S] acc. sg.
54. руша́ [SR] acc. sg.
55. голова́ [FR] acc. sg.
56. щёка́ [SR] acc. sg.
57. колбаса́ [S1] acc. sg.
58. вотобе́й [F]
59. ротосе́й [F] instr. sg. (mobile vowel in last syllable)

4

Adjectives

4.1. Declension of Adjectives

Adjective declension is simpler than that of nouns. Adjectives have only one set of endings, whose written form is determined by the same spelling rules given in Chapter 1. The only case/number indicator with more than one form is the nom. sg. masc., which has *-ой* when stressed, *-ый* when not; e.g., молодо́й but холо́дный.

The relevant rules are:

Spelling Rule 1 (in 1.1): *ы* becomes *и* after *к, г,* and *х*;

Spelling Rule 3 (in 1.3.5): after *ш ж ч щ* for underlying {a e i u] use the letters *a e u y*; see Rule 5 for *o* and *ё*;

Spelling Rule 4 (also in 1.3.5): after the letter *ц* use *a e ы y*; see Rule 5 for *o* and *ё*;

Spelling Rule 5 (in 1.7.3): applies to noun and adjective endings: if {o} is stressed after *ш ж ц ч щ*, spell it with the letter *o*, if not, spell it with the letter *e*.

Table 4-1. The Adjective Endings

	Sing.			Pl.
	Masc.	**Neut.**	**Fem.**	
Nom.	-ый/-ой	-ое	-ая	-ые
Acc.	= nom. or gen.	= nom.	-ую	= nom.or gen.
Gen.	-ого		-ой	-ых
Dat.	-ому		-ой	-ым
Instr.	-ым		-ой/ -ою	-ыми
Prep.	-ом		-ой	-ых

The adjective большо́й 'big' and the comparative бо́льший 'bigger' provide good examples of the application of Rule 5: gen. sg. m. большо́го 'big', бо́льшего 'bigger', prep. sg. m. большо́м 'big', бо́льшем 'bigger'. See also све́жий and чужо́й in 4.1.4.

Table 4-2. A Typical Hard-Stem Adjective: но́вый 'new'

	Sing.			Pl.
	Masc.	**Neut.**	**Fem.**	
Nom.	но́вый	но́вое	но́вая	но́вые
Acc.	= n. or g.	= nom.	но́вую	= n. or g.
Gen.	но́вого		но́вой	но́вых
Dat.	но́вому		но́вой	но́вым
Instr.	но́вым		но́вой/ -ою	но́выми
Prep.	но́вом		но́вой	но́вых

4.1.1. An end-stressed adjective such as молодо́й 'young' differs in the endings from но́вый only in the nom. sg. masc. If an ending has two syllables, the stress always falls on the first syllable of the ending: молодо́го, молодо́му, молода́я, молодо́е, молоды́е, молоды́ми.

4.1.2. Stems ending in a paired soft consonant never have end stress; most of them have /ŋ/ as the final consonant.

Table 4-3. A Typical Soft-Stem Adjective: си́ний 'blue'

	Sing.			Pl.
	Masc.	**Neut.**	**Fem.**	
Nom.	си́ний	си́нее	си́няя	си́ние
Acc.	= n. or g.	= nom.	си́нюю	= n. or g.
Gen.	си́него		си́ней	си́них
Dat.	си́нему		си́ней	си́ним
Instr.	си́ним		си́ней/ -ею	си́ними
Prep.	си́нем		си́ней	си́них

4.1.3. Adjectives which use Spelling Rule 1 include ди́кий 'wild' and глухо́й 'deaf'.

Table 4-4. A Stem-Stressed Velar Stem: ди́кий 'wild'

	Sing.			Pl.
	Masc.	**Neut.**	**Fem.**	
Nom.	ди́кий	ди́кое	ди́кая	ди́кие
Acc.	= n. or g.	= nom.	ди́кую	= n. or g.
Gen.	ди́кого		ди́кой	ди́ких
Dat.	ди́кому		ди́кой	ди́ким
Instr.	ди́ким		ди́кой/ -ою	ди́кими
Prep.	ди́ком		ди́кой	ди́ких

Table 4-5. An End-Stressed Velar Stem: глухо́й 'deaf'

	Sing.			Pl.
	Masc.	**Neut.**	**Fem.**	
Nom.	глухо́й	глухо́е	глуха́я	глухи́е
Acc.	= n. or g.	= n.	глуху́ю	= n. or g.
Gen.	глухо́го		глухо́й	глухи́х
Dat.	глухо́му		глухо́й	глухи́м
Instr.	глухи́м		глухо́й/ -о́ю	глухи́ми
Prep.	глухо́м		глухо́й	глухи́х

4.1.4. Adjectives which apply Spelling Rules 3 and 5 include све́жий 'fresh' and чужо́й 'foreign'.

Table 4-6. A Stem-Stressed Adjective in *ш ж ч щ*

	Sing.			Pl.
	Masc.	**Neut.**	**Fem.**	
Nom.	све́жий	све́жее	све́жая	све́жие
Acc.	= n. or g.	= nom.	све́жую	= n. or g.
Gen.	све́жего		све́жей	све́жих
Dat.	све́жему		све́жей	све́жим
Instr.	све́жим		све́жей/ -ею	све́жими
Prep.	све́жем		све́жей	све́жих

Table 4-7. An End-Stressed Adjective in *ш ж ч щ*

	Sing.			Pl.
	Masc.	**Neut.**	**Fem.**	
Nom.	чужо́й	чужо́е	чужа́я	чужи́е
Acc.	= n. or g.	= nom.	чужу́ю	= n. or g.
Gen.	чужо́го		чужо́й	чужи́х
Dat.	чужо́му		чужо́й	чужи́м
Instr.	чужи́м		чужо́й/ -о́ю	чужи́ми
Prep.	чужо́м		чужо́й	чужи́х

4.1.5. Spelling Rules 4 and 5 are used in ку́цый 'dock-tailed, short-tailed' (this type has only stem stress).

Table 4-8. An Adjective in *ц*

	Sing.			Pl.
	Masc.	**Neut.**	**Fem.**	
Nom.	ку́цый	ку́цее	ку́цая	ку́цые
Acc.	= n. or g.	= nom.	ку́цую	= n. or g.
Gen.	ку́цего		ку́цей	ку́цых
Dat.	ку́цему		ку́цей	ку́цым
Instr.	ку́цым		ку́цей/ -ею	ку́цыми
Prep.	ку́цем		ку́цей	ку́цых

4.1.6. In 1.8.4 the pronunciation of unstressed underlying {a} {e} {o} in noun and adjective endings was discussed with attention to nouns. Let us now consider adjectives.

4.1.6.1. As can be seen from Table 4-1 above, underlying {e} does not occur as the first or only vowel in adjective endings. The adjective endings with an underlying {o} or {a} as the first or only vowel are shown in Table 4-9 on the next page. The pronunciation of underlying {o} and {a} in adjective endings after soft and unpaired consonants depends partly upon the case form, with the nominative having one set of rules and the "oblique" cases having another. In the nominative, in both syllables of the ending, unstressed underlying {o} and {a} are always reduced to [ə], so синяя and синее are both realized as [şíŋəjə], both свежая and свежее as [syéžəjə], and both куцая and куцее as [kúcəjə].

The fem. and neut. sg. nom. endings are thus pronounced identically when unstressed: [əjə]. Note that the realization of the neut. sg. form as [ə] implies an underlying {o} in the second syllable. The nom. pl. is pronounced either [ɨji]/[iji] or [ɨjə]/ [ijə], with both variants heard among educated native speakers. This means that the underlying form for the first pronunciation has to be {iji}, and for the second {ijo} or {ija}. The second pronunciation ([ɨjə]), which is becoming less common, can be explained historically, but it is the ([ɨji]) which is of interest at the moment.

Table 4-9. Adjective Endings Beginning with {o} or {a}

	Sing.			Pl.
	Masc.	**Neut.**	**Fem.**	
Nom.	-ой	-ое	-ая	
Gen.	-ого		-ой	
Dat.	-ому		-ой	
Instr.			-ой/ -ою	
Prep.	-ом		-ой	

4.1.6.2. If we look at the endings of the fem. nom. sg., neut. nom. sg., nom. pl., and fem. acc. sg., what sort of generalization about their form can we make? To help you along, here are the endings listed: {aja}, {ojo}, {iji}, {uju}. Think before you go to the next paragraph.

The generalization is (roll of drums, breathless anticipation).... (see footnote).[1]

This interesting pattern can be explained historically, but that belongs to another course. At the moment, let's see if we can find a pattern in the masc. sg. nom. adjective ending. If our theory about the adjective endings is correct and the noun ends in {Ø}, then the adjective should end in {ØjØ}.

What would be the phonetic realization of {ØjØ}? Let's look at Chapter 2, where we have {Ø} as the ending in the nom. sg. and gen. pl.,

---

[1] The adjective endings of the fem. and neut. sg. and the pl. in the direct cases are the noun endings ({a}, {o}, {i}, {u}) doubled, with a {j} inserted between the two identical vowels.

of various nouns. Note that a final {Ø} produces a vowel before itself if the stem before the -Ø ends in two or more consonants. See the discussion of fill vowels in 2.2.5.

In effect, we have an alternation of vowel and Ø between the stem consonants. What would otherwise be CØCØ (where C = consonant) becomes CVC (where V = vowel). Thus сна, сну, сном, сны, etc. give a nom. sg. сон from {sØnØ}. If CØCØ gives CVC, then it is no surprise that the masc. nom. sg. adjective ending {ØjØ} gives {-oj}, spelled -ой. The only remaining questions are why the inserted vowel is /o/ instead of the expected /e/ before /j/, and where the form -ый comes from. The answers to both questions will be given in Appendix 1, Section 11.1.10, when we discuss Church Slavonicisms in Russian.

4.1.6.3. The pronunciation of the oblique case forms of adjectives after soft or unpaired consonants varies from speaker to speaker. The older pronunciation reduces underlying unstressed {o} to [ə], yielding [şíŋəvə], [şíŋəmu], [şíŋəm], [şíŋəj]. The newer, and spreading, pronunciation reduces underlying unstressed {o} to [i], thus acting as if the underlying vowel were {e}, and yielding [şíŋivə], [şíŋimu], [şíŋim], [şíŋij]. For details, see Avanesov 1968, §84. For a slightly different view, compare Panov 1967, §530 and 531.

4.2. Short Forms and Inserted Vowels

Qualitative adjectives (words like новый, чёрный, крепкий, узкий, высокий) may have a set of *short* forms when used in predicate position. These short forms have the same endings as nouns of the corresponding gender: {Ø, a, o, i}: нов, нова, ново, новы.

The masculine short forms in {Ø}, as the case with any forms with a zero ending, may produce inserted vowels, as discussed in 2.2.5 and 4.1.6.2. Examples are: злой ~ зол, интересный ~ интересен, резкий ~ резок, сильный ~ силён, смешной ~ смешон, стройный ~ строен, умный~умён, хитрый~ хитёр. In some words the expected inserted vowel does not appear: беглый~ бегл, быстрый ~ быстр, ветхий ~ ветх, мокрый ~ мокр, наглый ~ нагл, пёстрый ~ пёстр, рыхлый ~ рыхл, смуглый ~ смугл (for a list, see 4.5.3). This absence of the fill vowel is opposed to the more regular manifestation of the fill vowel in nouns: угол, уголь, окон, сестёр, земель. Most of the adjectives which do not use fill vowels have {r} or {l} at the end of the stem. We can denote the absence of an expected fill vowel with [f̶v̶]. The main environment where expected fill vowels do *not* appear in nouns is at the end of borrowed words in -*p*: театр [f̶v̶], Александр [f̶v̶]. For adjectives one can be sure that the fill vowel *will* appear with the suffixes {-n} and {-k}, which are the two most frequent suffixes.

4.3. Stress Patterns in Adjectives

4.3.1. The stress in a long form may fall on any syllable of the stem or the first syllable of the ending (see 4.1.1): вéчный, серéбряный, серебрúстый, холóдный, молодóй, смешнóй, немóй, молодóго, молодáя, молодóю, молодые, молодыми. The place of the stress does not change in declension or between genders.

Table 4-10. Disyllabic Adjective Endings (Underlined)

	Sing.			Pl.
	Masc.	**Neut.**	**Fem.**	
Nom.	немóй	немóе	немáя	немые
Acc.	= n. or g.	= nom.	немýю	= n. or g.
Gen.	немóго		немóй	немых
Dat.	немóму		немóй	немым
Instr.	немым		немóй/ -óю	немыми
Prep.	немóм		немóй	немых

4.3.2. Although the short forms of adjectives have noun endings, their stress patterns do not fully coincide with those of nouns. Like nouns, adjective short forms may have fixed stress. This is usually on the stem, but in some important lexical items is on the ending.

Examples of stem stress in the short forms are: вéчный ~ вéчен, вéчна, вéчно, вéчны; красúвый ~ красúв, красúва, красúво, красúвы.

Examples of ending stress in the short forms are: смешнóй /смешóн, смешнá, смешнó, смешны; хорóший/хорóш, хорошá, хорошó, хороши; тяжёлый/тяжёл, тяжелá, тяжелó, тяжелы.

Note that, as with nouns, you can't stress an ending that has a zero phonetic realization, so the fact that the masculine forms смешóн, хорóш, тяжёл have stress realized on the last syllable of the stem and that the feminine forms смешнá, хорошá, тяжелá have stress realized on the ending does not indicate a shift. By taking all four endings of each adjective into account, we see that the stress is fixed on the ending. (if it is not Ø).

4.3.2.1. Shifting stress does occur in the short forms. There is only one type, which always presents a stressed *ending* in the fem. form as opposed to a stressed *stem* for the masc., neut., and pl. (compare the stress of the past tense of verbs in Chapter 7; жил, жила́, жи́ло, жи́ли). Examples are но́вый~ нов, нова́, но́во, но́вы; сла́бый ~ слаб, слаба́, сла́бо, сла́бы; молодо́й ~ мо́лод, молода́, мо́лодо, мо́лоды, холо́дный~ хо́лоден, холодна́, хо́лодно, хо́лодны, немо́й ~ нем, нема́, не́мо, не́мы.

Since there is only one type of shifting stress, it can be denoted with [S]: но́вый [S], сла́бый [S], молодо́й [S], холо́дный [S] немо́й [S]. Since stress shifts only between the fem. ending and the *first or only* syllable of the stem, we need only the [S] notation, and not both [S] and [S1], which were necessary for nouns. Fixed stress on the stem (ве́чен, ве́чна, ве́чно, ве́чны) will be [F], and fixed stress on the endings (хоро́ш, хороша́, хорошо́, хоро́ший) will be [Fe].

4.3.2.2. At this point we come to an issue of descriptive methodology. In the preceding section, it was stipulated that the stress shifts only between the fem. ending and the *first or only* syllable of the stem, rather than just saying *the stem*.

In reality, the situation is not quite so simple. While the vast majority of adjectives with shifting stress have only one syllable in the stem (e.g., но́вый, нов, нова́, но́во, но́вы), there are eighteen adjectives with shifting stress and more than one syllable in the stem. We find the following:

Group A:
весёлый, ве́сел, весела́, ве́село, ве́селы
голо́дный, го́лоден, голодна́, го́лодно, го́лодны
дешёвый, дёшев, дешева́, дёшево, дёшевы
дорого́й, до́рог, дорога́, до́рого, до́роги
зелёный, зе́лен, зелена́, зе́лено, зе́лены
коро́ткий, ко́роток, коротка́, ко́ротко, ко́ротки
молодо́й, мо́лод, молода́, мо́лодо, мо́лоды
солёный, со́лон, солона́, со́лоно, со́лоны[2]

---

[2] Note the irregular stem change in the short form.

холо́дный, хо́лоден, холодна́, хо́лодно, хо́лодны
холосто́й, хо́лост, холоста́, хо́лосто, хо́лосты
развито́й, ра́звит, развита́, ра́звито, ра́звиты[3]

None of the ten (excluding развито́й) has an alternate stress pattern of either F or Fe in standard speech.

This group of ten has a noteworthy common property: all but two have the root formula: C + mid vowel (/e/ or /o/) + L (a liquid: /r/ or /l/) + mid vowel (usually the same) + C. Historically most belong to a pattern called "TORT formula"[4] or at least appear to (зелёный, зе́лен, зелена́, зе́лено, зе́лены and солёный, со́лон, солона́, со́лоно, со́лоны appear to belong, but don't; весёлый, ве́сел, весела́, ве́село, ве́селы and дешёвый, дёшев, дешева́, дёшево, дёшевы have the mid vowel surrounding a consonant, but the middle consonant is not a liquid).

Group B:
вели́кий, вели́к, велика́, вели́ко, вели́ки
жесто́кий, жесто́к, жестока́, жесто́ко, жесто́ки
уда́лый/удало́й,[5] уда́л, удала́, уда́ло, уда́лы
высо́кий, высо́к, высока́, высо́ко, высо́ки
глубо́кий, глубо́к, глубока́, глубо́ко́, глубо́ки
далёкий, далёк, далека́, далёко́, далёки
широ́кий, широ́к, широка́, широ́ко́, широ́ки

The first two items can be treated as having fixed stress on the stem of the short forms ([F]). The last four can be treated as having fixed stress on the endings of the short forms ([Fe]), leaving only уда́лый/удало́й, уда́л, удала́, уда́ло,уда́лы as having shifting accent but not retracting to the first syllable. We can even justify the lack of retraction in уда́л by citing the fact that prefixes are never stressed in regular adjectives

---

[3] This is treated by *Grammatika 1980* as a plain adjective, although it is historically a past passive participle, and the stress is typical of a certain type of verb. Since past passive participles have their own set of stress rules (see Chapter 9), we will exclude развито́й from further consideration in this section.

[4] Where T stands for any consonant, O for *o* or *e*, and R for *r* or *l*. This is the reconstructed form which preceded such Russian pairs as город vs. град (cf. Новгород but Ленинград, голова vs. глава, молочный vs. млечный, берег vs. брег, etc.) See Appendix 1 for additional information.

[5] Both accents are accepted.

(as opposed to past passive participles),[6] although of course historically удáлый/удалóй is a participle (*l*-participle, not past passive participle). We have a choice of forms for the shifting-stress rule: 1) state that retracted shifting stress falls on the first syllable of the stem or 2) state that it falls on the same syllable as in the long form (the second syllable). The first statement takes care of Group A, which is more numerous than Group B. The second approach takes care of group B, but not Group A.

Since group B can be taken care of by considering the first two items as fixed on the stem, the last four as fixed on the endings and applying the rule of no prefix stress in adjectives, there is no real need to consider any other formulation. If one does wish to include the shifting stress patterns of Group B and not consider them as [F] or [Fe], then either Group A or Group B must be considered irregular. Since Group A is more numerous, by ten to seven, approach 1 is more efficient, so we choose the formulation given in the last paragraph of 4.3.2.1: stress shifts between the fem. ending and the *first or only* syllable of the stem.

4.3.2.3. The short forms, especially the pl., frequently have variations in stress; for details and lists, see *Grammatika 1980*, §1360–64. A partial list of examples from adjectives cited above is: высóкó, высóки, глухи́, нóвы, óстёр, остро́, свёжи́, рéзки́, силён, си́льны́, стро́йны́, крéпки́, у́зки́, with the meaning 'too tight' also у́зко́, хитро́, хи́тры́. There are many, many more.

4.3.2.4. If the stress pattern of the short form is fixed, then the stress in the masc. sg. form remains on the same syllable as in the long form: вéчный ~ вéчен, вéчна, вéчно, вéчны; интерéсный ~ интерéсен, интерéсна, интерéсно, интерéсны; я́вный ~ я́вен, я́вна, я́вно, я́вны. If the stress pattern of the short form is shifting, then the stress in the masc. sg. form falls on the first or only syllable: рéзкий ~рéзок, резка́, рéзко, рéзки; я́ркий ~ я́рок, ярка́, я́рко, я́рки; холóдный ~ хóлоден, холодна́, хóлодно, хóлодны; корóткий, кóроток, коротка́, кóротко, кóротки. If the stress of the short form is fixed on the endings, then the fill vowel will normally show the stress: смешнóй ~ смешóн, смешна́, смешнó, смешны́; у́мный ~ умён, умна́, умнó, умны́; хи́трый ~ хитёр, хитра́, хитро́, хитры́; хмельнóй ~ хмелён, хмельна́, хмельнó, хмельны́.

---

[6] For details, see *Grammatika 1980*, pp. 566–72. This rule is part of the "fine print" that one needs for a full description of Contemporary Standard Russian (CSR).

For a full list of exceptions, see 4.5.6. Examples of the exceptions are: больно́й ~ бо́лен, больна́, больно́, больны́; до́лжный ~ до́лжен, должна́, должно́, должны́; лёгкий ~лёгок, легка́, легко́, легки́; о́стрый in the meaning 'witty, sharp (sarcastic)' has остёр, остра́, о́стро, о́стры, so the masc. sg. stress is irregular; in the meaning of 'sharp, honed (of a blade) it has остёр and остр, остра́, о́стро, о́стры, so остёр can be regarded as the regular result of остра́, остро́, остры́; тёмный ~ тёмен, темна́, темно́, темны́; тёплый ~тёпел, тепла́, тепло́, теплы́; чёрный ~ чёрен, черна́, черно́, черны́; шу́стрый has both шустёр and шустр, шустра́, шу́стро, and both шу́стры and шустры́. If the set is taken as шустра́, шу́стро, шу́стры then шустёр simply has irregular stress. If the set is taken as шустра́, шу́стро, шустры́, then шустёр can be regarded as regular with шу́стро irregular.

4.3.2.5. If we look at the combination of stress patterns between the long and short forms, we find that the two possible types of stress in the long form (fixed on stem, fixed on endings) and the three possible types of stress in the short form (fixed on stem, fixed on endings, shifting) produce five combinations:

1) fixed on the stem in both long and short forms: краси́вый, *-ая, -ое, -ые* ~ краси́в, краси́ва, краси́во, краси́вы;
2) fixed on the stem in the long forms and fixed on the endings in the short forms: хоро́ший, *-ая, -ее, -ие* ~ хоро́ш, хороша́, хорошо́, хороши́;
3) fixed on the stem in the long forms and shifting in the short forms: но́вый, *-ая, -ое, -ые* ~ нов, нова́, но́во, но́вы;
4) fixed on the endings in both long and short forms: смешно́й, *-áя, -óе, ы́е* ~ смешо́н, смешна́, снешно́, смешны́;
5) fixed on the ending in the long forms and shifting in the short forms немо́й, *-áя, -óе, -ы́е* ~ нем, нема́, не́мо, не́мы.

Adjectives of the final theoretically possible type, fixed on the endings in the long forms and fixed on the stem in the short forms, do not exist in Contemporary Standard Russian.

Type 1 is by far the most common. Most of the thousands of adjectives with the suffix *-н*, as well as adjectives with many other suffixes, belong to it. Type 3 is second most common; it contains many unsuffixed and suffixed basic adjectives such as бе́лый, но́вый, ди́кий, кра́ткий, ста́рый. Type 2 has about twenty members; type 4 about seven, and type 5 about eighteen.

Type 2 includes three sets of adjectives:

1) words with a monosyllabic stem: во́льный ~ во́лен, вольна́, вольно́, вольны́; до́лжный ~ до́лжен, должна́, должно́, должны́; лёгкий ~ лёгок, легка́, легко́, легки́; ма́лый ~ мал, мала́, мало́, малы́; по́лный ~ по́лон, полна́, полно́, полны́; све́тлый ~ све́тел, светла́, светло́, светлы́; тёмный ~ тёмен, темна́, темно́, темны́; тёплый ~ тёпел, тепла́, тепло́, теплы́; у́мный ~ умён, умна́, умно́, умны́; хи́трый ~ хитёр, хитра́, хитро́, хитры́; чёрный ~ чёрен, черна́, черно́, черны́. Note that the majority of these have an unexpected accent in the masc. short form: во́лен, до́лжен, лёгок, по́лон, све́тел, тёмен, тёпел, чёрен.

2) words with a disyllabic stem: горя́чий ~горя́ч, горяча́, горячо́, горячи́; здоро́вый (in colloquial meaning 'big, strong') ~ здоро́в, здорова́, здорово́, здоровы́; тяжёлый ~ тяжёл, тяжела́. тяжело́, тяжелы́; хоро́ший ~ хоро́ш, хороша́, хорошо́, хороши́;

3) words with a disyllabic stem and more than one stress pattern possible in the short forms: высо́кий ~ высо́к, высока́, высоко́, высоки́; глубо́кий ~ глубо́к, глубока́, глубоко́, глубоки́; далёкий ~ далёк, далека́, далеко́, далеки́; широ́кий, широ́к, широка́, широко́, широки́.

4) words like: смешно́й ~ смешо́н, смешна́, смешно́, смешны́; блажно́й (substandard) ~ блажо́н, блажна́, блажно́, блажны́; злой ~ зол, зла, зло, злы;[7] хмельно́й ~ хмелён, хмельна́, хмельно́, хмельны́; чудно́й ~ чудён, чудна́, чудно́, чудны́; шально́й ~ шалён, шальна́, шально́, шальны́.

5) words like: босо́й ~ бос, боса́, бо́со, бо́сы; гнило́й; живо́й; криво́й; младо́й; наго́й; немо́й; свято́й; седо́й; слепо́й; сыро́й; туго́й; хромо́й; худо́й; дорого́й ~ до́рог, дорога́, до́рого, до́роги; молодо́й ~ мо́лод, молода́, мо́лодо, мо́лоды; развито́й ~ ра́звит, развита́, ра́звито, ра́звиты; холосто́й ~ хо́лост, холоста́, хо́лосто, хо́лосты. Note that all the disyllabic stems in this type have the expected retraction to the first syllable.

---

[7] Of course, one can argue about the place of the stress in the forms of this word. Summarize the arguments.

4.3.2.6. If we use the nom. sg. masc. of the adjective as the citation form, as dictionaries normally do, then we know the stress on all of the long forms, since it does not change for number, gender, or case. We can mark the stresses of the short forms by a simple annotation; see 4.3.2.1 above. As we saw there, this annotation will include [F] for fixed stress on the stem, [Fe] for fixed on the endings, and [S] for shifting.

Here are the citation forms for some of the adjectives mentioned in this chapter: вели́кий [F] or [S] irregular; весёлый [S]; ве́чный [F]; высо́кий [Fe] or [S] irreg.; глухо́й [S]; ди́кий [S]; ку́цый [F]; злой— why is no stress indication needed?; интере́сный [F]; молодо́й [S]; но́вый [S]; ре́зкий [S]; све́жий [Fe]; краси́вый [F]; си́льный [S]; си́ний [S]; смешно́й [Fe]; тяжёлый [Fe]; холо́дный [S]; хоро́ший [F].

4.4. Suffixes of the Comparative

In addition to the ***analytical***[8] comparative made with бо́лее, Russian has a ***synthetic*** comparative made with the suffixes *-ee /-e /-ше*. The form with бо́лее can be used in either attributive or predicate position (хочу́ купи́ть бо́лее но́вую маши́ну; моя́ маши́на бо́лее но́вая чем твоя́). The suffixed form can only be used in predicate position (моя́ маши́на нове́е твое́й).

4.4.1. Three (historically related) suffixes are used to make the synthetic comparative: *-ee /-e /-ше*. The last, *-ше,* is restricted to a few lexical items which must be specified. The first, *-ee*, is used with the overwhelming majority of adjectives, but the second is used with many of the most common words.

The suffixes *-ee* and *-e* show opposing versions of two important characteristics: consonant mutation and stress.

1) the suffix *-ee never* causes mutation of the last consonant(s) of the stem, and it has stress on the first *e if and only if* the fem. sg. short form is end stressed; e.g., нове́е, трудне́е, беле́е, грубе́е, глупе́е. Its normal form is *-ee;* a variant *-ей* occurs, chiefly in spoken Russian and in poetry.

---

[8] ***Analytical*** – formed by a combination of words: R. бо́лее но́вый, English *more new*; ***synthetic*** – formed by inflection, by changing the form of the word: R. нове́е, E. *newer.* The means of expressing possession in English can be synthetic (the mother's book) or analytical (the book of the mother).

2) the suffix -*e always* causes mutation of the final consonant(s) of the stem (if the consonants can mutate), and stress is *always* on the final syllable of the stem, never on the -*e*; e.g., моло́же, доро́же, су́ше, бога́че, про́ще.

4.4.2. To a considerable extent one can predict which comparative suffix a given adjective will use.

4.4.2.1. Less than a dozen adjectives use -*ше*, and they can be listed:

вели́кий	→ бо́льше (with stem change)	до́лгий	→ до́льше
глубо́кий	→ глу́бже (with irregular voicing assimilation of *ш* to *ж*)	ма́ленький, малый	→ ме́ньше
		плохо́й	→ ху́же
		ра́нний	→ ра́ньше
го́рький	→ го́рче and го́рше	ста́рый	→ ста́рше
		то́нкий	→ то́ньше
далёкий	→ да́льше	хоро́ший	→ лу́чше

4.4.2.2. A substantial number of adjectives, including some of the most common ones, use -*e*. Adjectives which use -*e* may be unsuffixed, suffixed with -*к*, or suffixed with -*ок*. The suffix -*к* may or may not drop; this must be learned. The suffix -*ок* will always drop.

круто́й	→ кру́че	ги́бкий	→ ги́бче	
молодо́й	→ моло́же	гро́мкий	→ гро́мче	
твёрдый	→ тверже	дешёвый	→ деше́вле (note the change of *ё* to *e*)
густо́й	→ гу́ще			
просто́й	→ про́ще	пры́ткий	→ пры́тче	
то́лстый	→ то́лще	коро́ткий	→ коро́че	
ча́стый	→ ча́ще	га́дкий	→ га́же	
чи́стый	→ чи́ще	гла́дкий	→ гла́же	
дорого́й	→ доро́же	жи́дкий	→ жи́же	
стро́гий	→ стро́же	ре́дкий	→ ре́же	
туго́й	→ ту́же	жёсткий	→ жёстче	
ти́хий	→ ти́ше	бли́зкий	→ бли́же	
глухо́й	→ глу́ше	вя́зкий	→ вя́зче	
сухо́й	→ су́ше	ни́зкий	→ ни́же	
кре́пкий	→ кре́пче	ре́зкий	→ ре́зче	

у́зкий	→	у́же		я́ркий	→	я́рче
жа́лкий	→	жа́лче and жа́льче		лёгкий	→	ле́гче (note the change of *ё* to *е*)
ме́лкий	→	ме́льче		мя́гкий	→	мя́гче
мы́лкий	→	мы́лче and мы́льче		широ́кий	→	ши́ре
				высо́кий	→	вы́ше
жа́ркий	→	жа́рче				

4.4.2.3. Adjectives with *any* suffix *not* containing -*к* will always take the comparative suffix -*ee*:

тру́дный	→	трудне́е
леси́стый	→	леси́стее
дождли́вый	→	дождли́вее
забы́вчивый	→	забы́вчивее
вели́чественный	→	вели́чественнее
знамени́тый	→	знамени́тее
глаза́стый	→	глаза́стее
непреодоли́мый	→	непреодоли́мее

Exception: бога́тый ~ бога́т, бога́та gives бога́че, not the expected бога́тее. It is a question whether Russians think of бога́тый as being suffixed. See also below in 4.4.3, where бога́тый again behaves as if it were unsuffixed.

Examples of unsuffixed adjectives which take -*ee*:

скупо́й	→	скупе́е		си́зый	→	сизе́е
сла́бый	→	слабе́е		бе́лый	→	беле́е
но́вый	→	нове́е		весёлый	→	веселе́е

4.4.2.4. One can thus predict with a very high degree of accuracy which comparative suffix will be used by any specific adjective. If the adjective has a suffix containing *к* (either -*к* or -*ок*), then the comparative suffix will be -*e*. Unfortunately, one simply has to learn whether the *к* will drop or remain (with mutation to *ч*). If the adjective has any suffix other than *к* or *ок*, then the comparative will use -*ee*. If the adjective has no suffix, then stems ending in a labial consonant (*п б ф в м*) or the liquid *л* will normally take -*ee*. Stems ending in a velar (*к г x*) or in a dental other than *л* will normally take -*e*. The stems which take -*ше* must be learned.

4.4.3. Russian has a suffixed form in -*ейший* which is often incorrectly called "superlative" or "comparative". Its real meaning is 'manifesting the quality to a very high degree'. There is often no comparison involved.

This form is produced from a fairly large number of adjectives. The suffix -*ейший* is used after most consonants, e.g. новейший, грубейший, простейший, белейший, старейший. When the suffix is placed after velars (*к г x*), the velar mutates (*к → ч, г → ж, x → ш*) and the suffix becomes -*айший*: тихий ~ тишайший, строгий ~ строжайший.

When the form in -*ейший* is made from adjectives with a monosyllabic stem, the stress will always be on the suffix: новейший, грубейший, простейший, белейший, старейший, тихий ~ тишайший, строгий ~ строжайший. If the stem has more than one syllable, then the stress will be on the stem if the stem has fixed stem stress in the short forms (ужасный ~ ужаснейший,) and will be on the suffix if the stem has shifting or fixed end stress in the short forms: тяжёлый ~ тяжелейший, великий ~ величайший. Exceptions to the stress rule: богатый ~ богат, богата but богатейший; здоровый 'healthy' ~ здоров, здорова but здоровейший. See above in 4.4.2.3 for another instance of богатый behaving as if it were a monosyllable. The stem of здоровый is historically a monosyllable—it belongs to the so-called "TORT" group. See 4.3.2.2 and Appendix 1 for discussion of this pattern.

4.5. Exceptions

4.5.1. The following have a fill vowel where it is not expected:

долгий ~ долог   полный ~ полон

4.5.2. The following have a different fill vowel than expected:

достойный   ~   достоин (instead of достоен)
злой   ~   зол, зла, зло, злы
полный   ~   полон

4.5.3. The following do not have a fill vowel where it would be expected:

бе́глый	~	бегл	пёстрый	~	пёстр
бо́дрый	~	бодр	по́длый	~	подл
бо́рзый	~	борз	по́шлый	~	пошл
бы́стрый	~	быстр	ре́звый	~	резв
ве́тхий	~	ветх	ры́хлый	~	рыхл
го́рдый	~	горд	сму́глый	~	смугл
до́брый	~	добр	твёрдый	~	твёрд
кру́глый	~	кругл	трёзвый	~	трезв
мо́крый	~	мокр	хра́брый	~	храбр
му́дрый	~	мудр	хри́плый	~	хрипл
на́глый	~	нагл	щёдрый	~	щедр

4.5.4. The following have a different suffix than is expected in the comparative:

бога́тый → бога́че (see 4.4.2.3)
глубо́кий → глу́бже (irregular voicing assimilation of *ш* to *ж*)
го́рький → го́рше (note drop of *ь* in writing)
далёкий → да́льше (note retention of soft *л*)
дешёвый → деше́вле (see 4.4.2.4)
до́лгий → до́льше (note softening of *л*)
жёлтый → желте́е
лю́тый → люте́е
ра́нний → ра́ньше (note retention of soft *н*)
свято́й → святе́е
ста́рый → ста́рше (and regular старе́е, with differences in meaning)
сы́тый → сыте́е
то́нкий → то́ньше (note softening of *н*)
хоро́ший → лу́чше (with different stem)

4.5.5. The following have a different stem in the comparative (dropping of *-к* or *-ок* not included):

вели́кий	→	бо́льше
дешёвый	→	деше́вле (change of *ё* to *e*)
лёгкий	→	ле́гче (change of *ё* to *e*)
ма́ленький, малый	→	ме́ньше
плохо́й	→	ху́же
сла́дкий	→	сла́ще
хоро́ший	→	лу́чше

4.5.6. The following have an *irregular* stress in the short form (the hundreds of stress *variations* are not considered here):

больно́й	~	бо́лен, больна́, больно́, больны́;
во́льный	~	во́лен, вольна́, вольно́, вольны́;
до́лжный	~	до́лжен, дожна́, должо́, должны́;
лёгкий	~	лёгок, легка́, легко́, легки́;

о́стрый in the meaning 'witty, sharp (sarcastic)' has остёр, остра́, о́стро, о́стры, so the masc. sg. stress is irregular; in the meaning of 'sharp, honed (of a blade) it has остёр and остр, остра́, о́стро́, о́стры́, so остёр can be regarded as the regular result of остра́, остро́, остры́

по́лный	~	по́лон, полна́, полно́, полны́
све́тлый	~	све́тел, светла́, светло́, светлы́
счастли́вый	~	сча́стлив, сча́стлива, сча́стливо, сча́стливы or

(archaic) счастли́в, счастли́ва, счастли́во, счастли́вы. Comparative счастли́вее from either.

тёмный	~	тёмен, темна́, темно́, темны́
тёплый	~	тёпел, тепла́, тепло́, теплы́
чёрный	~	чёрен, черна́, черно́, черны́

шу́стрый has both шустёр and шустр, шустра́, шу́стро, and both шу́стры and шустры́. If the set is taken as шустра́, шу́стро, шу́стры then шустёр simply has irregular stress. If the set is taken as шустра́, шу́стро, шустры́, then шустёр can be regarded as regular with шу́стро irregular.

4.5.7. Many adjectives do not have short forms. The largest single group is all adjectives in *-ский*, such as ру́сский. Adjectives other than qualitative do not normally have short forms, so деревя́ный 'wooden', соба́чий 'dog's, canine', сего́дняшний 'today's', тепе́решний 'of the present time', etc. exist only in the long forms.

Soft stems, even in qualitative adjectives, do not show short forms, so ра́нний 'early', по́здний 'late' lack short forms. The only two soft adjectives which show short forms are си́ний 'blue' (синь, синя́, си́не, си́ни) and и́скренний 'sincere' (и́скренен, и́скренна, with a hard final consonant).

The active participles, both present and past, do not have short forms. There are several other less numerous groups that lack short forms: 1) ordinal numerals, such as пе́рвый, шесто́й; 2) forms with the suffixes *-ущий*, *-енный*, *-ейший*, or the prefixes *пре-*, *раз-*, such as большу́щий, здорове́нный, краси́вейший, преспоко́йный, развесёлый; 3) words denoting the color of animals, such as вороно́й, пе́гий. For the complicated details, see *Грамматика 1980*, §1331–38.

Two adjectives exist only in short forms: рад 'glad' and гора́зд 'good at' (colloquial).

4.5.8. Either morphological or semantic factors may prevent the formation of short forms, Both types of factors may also prevent the formation of the comparative. Some of the factors differ in the two categories, but one that is the same is the suffix *-ский*, which prevents the formation of comparatives. For details on this complicated topic, see *Грамматика 1980*, §1344–47.

However, counter-examples to the rules laid down spring easily to mind. In §1344, paragraph 1), *Грамматика 1980* states that живо́й in the meaning 'alive, not dead' has no comparative, but in Communist times the slogan (Ленин) Живе́е всех живы́х! was to be seen in many places, from large posters to *значки*.

4.5.9. Certain adjectives exhibit a variety of unclassifiable irregularities:

бли́зкий	~	ближа́йший (consonant mutation)
бога́тый	~	бога́т, бога́та but богате́йший (stress)
глубо́кий	→	глу́бже (irregular voicing assimilation: *ш* → *ж*)
здоро́вый	~	здоро́в, здоро́ва but здорове́йший (stress)
по́здний	→	по́зже (the *н* is dropped)
сла́дкий	→	сла́ще (сла́дке → сладче → слатче; (*т* assimilates to *ш* before *ч*, producing the cluster *шч*, written *щ*)
солёный	~	со́лон, солона́, со́лоно, со́лоны, with *ё* to *о*.

Exercises

I.   Decline the following long-form adjectives in six cases in all three genders and the plural:

1. бе́лый
2. ру́сский
3. ку́цый
4. круто́й
5. по́здний
6. дорого́й
7. кудря́вый
8. рабо́чий

9. плохо́й
10. слепо́й
11. небольшо́й
12. ры́жий
13. жесто́кий
14. га́дкий
15. многосторо́нний

II.   Give the the nom. sg. (m, f, n) and pl. short forms, *with stress*, for the following adjectives. Also give the comparative with *-ee/-e*. A few are real, most are invented.

1. во́пный [S]
2. луси́стый [F]
3. рого́й [S]
4. во́стрый [S]
5. судло́стый [F]
6. блысто́й [Fe]
7. гу́ркий [Fe]
8. сёплый [S]
9. будрёный [Fe]
10. наго́й [Fe]
11. о́стрый [S]
12. холо́стый [S]
13. гру́стый [S]
14. стро́йкий [F]
15. резо́й [S]

16. са́жий [S]
17. гла́бый [Fe]
18. слухо́й [S]
19. ши́дный [S]
20. гло́бный [F]
21. золо́гий [S]
22. свистли́вый [F]
23. говори́стый [F]
24. голова́тый [F]
25. торго́й [S]
26. но́ский [S]
27. тарова́тый [F]
28. хро́мкий [F]
29. дуро́кий [Fe]
30. противи́тельный [F]

5

Pronominals

5.0. Introduction

Pronominals are defined as a class by morphology. They encompass several different categories in traditional grammatical description: personal pronouns (он); demonstrative pronouns (тот, э́тот); interrogative pronouns (кто, что, чей), other non-personal pronouns (весь); possessive pronouns (наш); adjectives derived from the names of animals (ли́сий, ли́сья); the numeral оди́н, etc. At the end of this chapter we will consider possessive adjectives in *-ин* and *-ов* (ма́мин, па́пин, Ни́нин; отцо́в) and family names in *-ов-* and *-ин-*. which resemble pronominals but lack at least one typical feature.

The *first*, most obvious morphological trait of pronominals is that they take noun endings in the *direct* (nom., acc.) cases (оди́н, одна́, одно́, одну́) and adjective endings in the *oblique* cases (gen., dat., instr., prep.) (одного́, одному́, одно́й).

A *second* feature is that where adjectives would have *ы* in the ending, pronominals have either *u* (most) or *e* (те, все).

The *third* is that in the masc. and neut. gen. and dat sg. of stems with end stress, the second syllable of the ending is stressed, as opposed to the first syllable of the ending in adjectives (одного́, одному́ vs. немо́го, большо́го).

A *fourth* feature: after a soft consonant, the feminine ending {oj} of the gen./dat./instr./prep. goes to /ej/: всей vs. одно́й.

The *fifth* is that many of them do something unexpected in the *unmarked* form, which is the nom. sg. masc. for т(от), эт(от), од(и́)н, к(то), and the nom. sg. neut. for ч(то), which does not have a masculine form.

5.1. Demonstrative Pronouns

5.1.1. The numeral оди́н (see Table 5-1) incorporates all of the above features except number four. Feature one is shown throughout the declension, with nom. and acc. opposed to gen., dat., instr., and prep. Feature two appears in the instr. sg. masc./neut. and in all cases of the plural. Three shows in the gen. and dat. sg. masc. and neuter. Observe that the instr. sg. disyllabic endings -ою and -ими are not end-stressed.[1] Feature five is of course seen in the nom. sg. masc. один.

Table 5-1. The Declension of один 'one'

	Masc.	**Neut.**	**Fem.**	**Pl.**
Nom.	один	одно́	одна́	одни́
Acc.	= n. or g.	= nom.	одну́	= n. or g.
Gen.	одного́		одно́й	одни́х
Dat.	одному́		одно́й	одни́м
Instr.	одни́м		одно́й/ -о́ю	одни́ми
Prep.	одно́м		одно́й	одни́х

Table 5-2. The Forms of тот 'that'

	Masc.	**Neut.**	**Fem.**	**Pl.**
Nom.	тот	то	та	те
Acc.	= n. or g.	= nom.	ту	= n. or g.
Gen.	того́		той	тех
Dat.	тому́		той	тем
Instr.	тем		той/ то́ю	те́ми
Prep.	том		той	тех

5.1.2. Where does the form тот come from? If the stem is {т+}, then in the nom. sg. masc. we would expect *{тØ}, yielding a surface form *т, which would be difficult to perceive and to pronounce, especially before any word which begins with more than one consonant, or with even a single dental consonant. Try pronouncing т князь, т дом. In order to have something pronounceable, Russian *reduplicated* the stem to *тØтØ, which yields тот. For the change of -ØCØ- to -оC-, see 4.1.6.2.

---

[1] Remember that nouns never stress {-ju} in the instr. sg. (see 2.3.2): nom. любо́вь, глушь, gen./dat./prep. любви́, глуши́, both nouns with fixed end stress, but instr. любо́вью, глу́шью.

Table 5-3. The Forms of э́тот 'this'

	Masc.	**Neut.**	**Fem.**	**Pl.**
Nom.	э́тот	э́то	э́та	э́ти
Acc.	= n. or g.	= nom.	э́ту	= n. or g.
Gen.	э́того		э́той	э́тих
Dat.	э́тому		э́той	э́тим
Instr.	э́тим		э́той/ -ою	э́тими
Prep.	э́том		э́той	э́тих

5.1.3. The pronominal э́тот 'this' is originally derived from тот by prefixing the particle э 'this nearby.' Compare such words as этако́й 'of this sort right here' in colloquial Russian. In modern standard Russian э́тот differs from тот in the vowel which replaces *ы* in the instr. sg. and in the plural. While э́тот has *и*, тот has *е*. Whence the difference? At an earlier stage, the forms were instr. sg. тѣмь, pl. ти, тѣхъ. тѣмъ. тѣми, тѣхъ. The vowel *ѣ*, called "ять," became *е* (but normally not *ё*) in modern Russian, and the "jers" (*ь* and *ъ*, which were high or mid-high short vowels) were lost. This would have given тем, ти, тех, тем, теми, тех, but Russian *leveled out* the vowel by *analogy*. The nom. pl. ти was made те by analogy to the other forms of the plural, and the oblique case forms of э́тот acquired *и* instead of *е* by analogy to the nom. pl., which is used much more commonly than any single oblique case form, and is also the *unmarked* form.

5.2. Possessive Pronouns

5.2.1. Мой, твой, and свой, the "possessive pronouns" in traditional grammatical terms, show features one, three, and four.

Table 5-4. The Declension of мой, твой, свой 'my, your, own'

	Masc.	**Neut.**	**Fem.**	**Pl.**
Nom.	мой	моё	моя́	мои́
Acc.	= n. or g.	= nom.	мою́	= n. or g.
Gen.	моего́		мое́й	мои́х
Dat.	моему́		мое́й	мои́м

	Masc.	Neut.	Fem.	Pl.
Instr.	мои́м		мое́й/ -е́ю	мои́ми
Prep.	моём		мое́й	мои́х

5.2.2. The possessive pronouns наш, ваш have stem stress.

Table 5-5. The Declension of наш, ваш 'our, your'

	Masc.	Neut.	Fem.	Pl.
Nom.	наш	на́ше	на́ша	на́ши
Acc.	= n. or g.	= nom.	на́шу	= n. or g.
Gen.	на́шего		на́шей	на́ших
Dat.	на́шему		на́шей	на́шим
Instr.	на́шим		на́шей/ -ею	на́шими
Prep.	на́шем		на́шей	на́ших

5.2.3. The stem of чей is {čj+}; the nom. sg. masc. is {čjØ} → /čej/ by the fill vowel rules discussed in 2.2.5.

Table 5-6. The Forms of чей 'whose'

	Masc.	Neut.	Fem.	Pl.
Nom.	чей	чьё	чья	чьи
Acc.	= n. or g.	= nom.	чью	= n. or g.
Gen.	чьего́		чьей	чьих
Dat.	чьему́		чьей	чьим
Instr.	чьим		чьей чье́ю	чьи́ми
Prep.	чьём		чьей	чьих

5.3. Additional Pronouns

5.3.1. The fem. acc. sg. of сам has a unique alternative ending: самоё. It is archaic and not much used today. You should be able to recognize it but not use it. The nom. pl. form has an unexpected accent: са́ми.

Table 5-7. The Declension of сам 'one's self'

	Masc.	**Neut.**	**Fem.**	**Pl.**
Nom.	сам	само́	сама́	са́ми
Acc.	= n. or g.	= nom.	саму́ <u>самоё</u>	= n. or g.
Gen.	самого́		само́й	сами́х
Dat.	самому́		само́й	сами́м
Instr.	сами́м		само́й/ -о́ю	сами́ми
Prep.	само́м		само́й	сами́х

5.3.2. The forms of весь showing features one through four.

Table 5-8. The Declension of весь 'all'

	Masc.	**Neut.**	**Fem.**	**Pl.**
Nom.	весь	всё	вся	все
Acc.	= n. or g.	= nom.	всю	= n. or g.
Gen.	всего́		всей	всех
Dat.	всему́		всей	всем
Instr.	всем		всей все́ю	все́ми
Prep.	всём		всей	всех

5.3.3. The distinction between кто and что is *animate* vs. *inanimate*, which is why the acc. of кто is always кого́.

Table 5-9. The Forms of кто 'who' and что 'what'

	Sing.	
	Masc.-Fem. (Animate)	**Neut. (Inanimate)**
Nom.	кто	что
Acc.	кого́	что
Gen.	кого́	чего́
Dat.	кому́	чему́
Instr.	кем	чем
Prep.	ком	чём

5.4. Personal Pronouns

The declensional forms of the personal pronouns are the most irregular items in the Russian language. All six personal pronouns show *suppletion*, which means that not all case forms are made from the same stem. Я has stems мен- and мн- in the oblique cases; ты uses теб- and тоб-. In the plural мы and вы use на- and ва- respectively. The reflexive has себ- and соб-.

Table 5-10. The First and Second Person Pronouns

	Singular		Plural		Reflexive
	First	**Second**	**First**	**Second**	
Nom.	я	ты	мы	вы	(none)
Acc.	меня	тебя	нас	вас	себя
Gen.	меня	тебя	нас	вас	себя
Dat.	мне	тебе	нам	вам	себе
Instr	мной	тобóй	нáми	вáми	собóй
Prep.	мне	тебе	нас	вас	себе

The 3rd person pronoun is also suppletive, with a stem of {on+} in the nominative and {j+} in the oblique cases. Note that the acc. sg. and pl. of all three genders are always the same as the genitive, even for inanimates. This is the only situation in Russian where this is true. The accusative of кто is always когó, but the form is used only for animates.

The stem {j+} usually is not pronounced in the plural before /i/ for the same reason that initial и is normally pronounced [i] in other lexical items (e.g., и́ва, и́го): Russian turns underlying {#ji-} and {#i} both into [i].[2] This does not apply when the surface [i] comes from an underlying {#jo} or {#je}, so ёж {jož} 'hedgehog' has a genitive ежá [jižá]; едá {jedá} (cf. ел 'ate') → [jidá]; gen. sg. егó {jovó} → [jivó], её {jejó} → [jijó].

As discussed in 1.6.4 and 1.9.2, in the past some Russians pronounced the plural forms [jix, jim, jíi, jix].

The form éю is prescribed as obligatory when the fem. instr. sg. is used without a preposition: мать горди́тся éю "her mother is proud of her." When used with a preposition, the shorter form is usual: Мать говори́т с ней, although the two-syllable form is usable in the same situations as

---

[2] The sign # means a word boundary: #стол#.

apply to the use of the long form with all other words: poetry, rhythmic considerations, etc.

Almost all of the forms of the 3rd person pronoun can be derived from the stems {on+} and {j+} plus the expected endings. For example, {on+a} → она́; {j+ovo} → его́; {j+omu} → ему́; {j+im} → им; {j+oj} → ей (feature four); {j+oj(u)} → е́ю; {j+ix} → их. The only truly unexpected form is gen. sg. fem. её. We would also expect *{j+u} in the acc. sg. fem., but it is replaced by the gen. sg. её, just as in the masc., neut., and pl. the form of the gen. is used for both animates and inanimates.

Table 5-11. The Third Person Pronouns.

	Masc.	**Neut.**	**Fem.**	**Pl.**
Nom.	он	оно́	она́	они́
Acc.	его́		её	их
Gen.	его́		её	их
Dat.	ему́		ей	им
Instr.	им		ей е́ю	ими
Prep.	нём		ней	них

5.5. Possessive Adjectives

5.5.1. The first group of adjectives (in *-ий, -ья,* and *-ье*) add the suffix {j} to the stem of the underlying noun and are declined as pronominals. The group is comprised primarily of adjectives derived from the names of animals. The last consonant of the stem may mutate (e.g., соба́чий 'dog's'; медве́жий 'bear's') or not (e.g., ли́сий 'fox's'; коро́вий 'cow's'). A small number of words in this group are derived from words for persons: вдо́вий 'widow's'; каза́чий 'Cossack's'. Falling into neither category are Бо́жий 'God's, divine' and тре́тий 'third.'

Stress is always on the stem, never the ending. The fill vowel {e} before {jØ} in the masc. sg. is spelled *-и-* (see 2.2.5), which is why the nom. sg. of these words looks like the nom. sg. of such adjectives as си́ний, ди́кий, све́жий. The other case forms show a stem which is clearly not the same as the stem of си́ний, ди́кий, све́жий. Table 12b gives the same material in transcription, in order to show better the stem-final {-j+}.

Table 5-12a. The Declension of лисий 'fox's'

	Masc.	**Neut.**	**Fem.**	**Pl.**
Nom.	лисий	лисье	лисья	лисьи
Acc.	= n. or g.	= nom.	лисью	= n. or g.
Gen.	лисьего		лисьей	лисьих
Dat.	лисьему		лисьей	лисьим
Instr.	лисьим		лисьей/ -ею	лисьими
Prep.	лисьем		лисьей	лисьих

Table 5-12b. The Declension of {l̦ísj+∅} 'fox's'

	Masc.	**Neut.**	**Fem.**	**Pl.**
Nom.	{l̦ísj∅}	{l̦ísjo}	{l̦ísja}	{l̦ísji}
Acc.	= n. or g.	= nom.	{l̦ísju}	= n. or g.
Gen.	{l̦ísjovo}		{l̦ísjoj}	{l̦ísjix}
Dat.	{l̦ísjomu}		{l̦ísjoj}	{l̦ísjim}
Instr.	{l̦ísjim}		{l̦ísjoj/ -oju}	{l̦ísjimi̦}
Prep.	{l̦ísjom}		{l̦ísjoj}	{l̦ísjix}

5.5.2. A second group of adjectives (in *-ин* and *-ов*) is used primarily in the spoken language. The ones in *-ин* are made chiefly from personal names (especially *hypocoristics* in *-a*) and from words for relatives: мамин, папин, дядин, тётин, Нинин, Сашин, Володин. The ones in *-ов* are made, but by no means exclusively, from names for male relatives: отцов, дедов, but царёв.

The pattern of declension fits pronominals in general, but with the major difference that feature two (*ы* → *и/е*) is absent:

Table 5-13a. The Forms of Нинин 'Nina's'

	Masc.	**Neut.**	**Fem.**	**Pl.**
Nom.	Нинин	Нинино	Нинина	Нинины
Acc.	= n.or g.	= nom.	Нинину	= n. or g.
Gen.	Нининого		Нининой	Нининых
Dat.	Нининому		Нининой	Нининым

	Masc.	**Neut.**	**Fem.**	**Pl.**
Instr.	Ни́ниным		Ни́ниной/ -ою	Ни́ниными
Prep.	Ни́нином		Ни́ниной	Ни́ниных

Forms in *-ов, -ёв* have the same endings as those in *-ин*, except that the gen. and dat. sg. masc. and neut. use nominal forms; see Table 5-13b. In the nineteenth century, adjectives in *-ин* optionally had nominal endings in the gen. and dat. sg. masc. and neut. For further not-always-clear information, see *Грамматика 1980*, §§1324, 1326, 1327.

Table 5-13b. The Forms of де́дов 'grandfather's'

	Masc.	**Neut.**	**Fem.**	**Pl.**
Nom.	де́дов	де́дово	де́дова	де́довы
Acc.	= n. or g.	= nom.	де́дову	= n. or g.
Gen.	де́дова		де́довой	де́довых
Dat.	де́дову		де́довой	де́довым
Instr.	де́довым		де́довой/ -ою	де́довыми
Prep.	де́довом		де́довой	де́довых

5.5.3. Russian family names in *-ов* and *-ин* decline like pronominals in all forms of the fem. and pl., but only in the instr. sg. of masculines. Note that feature two (*ы → и/е*) is absent.

Table 5-14a. The Forms of Пу́шкин

	Masc.	**Fem.**	**Pl.**
Nom.	Пу́шкин	Пу́шкина	Пу́шкины
Acc.	Пу́шкина	Пу́шкину	Пу́шкиных
Gen.	Пу́шкина	Пу́шкиной	Пу́шкиных
Dat.	Пу́шкину	Пу́шкиной	Пу́шкиным
Instr.	Пу́шкиным	Пу́шкиной/ -ою	Пу́шкиными
Prep.	Пу́шкине	Пу́шкиной	Пу́шкиных

Table 5-14b. The Forms of Ива́но́в

	Masc.	**Fem.**	**Pl.**
Nom.	Ива́но́в	Ива́но́ва	Ива́но́вы
Acc.	Ива́но́ва	Ива́но́ву	Ива́но́вых
Gen.	Ива́но́ва	Ива́но́вой	Ива́но́вых
Dat.	Ива́но́ву	Ива́но́вой	Ива́но́вым
Instr.	Ива́но́вым	Ива́но́вой/ -ою	Ива́но́выми
Prep.	Ива́но́ве	Ива́но́вой	Ива́но́вых

Stress in this name is found both on the middle syllable of the stem and on the last stem syllable: Ива́нов and Ивано́в.

Place names ending in *-ов* and *-ин* have the instr. sg. ending *-ом*: за Пу́шкином, над Сара́товом.

Exercises

I. Which of the following are pronominals?

1. го́стья 'female guest'
2. столо́в 'tables' (gen. pl.)
3. царёва 'Tsar's' (сестра)
4. воробе́й 'sparrow'
5. Ма́шин 'Maria's' (муж)
6. (в) том 'that'
7. ниче́й 'nobody's'
8. бей! 'beat'
9. том 'volume'
10. маши́н 'machines' (gen. pl.)

6

Numerals

6.0. Introduction

Numerals are not as neatly defined a morphological category as are nouns, adjectives, and even pronominals. Nouns can be characterized, among other ways, as having inherent gender, showing animacy, requiring agreement from adjectives, etc. Adjectives show agreement in case, number, and gender with the word they modify. Pronominals are defined by several factors, of which the most obvious is the system of endings.

Among numerals only один/одна/одно, два/две, оба/обе, and полтора/полторы distinguish gender. No numeral distinguishes animacy independently. Only один has a number distinction. Some numerals distinguish as few as two cases. Numerals are gathered into a single grammatical category primarily on the basis of 1) meaning, and 2) what they are not: nouns, adjectives, pronominals, verbs, adverbs, conjunctions, exclamations, or particles.

6.1 Cardinal Numerals

6.1.1. 'Zero' is нуль/ноль [Fe], a masculine soft stem with fixed end stress like рубль. For usage, see Wade §192. The forms of оди́н 'one', a pronominal, were given in Table 5-1.

Table 6-1. The Forms of два, три, четы́ре

Nom.	Masc./Neut. Два, Fem. Две	Три	Четы́ре
Acc.	= n. or g.	= n. or g.	= n. or g.
Gen.	двух	трёх	четырёх
Dat.	двум	трём	четырём
Instr.	двумя́	тремя́	четырьмя́
Prep.	двух	трёх	четырёх

6.1.2. The choice of nom. or gen. in the acc. depends upon the animacy of the noun: я видел два/три/четыре столá, but я видел двух/трёх/ четырёх конéй/лошадéй/дуракóв.

6.1.3. Óба is the only numeral in Russian besides одúн to show a gender distinction in all cases. Similar to полторá is полторáста '150', oblique form полýтораста.

Table 6-2. The Forms of óба, полторá

	Masc./ Neuter	Fem.	Masc./ Neuter	Fem.
Nom.	óба	óбе	полторá	полторы́
Acc.	= n. or g.	= n. or g.	= n. or g.	= n. or g.
Gen.	обóих	обéих	полýтора	
Dat.	обóим	обéим		
Instr.	обóими	обéими		
Prep.	обóих	обéих		

6.1.4. The numerals шесть, семь, вóсемь, дéвять, дéсять, двáдцать, трúдцать all decline like пять, with stress on the ending in all forms.

Table 6-3. The Forms of пять, вóсемь, пятнáдцать, двáдцать

Nom.	пять	вóсемь	двáдцать	пятнáдцать
Acc.	пять	вóсемь	двáдцать	пятнáдцать
Gen.	пятú	восьмú	двадцатú	пятнáдцати
Dat.	пятú	восьмú	двадцатú	пятнáдцати
Instr.	пятью́	восемью́	двадцатью́	пятнáдцатью
Prep.	пятú	восьмú	двадцатú	пятнáдцати

This alternation of stress in the singular of a disyllabic stem between the first syllable in the nominative and the ending in the other cases does not occur in third- declension noun stems; the few with end stress are monosyllabic stems (such as грудь, ось, Русь, Тверь; see 3.4.5 and *Грамматика 1980*, §1262 & 1263). The nouns also never have an end accent in the instr. sg.: грýдью, óсью, Рýсью, Твéрью, while the instr.

sg. of numerals can be stressed; see 2.3.2. Only во́семь has a moble vowel. There is also a colloquial form восьмью́.

The numerals оди́ннадцать, двена́дцать, трина́дцать, четыр–надцать, шестна́дцать, семна́дцать, восемна́дцать, девятна́дцать, all decline like пятна́дцать, with оди́ннадцать and четы́рнадцать having stress on a vowel other than the -на́-. In оди́ннадцать through девятна́дцать the stress remains on the same syllable in all forms, in-stead of going to the endings in the oblique cases, as it does in пять through де́сять, два́дцать, and три́дцать.

6.1.5. Сто does have other separate forms as part of compound numer-als for hundreds, such as две́сти, три́ста, пятьсо́т, etc.; see Tables 6-7 and 6-8 below. It also has regular oblique case forms (сот, стам, ста́ми, стах) when used with the indefinite numerals мно́го and не́сколько and a noun in the gen. pl. For details, see *Грамматика 1980*, §1373, note.

Со́рок, девяно́сто, and сто join полтора́ in having only two case forms (see Table 6-2 above). In fact, although девяно́сто has two forms in writing, vowel reduction leaves only one in speech: [dˌivˌinóstə].

Table 6-4. The Forms of со́рок, девяно́сто, and сто

Nom./Acc.	со́рок	девяно́сто	сто
Gen./Dat./ Instr./Prep.	сорока́	девяно́ста	ста

6.1.6. In the following table note the irregular (from the point of view of nouns) shift of accent from the last syllable back to a medial syllable, as well as the change of stem from hard in the nom./acc. to soft in the oblique cases.

Table 6-5. The Forms of пятьдеся́т, шестьдеся́т

Nom.	пятьдеся́т	шестьдеся́т
Acc.	пятьдеся́т	шестьдеся́т
Gen.	пяти́десяти	шести́десяти
Dat.	пяти́десяти	шести́десяти
Instr.	пятью́десятью	шестью́десятью
Prep.	пяти́десяти	шести́десяти

6.1.7. Note once again the shift of the stress, in this case from the initial to a medial syllable, and the alternation of the hard and soft stems. There is a colloquial variant of the instr. for 'eighty': восьмью́десятью. Cf. восьмью́ in 6.1.3 above and in 6.1.7 below.

Table 6-6. The Forms of се́мьдесят, во́семьдесят

Nom.	се́мьдесят	во́семьдесят
Acc.	се́мьдесят	во́семьдесят
Gen.	семи́десяти	восьми́десяти
Dat.	семи́десяти	восьми́десяти
Instr.	семью́десятью	восемью́десятью
Prep.	семи́десяти	восьми́десяти

6.1.8. In the above table *ё* in трёхсо́т, четырёхсо́т, etc. indicates a light secondary stress on the first part of the compound.

Table 6-7. The Forms of две́сти, три́ста, четы́реста, пятьсо́т

Nom.	две́сти	три́ста	четы́реста	пятьсо́т
Acc.	две́сти	три́ста	четы́реста	пятьсо́т
Gen.	двухсо́т	трёхсо́т	четырёхсо́т	пятисо́т
Dat.	двумста́м	трёмста́м	четырёмста́м	пятиста́м
Instr.	двумя́ста́ми	тремя́ста́ми	четырьмя́ста́ми	пятьюста́ми
Prep.	двухста́х	трёхста́х	четырёхста́х	пятиста́х

The numerals шестьсо́т, семьсо́т, восемьсо́т, and девятьсо́т decline and are stressed like пятьсо́т. As we would expect from 6.1.3 and 6.1.6, восемьсо́т has both восемьюста́ми and the colloquial восьмьюста́ми.

6.1.9. The numerals ты́сяча 'thousand', миллио́н 'million', биллио́н 'billion' (= one thousand million), миллиа́рд 'billion', триллио́н 'trillion', and квадрильо́н 'quadrillion' are all nouns and decline as such, with the quantified object in the gen. pl.: cf. к ты́сяче/миллио́ну/ биллио́ну/миллиа́рду/триллио́ну/квадрильо́ну рубле́й; в ты́сяче/ миллио́не/биллио́не/миллиа́рде/триллио́не/квадрильо́не рубле́й. In the instr. sg. тысяча has both тысячью and тысячей; see *Грамматика 1980*, §1378 and Wade, §197.

6.2. Ordinal Numerals

The ordinal numerals are morphologically simply ordinary adjectives: пе́рвый, пя́тый, двадца́тый, со́тый. The only exception is тре́тий, which is a pronominal (see 5.12).

The ordinals are formed from the cardinals, either with or without change of stem, except for пе́рвый 'first' and второ́й 'second.' The ordinals for 'first' to 'trillionth' are:

пе́рвый	восьмидеся́тый
второ́й	девяно́стый
тре́тий	со́тый
четвёртый	сто пе́рвый
пя́тый	двухсо́тый
шесто́й	трёхсо́тый
седьмо́й	четырёхсо́тый
восьмо́й	пятисо́тый
девя́тый	шестисо́тый
деся́тый	семисо́тый
оди́ннадцатый	восьмисо́тый
двена́дцатый	девятисо́тый
трина́дцатый	ты́сячный
четы́рнадцатый	ты́сяча пе́рвый
пятна́дцатый	двухты́сячный
шестна́дцатый	трёхты́сячный
семна́дцатый	десятиты́сячный
восемна́дцатый	двухсотты́сячный
девятна́дцатый	пятисотты́сячный
двадца́тый	миллио́нный
двадца́ть пе́рвый	десятимиллио́нный
тридца́тый	шестидесятитрёхмиллио́нный
сороково́й	миллиа́рдный
пятидеся́тый	биллио́нный
шестидеся́тый	триллио́нный
семидеся́тый	

6.3. Collective Numerals

Russian has the collective numerals дво́е, тро́е, че́тверо, пя́теро, ше́стеро, се́меро, во́сьмеро, де́вятеро, де́сятеро. Their usage is limited to four categories of words: 1) nouns denoting male persons, e.g., пя́теро враче́й/ мальчиков, or epicene nouns, e.g., че́тверо сиро́т/пья́ниц; 2) with the nouns де́ти, ребя́та, лю́ди, ли́ца (in the meaning 'person'), with designations of immature animals (in -*ята*), and with substantivized adjectives and participles, e.g., ше́стеро дете́й/ люде́й/изве́стных лиц/теля́т/щеня́т/знако́мых/отдыха́ющих; 3) with the personal pronouns мы, вы, они́, e.g., оста́лись мы тро́е, нас бы́ло тро́е, я ви́дел их двои́х; 4) with *pluralia tantum*, e.g. тро́е сане́й/су́ток/но́жниц; for details and limitations, see *Грамматика 1980*, §1369.

Animacy is determined by the noun or pronoun and the collective numeral follows: я ви́дел двои́х враче́й/дете́й/теля́т/ отдыха́ющих, я ви́дел дво́е сане́й, я ви́дел их двои́х.

Table 6-8. Forms of the Collective Numerals

Nom.	дво́е	че́тверо	пя́теро
Acc.	= n. or g.	= n. or g.	= n. or g.
Gen.	двои́х	четверы́х	пятеры́х
Dat.	двои́м	четверы́м	пятеры́м
Instr.	двои́ми	четверы́ми	пятеры́ми
Prep.	двои́х	четверы́х	пятеры́х

Тро́е declines and is stressed like дво́е; ше́стеро, се́меро, во́сьмеро, де́вятеро, де́сятеро decline and are stressed like пя́теро.

6.4. The Indefinite Numerals

This group includes мно́го, немно́го, ско́лько, не́сколько, сто́лько. Morphologically these are essentially identical to the collective numerals, but there is a difference in the animacy rules. In modern Russian both я посети́л мно́го друзе́й and я посети́л мно́гих друзе́й are possible. According to *Грамматика 1980*, §1379, мно́го is the predominant form.

Table 6-9. Indefinite Numerals

Nom.	мно́го	немно́го	ско́лько
Acc.	= n. or g.	= n. or g.	= n. or g.
Gen.	мно́гих	немно́гих	ско́льких
Dat.	мно́гим	немно́гим	ско́льким
Instr.	мно́гими	немно́гими	ско́лькими
Prep.	мно́гих	немно́гих	ско́льких

6.5. Animacy in Numerals

An issue of description: *Грамматика 1980*, §1370, states that два, три, четы́ре show animacy on the basis of their behavior in the accusative. If we look at the forms of these with nouns in all six cases, we could state that the numerals agree in case with the noun they modify (except in the nom./acc.), just like adjectives: два стола́ стоя́ло здесь; я ви́дел два стола́; я ви́дел двух коне́й/лошаде́й/дурако́в; я стоя́л недалеко́ от двух столо́в; я подошёл к двум стола́м; я стоя́л под двумя́ стола́ми; я стоя́л на двух стола́х.

But there is a crucial difference for such numerals as пять 'five': пять столо́в стои́т здесь; я ви́дел пять столо́в; я стоя́л недалеко́ от пяти́ столо́в; я подошёл к пяти́ стола́м; я стоя́л под пятью́ стола́ми; я стоя́л на пяти́ стола́х, but я ви́дел пять коне́й/лошаде́й /дурако́в, not *пяти́ коне́й/лошаде́й/дурако́в.

There is yet another set of relations for such numerals as миллиа́рд (see 6.1.8): миллиа́рд столо́в стои́т здесь; я ви́дел миллиа́рд столо́в; я стоя́л недалеко́ от миллиа́рда столо́в; я подошёл к миллиа́рду столо́в; я стоя́л под миллиа́рдом столо́в; я стоя́л на миллиа́рде столо́в, as well as я ви́дел миллиа́рд коне́й/ лошаде́й/ дурако́в, not *миллиа́рда коне́й/лошаде́й/дурако́в.

For два, три, четы́ре, the animate acc. is valid only when the numeral is not part of a larger number, so one must say я ви́дел двух студентов, я ви́дел два́дцать два/три́дцать три/во́семьдесят четыре/сто два/ миллио́н и три студе́нта. For details, see *Грамматика 1980*, §1370.

Finally we must take into account the behavior of мно́го, немно́го, ско́лько, не́сколько, сто́лько (see 6.4 above).

The issue is: do we conclude that animacy is manifested in the cardinal numerals only in два/три/четы́ре and only when they are not the last component of a number larger than 20, and not in пять, миллиа́рд etc., or do we conclude that agreement works three or four or five different ways in the different sets of numerals?

Verbs, Part 1

Present, Past, Imperative, and Infinitive

7.0. Introduction

Textbook writers and scholars have advocated various widely differing systems for describing the forms of the Russian verb. A traditional approach often starts out with verbs of the де́лать/чита́ть class and formulates a set of rules for the present tense that begins with "Remove the *-ть* of the infinitive and add the present tense endings *-ю, -ешь, ет, -ем, -ете, -ют.*" For verbs in *-ить*, such as говори́ть, a similar but confusingly different formula is applied: "Remove the *-ить*, not just the *-ть*; the endings are *-ю, -ишь, -ит, -им, -ите, -ят.*"

Of course, as soon as the learner encounters писа́ть or бить, the rules just given are no longer valid, and the books begin to talk about learning a "present stem" and a "past stem." For verbs like вести́, веду́, ведёшь, вёл, вела́, вели́, веди́! 'lead', one is advised to learn not just a present stem and a past stem, but to memorize at least two forms of the present tense and three of the past, plus the imperative and infinitive.

The student begins to wonder how anybody can master such a complicated system. Isn't there a simpler way of describing the forms of a Russian verb? There is, but most textbook authors have not paid much attention to it. Most textbooks continue to use a two-or-more-stem system, in which some forms are made from the present stem and some from the infinitive/past stem. Such systems require additional information or another stem to take into account some forms of such verbs as вести́, where the past, infinitive, and present each apparently use different stems: past вёл, вела́, вели́; infinitive вести́; present веду́, ведёшь.

In 1948 Roman Jakobson published "Russian Conjugation," in which he showed that a single stem (= base form, underlying form), if properly chosen, could by application of carefully specified and ordered rules produce all the forms of the present, past, imperative, and infinitive of all Russian verbs, with only a handful of irregularities left over.

Since the article was written in Jakobson's typical terse style, it was read primarily by scholars and advanced students of Slavic linguistics. Similar "single-stem" descriptions of other Slavic languages were published, but all were treated basically as intriguing demonstrations that such a description could be made. Nobody seemed to see any real pedagogical applications until the late 1950s, when Alexander Lipson introduced a one-stem approach in his own textbook, which he used for teaching at the Massachusetts Institute of Technology and for his private Russian language classes.

After Sputnik went aloft in 1957, large numbers of Americans tried to learn Russian, and the existing textbooks were not adequate, to put it as charitably as possible. Lipson's book was humorous, enabled students to talk at an early stage, and was quite sophisticated both pedagogically and linguistically. He soon acquired a large and eager audience in the Boston area. Other teachers in North America and Europe adopted and adapted some of Lipson's advances, including the use of a single-stem verb system.

Many textbooks and reference books approach the problem of verb forms by giving model verbs as patterns. This means learning quite a few forms in each of a substantial number of patterns. Zaliznjak 1977, for example, sets up sixteen basic types, each with several subtypes (typically from six to twelve). Just his tables of conjugation patterns take up forty-five pages, not including notes. Zaliznjak's listing of forms may be the most exhaustive, but it is also exhausting.

The Forms of Russian gives a modified and expanded version of the one-stem system, based primarily on the work of Lipson and Jakobson. It offers numerous examples and tries to avoid confusing terseness. Repetition is utilized when it seems to be useful; повторение—мать учения.

7.0.1. Note that from here on we will be dealing with verb **stems**, which are the underlying starting point. When stems are processed correctly through the proper set of ordered rules they produce the real forms of the verb. Rules for finding a stem form are given below, but you will find that you recognize patterns, just as you do in English (see the discussion of *bink* in Chapter 1).

As stated above, a stem is the base from which all of the "real" (occurring) forms of a word can be made by the correct application of a set of ordered rules. How, then, does one get the stem? For a quick and usually correct answer, take the present tense third person plural and past tense feminine sg. forms, remove the endings, and compare the two results. The longer of the two will be the stem (sometimes they are of equal length). The stress pattern can be ascertained by using information supplied in Chapter 8. For examples of finding stems, see 7.6 at the end of this chapter.

The real answer is that you recognize a pattern that the word fits into, just as you do with new words in English. If faced with the need to use the plural of an unknown word *blig*, you fit it into the pattern of *twig, fig, pig, swig*, etc. and make *bligs*, pronounced /bligz/. There are only about twenty patterns for Russian verbs, and they will all be treated in Chapter 8. The rules given in the first part of Chapter 8 are just a way of working out the forms if the pattern doesn't click.

7.0.2. The following sets with similar or identical infinitive forms but completely different present/future forms illustrate the fact that the infinitive does not give enough information in many or even most Russian verbs.

ма́зать	~	ма́жет		нести́	~	несёт
де́лать	~	де́лает		вести́	~	ведёт
конча́ть	~	конча́ет		скрести́	~	скребёт
крича́ть	~	кричи́т		плести́	~	плетёт
нача́ть	~	начнёт				
				печь	~	печёт, пёк
жить	~	живёт		стричь	~	стрижёт, стриг
шить	~	шьёт				
реши́ть	~	реши́т		плыть	~	плывёт
				крыть	~	кро́ет
лежа́ть	~	лежи́т				
меша́ть	~	меша́ет		кри́кнуть	~	кри́кнул
				кре́пнуть	~	креп
жать	~	жмёт				
жать	~	жнёт		маха́ть	~	ма́шет
				маха́ть	~	маха́ет
боле́ть	~	боле́ет				
боле́ть	~	боли́т				

7.1. Definitions

It will be useful to categorize verb stems by various characteristics.

Vowel stems, such as ходи+,[1] сиде+, лежа+, писа+, *end* in a vowel (surprise!).

Consonant stems *end* in a consonant. Consonant stems are divided into *resonant* stems and *obstruent* stems.

Resonant stems end in *в, й, м, н, р, л*:[2] жив+, знай+, стан+, жм+, жн+, тр+.

Obstruent stems end in any consonant other than *в, й, м, н, р, л*: пас+, полз+, раст+, пад+, клад+, скрёб+,[3] пёк+,[3] стриг+.

Syllabic stems have one or more vowels in the root, the suffix, or both: ходи+, сиде+, лежа+, писа+, жив+, знай+, пас+, полз+, раст+, пад+, клад+, скрёб+, пёк+, стриг+, зва+, лга+, спа+; *non-syllabic stems* do not: жм+, жн+, тр+, жг+.

Similarly, *syllabic roots* have a vowel in the root: ход-,[4] сид-, пис-, жив-, знай-, пас-, полз-, раст-, пад-, клад-, скрёб-, пёк-, стриг-, and *non-syllabic roots* do not: жм-, жн-, тр-, жг-, зв-, лг- сп- (although they may have a vowel in a suffix, thus becoming *syllabic stems*: зва+, лга+, спа+).

Suffixed stems have a suffix: ходи+, сиде+, молча+, писа+, зва+, лга+, спа+, бде+; *non-suffixed* stems do not: пас+, полз+, раст+, пад+, клад+, скрёб+, пёк+, стриг+, жив+, знай+.

In some books you may encounter the term *primary* instead of *non-suffixed* and *secondary* instead of *suffixed.*

7.2. The Present Tense

In Chapter 8 we will give a catalog of verb types and a set of rules for making forms; let us first now consider the endings of the present tense (sometimes called *non-past*, which is more accurate but also is unwieldy).

---

[1] The plus sign means that a form is a *stem*; that is, endings must be added to produce a word form.

[2] Although *л* belongs with the other resonant consonants because of its phonetic and phonological properties in Russian, there are no CSR verb stems ending in -*л*.

[3] The letter *ё* means that when stressed, it will be *ё*, not *e*: я скребу́, пеку́; ты скребёшь, печёшь, она́ скребла́, пекла́, but он скрёб, он пёк.

[4] The hyphen at the end shows that the form is a *root*, to which one or more prefixes and/or suffixes (including) must be added to form a *stem*, e.g. пре-вос-ход-и-тель-н+ый, о-пис-а-тель-н+ый.

7.2.1. If we take the most simple type of verbs, non-suffixed ones such as жив+ 'live', пас+ 'graze, shepherd', клад+ 'place, put', пёк+ 'bake', etc., we see a simple addition of ending to stem, with the stress automatically on the ending:

Table 7-1. The Present Tense of жив+, пас+, клад+, пёк+

	Sg.	**Pl.**
1st Person	живу́, пасу́ кладу́, пеку́	живём, пасём кладём, печём
2nd Person	живёшь, пасёшь кладёшь, печёшь	живёте, пасёте кладёте, печёте
3rd Person	живёт, пасёт кладёт, печёт	живу́т, пасу́т кладу́т, пеку́т

From these forms we may abstract a set of endings: {*-у, -ёшь, -ёт, -ём, -ёте, -ут*}, or, in transcription, {u, ̦oš, ̦ot, ̦om, ̦oțe, ut}, where the symbol ̦ denotes palatalization of the preceding consonant, unless that consonant occurs only hard (*ж, ц, ш*). The change of *к* → *ч* and *г* → *ж* before the *ё* will be accounted for in our rules later, in Rule 17, section 8.1.3.4.

7.2.2. If we next consider another group of common basic verbs, those with a stem in *-a*, such as плака+ 'cry', паха+ 'plow', рва+ 'tear', we find the same endings, except that unstressed *ё* is replaced by *e*, as we would expect:

7.2.3. Table 7-2 shows all three possible present tense stress patterns for Russian verbs: 1) stress always on the stem (пла́чу, пла́чешь, пла́чет, пла́чем, пла́чете, пла́чут); 2) stress always on the ending (рву, рвёшь, рвёт, рвём, рвёте, рвут);[5] and 3) stress on the ending in the first person sg. and shifting to the syllable before the ending in the other five forms (пашу́, па́шешь, па́шет, па́шем, па́шете, па́шут).

---

[5] To be sure, the stress here can only be on the endings, but consider also опа́+ 'yell': ору́, орёшь, орёт, орём, ору́т.

Table 7-2. The Present Tense of плака+, паха+, рва+

	Sg.	**Pl.**
1st Person	плáчу, пашý, рву	плáчем, пáшем, рвём
2nd Person	плáчешь, пáшешь, рвёшь	плáчете, пáшете, рвёте
3rd Person	плáчет, пáшет, рвёт	плáчут, пáшут, рвут

As with the noun, we can denote fixed stem stress with the note [F] following the stem, or we may put an acute accent over the vowel: плáка+. Fixed ending stress can be noted with [Fe] or an acute accent over the suffix: сидé+[6] and shifting stress with [S] or a grave accent over the vowel: пахà+. There is only one shifting type; see 7.2.11 and Chapter 8.

7.2.4. In some verbs the last consonant before the endings is soft in the present tense, and then of course the first sg. and third pl. endings are spelled with *ю* rather than *у*: so крáпа+ [F] 'sprinkle (rain)' and дремà+ [S] 'doze' have the following forms:

Table 7-3. The Present Tense of крáпа+ and дремà+

	Sg.	**Pl.**
1st Person	крáплю, дремлю́	крáплем, дрéмлем
2nd Person	крáплешь, дрéмлешь	крáплете, дрéмлете
3rd Person	крáплет, дрéмлет	крáплют, дрéмлют

Forms of крáпа+ other than the 3rd person require some imagination, but they do exist and illustrate my points.

7.2.5. If we move to one more large group of first conjugation verbs, those in -нуть, such as вёрнý+ [F] 'return' and трóну+ [F] 'touch', we again see the same endings:

---

[6] Fixed end stress in verbs ending in a consonant will be marked with an acute accent over the last consonant: пáс+, пёќ+, плёѓ+.

Table 7-4. The Present Tense of вёрну+, тро́ну+

	Sg.	**Pl.**
1st Person	верну́, тро́ну	вернём, тро́нем
2nd Person	вернёшь, тро́нешь	вернёте, тро́нете
3rd Person	вернёт, тро́нет	верну́т, тро́нут

7.2.6. Two major groups of first-conjugation verbs remain. One comprises those which end in *-a* or *-e* which does not drop in the present tense: знать/зна́ю 'know', де́лать/де́лаю 'do', чита́ть/чита́ю 'read', греть/ гре́ю 'warm', красне́ть/красне́ю 'blush'. The other is verbs in -овать, such as адресова́ть 'address'.

In these verbs one might propose *-ю, -ёшь, -ёт, -ём, -ёте, -ют* as the set of endings, based upon the orthography (the *ё* rather than *e* is again based on the nature of the vowel after {j} when stressed, as in узна́ть ~ узна́ет but узнава́ть ~ узнаёт, смея́ться ~ смеётся, гнить ~ гниёт, бить ~ бьёт). If, however, we look at the same words in transcription, we see the underlying endings are still {u, ˌoš, ˌot, ˌom, ˌoțe, ut}.

Table 7-5a. The Present Tense of знать ~ зна́ю, де́лать ~ де́лаю, чита́ть ~ чита́ю, греть ~ гре́ю, красне́ть ~ красне́ю

	Sg.	**Pl.**
1st Person	зна́ю, де́лаю, чита́ю, гре́ю, красне́ю	зна́ем, де́лаем, чита́ем, гре́ем, красне́ем
2nd Person	зна́ешь, де́лаешь, чита́ешь, гре́ешь, красне́ешь	зна́ете, де́лаете, чита́ете, гре́ете, красне́ете
3rd Person	зна́ет, де́лает, чита́ет, гре́ет, красне́ет	зна́ют, де́лают, чита́ют, гре́ют, красне́ют

Table 7-5b. The Present Tense of знать ~ зна́ю, де́лать ~ де́лаю, чита́ть ~ чита́ю, гре́ть ~ гре́ю, красне́ть ~ красне́ю in Transcription

	Sg.	Pl.
1st Person	znáju, délaju, čitáju, gréju, krasnéju	znájom, délajom, čitájom, gréjom, krasnéjom
2nd Person	znájoš, délajoš, čitájoš, gréjoš, krasnéjoš	znájoţe, délajoţe, čitájoţe, gréjoţe, krasnéjoţe
3rd Person	znájot, délajot, čitájot, gréjot, krasnéjot	znájut, délajut, čitájut, gréjut, krasnéjut

The reality of stems ending in {j} and Russians' perception of them is illustrated by such words as всезна́йка 'know-it-all', незна́йка 'know-nothing', водогре́й 'vessel for heating water', водогре́йка 'vessel or building for heating water', водогре́йня 'building for heating water', водогре́йный 'pertaining to the heating of water', where the suffixes -ка, -Ø, -ня, and -ный are clearly added to a stem ending in {j}. We also see the {j} in the imperative: знай!, де́лай!, чита́й!, грей!, красне́й!

Note that if the stem ends in {j}, the {j} is lost before the infinitive suffix. This is part of a more general rule about verbs which also explains the loss of the {v} in жив+ and the {n} in стан+ before the -*ть* of the infinitive and the -*л* of the past tense; see Rule 8 in 8.1.3.2.

7.2.7. The final major group is verbs in -ов-ать, such as атакова́ть. In -ов-ать verbs the suffix -а- drops, as in писа́ть and орать, and the -ов becomes -уй- before a vowel ending, giving present forms -ую, -уёшь, -уёт, -уём, -уёте, -уют. Verbs ending in -ов-ать all have fixed stress, which subdivides into three accent patterns: 1) stress on the stem (тре́бовать 'demand'), 2) stress on the -а- where the -ов- is a suffix (атакова́ть 'attack'), in which case present-tense stress is on the -уй- (атаку́ю), and 3) stress on the -а- where the -ов- is part of the root (кова́ть 'hew, forge'; compare the etymologically connected English *hew*), in which case present-tense stress is on the endings (кую́, куёшь). This last pattern only includes seven verbs: блева́ть (блюю́) 'vomit', жева́ть (жую́) 'chew', клева́ть (клюю́) 'peck', кова́ть (кую́) 'hew, forge', плева́ть (плюю́) 'spit', сновáть (сну́ю) 'warp (textiles); scurry about', совáть (су́ю) 'shove, poke', whereas the verbs of the first two types are to be numbered in the thousands.

In this group of verbs we again see the consonant {j} plus a vowel being written with a soft vowel letter: {uj+u} → ую, {uj+ͺoš} → уёшь, etc.

Table 7-6. The Present of трéбова+, атаковá+, ковá+.

	Sg.	**Pl.**
1st Person	трéбую, кую́ атаку́ю	трéбуем, куём атаку́ем
2nd Person	трéбуешь, куёшь атаку́ешь	трéбуете, куёте атаку́ете
3rd Person	трéбует, куёт атаку́ет	трéбуют, кую́т атаку́ют

Although several other not-very-numerous types of first conjugation verbs remain, their treatment does not differ in principle from that of the groups we have examined, so let us remember the set of endings that we have deduced ({-у, -ёшь, -ёт, -ём, -ёте, -ут}, or, in transcription, {u, ͺoš, ͺot, ͺom, ͺoͺe, ut}) and turn to the second conjugation.

7.2.8. *Second conjugation* verbs include three major groups: 1) verbs with the suffix *-u-* in the infinitive, such as ходи́ть 'go' (but not пить, вить, лить, бить, шить, гнить, брить, where the *u* is part of the root); 2) verbs which in the infinitive have a suffix *-e-* that drops in the present, such as сидéть 'sit'; 3) verbs with the suffix *-a-* after *ж/ш/ч/щ* in the infinitive and the *-a-* drops in the present, such as лежáть 'lie'.

Table 7-7. The Present of ходи́+, сидé+, лежá+.

	Sg.	**Pl.**
1st Person	хожу́, сижу́, лежу́	хóдим, сиди́м лежи́м
2nd Person	хóдишь, сиди́шь, лежи́шь	хóдите, сиди́те лежи́те
3rd Person	хóдит, сиди́т, лежи́т	хóдят, сидя́т, лежа́т

The endings are obviously different from those of the first conjugation in all but the first person singular, but if we substitute *u* for *ë* and *ят* for *ym*, we get a set of endings that seem adequate to describe the facts observed. One might ask whether the *-ишь, -ит, -им, -ите* are that or really *-шь, -т, -м, -те* appended to the stem ходи+. Since in the first singular and the third plural the *-y* and *-ят* clearly replace the *-и-* of the stem, and since the *-и-* in the four forms хо́дишь, хо́дит, хо́дим, хо́дите from ходи́ть is not stressed, whereas in the infinitive it is, it seems better to posit the *-и-* as part of the ending. Decisive evidence is supplied by сиде́+, where all six forms of the present clearly replace the é of the stem with the vowels of the present tense endings: сижу́, сиди́шь, сиди́т, сиди́м, сиди́те, сидя́т. Moreover, taking the endings as *y, ишь, ит, им, ите, ят* makes the present endings of the first and second conjugations parallel:

1st	-у	-ёшь	-ёт	-ём	-ёте	-ут
2nd	-у	-ишь	-ит	-им	-ите	-ят

A more subtle and more difficult question is whether the palatalization of the stem-final consonant in the various forms of the second conjugation is due to the endings of the present or is 'left over' from the infinitive. We will tackle this later.

7.2.9. Let us now review the verbs that we have considered so far and how they combine with the endings. Verbs whose stem ends in a consonant simply add the vowel endings of the present to the stem: жив+, пас+, клад+, пёк+, знай+, делай+, читай+, грей+, красней+ give present tense живу́, пасу́, пеку́, кладу́, зна́ю, де́лаю, чита́ю, гре́ю, красне́ю. See Rule 18 in 8.1.3.4.

We can even make a generalization about the place of the accent in the present tense: if the stem ends in any consonant other than {j} or {n},[7] then the present tense stress will be on the endings. If the stem ends in {j} or {n}, then the stress is on the stem (which syllable of the stem must be learned, as shown by де́лай+ vs. чита́й+). When we do a systematic survey later, we will find only a few exceptions to this rule for automatic placement of the stress in the present tense.

---

[7] See 8.1.3.1. There are only four syllabic stems in {н}: де́н+ 'place, put'; ста́н+ 'become'; сты́н+ 'cool, become cold'; (за-) стря́н+ 'get stuck'.

If the stem ends in a vowel, such as пла́ка+, паха̀+, рва̀+, кра́па+, дрема̀+, вёрну́+, тро́ну+, тре́бова+, атакова̀+, кова̀+, ходѝ+, сиде́+, лежа́+, then the vowel at the end of the stem is *truncated* (cut off, dropped) before the vowel of the present tense endings, giving in the third person singular пла́чет, па́шет, рвёт, кра́плет, дре́млет, вернёт, тро́нет, тре́бует, атаку́ет, куёт, хо́дит, сиди́т, лежи́т. See Rule 19 in 8.1.3.4.

7.2.10. We see two other things happening in the present tense forms. First, the consonant before the final vowel of the stem *may* mutate, as it does in all six forms of пла́ка+ ~ пла́чу ~ пла́чет, паха̀+ ~ пашу́ ~ па́шет, кра́па+ ~ кра́плю ~ кра́плет, дрема̀+ ~ дремлю́ ~ дре́млет, but only in the first singular of ходѝ+ ~ хожу́ ~ хо́дит, сиде́+ ~ сижу́ ~ сиди́т. In тре́бова+, all six forms change, but there is an unexpected transformation of -ов- to -уй- ~ тре́бую ~ тре́бует, атакова̀+ ~ атаку́ю ~ атаку́ет, кова̀+ ~ кую́ ~ куёт. There is no mutation, only softening before {о} in рва̀+ ~ рву́ ~ рвёт, верну+ ~ верну́ ~ вернёт, тро́ну+ ~ тро́ну ~ тро́нет. In лежа́+ ~ лежу́ ~ лежи́т, the *ж* is already a mutated consonant.

In general, mutation *may* occur if the **dropped** vowel is {а, е, i, о}, but not if the vowel is {u}. It usually *will* occur if the **first vowel of the ending** is a **rounded** vowel {о} or {u}, but usually will not if it is {а} or {i} (the vowel {е} does not occur as the first element of a verb ending). The verb рва̀+ is apparently exceptional here also: in spite of the {а} dropping, mutation does not occur. This in its turn is according to another rule which says that verbs with a non-syllabic root and the suffix -*a*+ do not have consonant mutation in the present; cf. жда̀+, вра̀+, зва̀+, рва̀+, etc. This will be covered systematically in Chapter 8; at this point I am only indicating some issues. Verbs like рва̀+ (and опа́+, which is irregular) were chosen deliberately in order to illustrate the variety of Russian verbs.

7.2.11. The second thing that *may* happen in the present tense forms is stress shift. Verb stems ending in a consonant have automatic stress placement in the present tense, as explained above in 7.2.9 and later in Rule 1 of 8.1.3.1. They never have shifting stress in the present tense (except for мог+ 'be able': могу́, мо́жешь, мо́жет, мо́жем, мо́жете, мо́гут). Verbs with a stem ending in a vowel may have a present tense with 1) fixed stem stress (пла́ка+, ка́па+, тро́ну+, тре́бова+); 2) fixed end stress (рва́+, ве́рну́+, кова́+, сиде́+, лежа́+), or 3) shifting stress (паха̀+, ходѝ+).

With vowel-stem verbs we will use an acute accent (´) to denote fixed present-tense accent, and a grave accent (`) to denote shifting present-tense accent.

Since рва̀+ has a present tense stem рв+, and the present tense stress is therefore automatically on the endings (рву, рвёшь, рвёт...), the stress mark in non-syllabic roots with the suffix -à refers, as an exception, to the past tense: рвал, рвала́, рва́ло; ждà+ ~ ждал, ждала́, жда́ло.

Which type of stress a given verb has must be shown and learned. When we do the systematic inventory of verbs we will see that it is often possible to predict the type of stress, or at least guess fairly accurately (e.g., verbs in -*e*+ or husher plus -*a*+ normally have fixed end stress, as in сиде́+ and лежа́+).

7.3. The Past Tense

Let us now turn to the past tense forms of the verbs discussed earlier:

Table 7-8. The Past of пла́ка+, паха̀+, кра́па+, дрема̀+

	Sg.	Pl.
Masc.	пла́кал, паха́л, кра́пал, дрема́л	пла́кали, паха́ли, кра́пали, дрема́ли
Fem.	пла́кала, паха́ла, кра́пала, дрема́ла	
Neut.	пла́кало, паха́ло, кра́пало, дрема́ло	

Table 7-9. The Past of ве́рну́+, тро́ну+, тре́бова+, атакова́+, кова́+

	Sg.	Pl.
Masc.	верну́л, тро́нул, тре́бовал, атакова́л, кова́л	верну́ли, тро́нули, тре́бовали, атакова́ли, кова́ли
Fem.	верну́ла, тро́нула, тре́бовала, атакова́ла, кова́ла	
Neut.	верну́ло, тро́нуло, тре́бовало, атакова́ло, кова́ло	

Table 7-10. The Past of ходи́+, сиде́+, лежа́+

	Sg.	Pl.
Masc.	ходи́л, сиде́л, лежа́л	ходи́ли, сиде́ли, лежа́ли
Fem.	ходи́ла, сиде́ла, лежа́ла	
Neut.	ходи́ло, сиде́ло, лежа́ло	

7.3.1. As we see, the past tense uses compound suffixes. The tense suffix is {-l-}, and it is followed by pronominal endings: {-∅, -a, -o, -i}. As expected in pronominals, the {i} is realized as *-u*, so the surface forms are: *-л, -ла, -ло, -ли.*

7.3.2. As shown in 7.2.9, consonant plus vowel join smoothly in forming the present tense, whereas vowel joining vowel causes truncation of the first element. Since all four of the past tense forms begin with a consonant, we expect, and find, that stems ending in a vowel will undergo no changes and that stems ending in a consonant will have something happen. The principle is "unlikes combine smoothly," as do opposite poles of magnets, whereas "likes clash" as do similar poles of magnets. See Rule 7 and Rules 8 through 12 of 8.1.3.3.

7.3.3. *Stress shift can* (but does not *necessarily*) occur only when *truncation* takes place, and truncation takes place only when V+V or C+C occurs. Consonant mutation occurs *only* when V+V truncation has taken place. Therefore consonant mutation and stress shift can occur in the present tense of vowel stems (V+V), and stress shift can occur in the past tense of consonant stems (C+C).

Thus truncation occurs in the present of паха́+ (я пашу́), дрема́+ (я дремлю́), вёрну́+ (я верну́), атакова́+ (я атаку́ю), кова́+ (я кую́), ходи́+ (я хожу́), сиде́+ (я сижу́), and лежа́+ (я лежу́), but stress shift is found only in паха́+ (ты па́шешь), дрема́+ (ты дре́млешь), and ходи́+ (ты хо́дишь).

Consonant mutation occurs in the first sg. present of паха́+, (я пашу́), дрема́+ (я дремлю́), ходи́+ (я хожу́), and сиде́+ (я сижу́), but not in the first sg. of вёрну́+ (я верну́).

7.3.4. There are minor exceptions to the generalizations in 7.3.2 and 7.3.3; the past tense stress of рва́+ is one (see 7.2.11 and Table 7-12); the lack of truncation in the past of па́с+ and пёк+ is another (see Table 7-11).

The resonant consonants {j}, {n}, and {v} will always truncate before any consonant; {t} and {d} truncate before {l}; other combinations will be discussed later. See Rules 8 through 12 in 8.1.3.3.

Table 7-11. The Past Tense of жив+, пас+, клад+, пёк+

	Sg.	**Pl.**
Masc.	жил, пас клал, пёк	жи́ли, пасли́ кла́ли, пекли́
Fem.	жила́, пасла́ кла́ла, пекла́	
Neut.	жи́ло, пасло́ кла́ло, пекло́	

Table 7-12. The Past Tense of рва+, знай+, делай+,
читай+, грей+, красней+

	Sg.	**Pl.**
Masc.	рвал, знал, де́лал чита́л, гре́л, красне́л	рва́ли, зна́ли, де́лали чита́ли, гре́ли, красне́ли
Fem.	рвала́, зна́ла, де́лала чита́ла, гре́ла, красне́ла	
Neut.	рва́ло, зна́ло, де́лало чита́ло, гре́ло, красне́ло	

Table 7-13. The Past Tense of ходи+, сиде+, лежа+

	Sg.	**Pl.**
Masc.	ходи́л, сиде́л, лежа́л	ходи́ли, сиде́ли, лежа́ли
Fem.	ходи́ла, сиде́ла, лежа́ла	
Neut.	ходи́ло, сиде́ло, лежа́ло	

The past tense is thus rather simple in outline, although the stress patterns and the details of C+C truncation add some points which we will examine in the systematic survey.

7.4. The Imperative

Russian uses suffixes (endings and particles—see below) to make imperative forms for the second person singular and plural. Forms for the other persons are made in other ways; e.g., пусть читáет, давáйте читáть.

Table 7-14. The Imperative

Stem	2nd Sg.	2nd Pl.
жѝв+	живѝ	живѝте
пас́+	пасѝ	пасѝте
клáд+	кладѝ	кладѝте
пёќ+	пекѝ	пекѝте
плáка+	плачь	плáчьте
пахà+	пашѝ	пашѝте
рвà+	рвѝ	рвѝте
дремà+	дремлѝ	дремлѝте
вёрну́+	вернѝ	вернѝте
трóну+	тронь	трóньте
знáй+	знай	знáйте
дéлай+	дéлай	дéлайте
читáй+	читáй	читáйте
грéй+	грéй	грéйте
краснéй+	краснéй	краснéйте
трéбова+	трéбуй	трéбуйте
атаковá+	атакýй	атакýйте
ковá+	куй	кýйте
ходѝ+	ходѝ	ходѝте
сидé+	сидѝ	сидѝте
лежá+	лежѝ	лежѝте

The correct imperative from крáпа+ is probably крáпли.

7.4.1. By examining the forms we see that the most common ending for the imperative is -*u*, as in живѝ, пасѝ, кладѝ, пекѝ, пашѝ, рвѝ, крáпли, дремлѝ, вернѝ, ходѝ, сидѝ, лежѝ. A second ending is apparently -Ø, seen in плачь, тронь, знай, де́лай, чита́й, гре́й, красне́й, тре́буй, атаку́й, куй.

The verbs which seem to have -Ø as the ending nonetheless show stem changes like those caused by vowel endings in the present tense: the к in пла́ка+ goes to ч; the н in тро́ну+ goes to нь ; the -ова- in тре́бова+, атакова́+, кова́+ goes to -уй-. However, in other places we have seen that the Ø ending normally does not cause changes (го́род plus Ø = го́род [nom. sg.]; рука́ minus -a plus Ø = рук [gen. pl.]; in deverbal nouns Ø does not affect the consonant: перехо́д, приве́т), This calls into question the accuracy of considering Ø as an ending of the imperative.

It seems as if something evoked the changes and then disappeared, leaving behind only the results of its presence. The obvious candidate is the -и which appears in the imperative of other verbs. When does the -и get lost? Apparently when it follows only a single consonant and is not stressed: consider плачь, тронь, знай, де́лай, чита́й, гре́й, красне́й, тре́буй, атаку́й. If it follows two consonants, the -и remains even when unstressed: кра́пли, по́мни.

7.4.1.1. The only form not accounted for by this rule is куй, where the present tense stress кую́, куёшь would argue for an imperative *куи́. Further investigation shows that the imperative ending -и always drops when it follows a stem-final -й. Compare стоя́+ ~ стою́ ~ стой!, смея́+-ся ~ смею́сь ~ сме́йся!.

7.4.1.2. Unaccounted for is the fact that the -и of the imperative produces consonant mutation in verbs of the пла́ка+, паха̀+, кра́па+, and дрема̀+ type, but not in the ходи́+ and сиде́+ types. It thus acts like a rounded vowel in the first type, but not in the last two (see above in the discussion of the present tense, 7.2.10). There is no obvious solution to the contradiction, so we will simply have to note that mutation of the consonant takes place in the imperative of verbs in hard consonant plus -a, just as it does in the present tense.

7.4.1.3. Note also the verb пий+ (and the other four conjugated like it, вий+, лий+, бий+, ший+) drops the и of the stem when a vowel ending is added, giving present tense пью, пьёшь, etc. ({pij+} plus {u} → / pju/). In the imperative adding -и should give *пьи, but after /j/ и → Ø, leaving /pj/, but since a phonologically independent word (as distinguished from most prepositions, particles, etc.) must have a vowel, the fill vowel *e* is inserted according to the rules, giving the actual form, пей. Observe that proper application of the ordered rules makes these five verbs completely regular.

7.4.1.4. The only exceptions to the rule in 7.4.1.1 that *-u* in the imperative drops after /j/ are eleven verbs in *-ой+* and their compounds, for most of which the imperative is prescribed as *-ой*, although there is in fact some vacillation between *-ой* and *-ой*. The verb тай+ 'secrete, hide' is also an exception, with тай! as the imperative. Note that because of unstressed vowel reduction, all twelve verbs have the spoken form /C(C) ají/ for the imperative, where $C = consonant$.

The eleven are: сбой+ 'cause or allow a stoppage or interruption', гной+ 'let rot or decay', двой+ 'double, divide into two', дой+ 'milk', крой+ 'cut (cloth)', плой+ 'pleat; wave hair', пой+ 'give to drink, water', рой+ 'swarm', слой+ 'layer, stratify', трой+ 'treble, divide into three', хвой+ 'cover with pine needles'. According to some the verbs тай+ and пой+ have orthoepic forms only in *-й* (тай! and пой!), which is probably to avoid homonymy with the imperatives тай! from тая+ 'melt' and пой! from поя+ (irregular present) 'sing'.

7.4.1.5. A further interesting point about the imperative is that the plural suffix *-те* does not affect preceding consonants, so from знай+, делай+, читай+, грей+, краснёй+ we have infinitives знать, делать, читать, греть, краснеть with the *й* dropped by C+C truncation, but imperatives знайте, делайте, читайте, грейте, краснейте; similarly плака+ gives плачьте, реза+ gives режьте, ответи+ gives ответьте, and стан+ gives станьте. This same particle *-те*, meaning 'second person included in statement', can also be hung on a first person plural verb form without causing truncation: пойдёмте 'let's go and you're included in the exhortation'. The particle *-ка*, which expresses softening of command, politeness, exhortation (Isačenko 1960: 490–91), exhibits the same behavior toward preceding consonants: читай-ка 'please read', стань-ка 'stand/become, please', ответь-ка 'be so kind as to answer', режь-ка 'cut (some), please'.

7.4.1.6. Imperative stress is the same as that of the first person singular, except when the rule about stems ending in {j} (see 7.4.1.1) interferes:

жив+ ~ живу, живи!   пас+ ~ пасу, паси!

кла́д+	~	кладу́, клади́!	красне́й+	~ красне́ю,
пёќ+	~	пеку́, пеки́		красне́й!
пла́ка+	~	пла́чу, плачь!	тре́бова+	~ тре́бую, тре́буй!
паха̀+	~	пашу́, паши́!	атакова́+	~ атаку́ю, атаку́й!
рва̀+	~	рву́, рви́!	кова́+	~ кую́, куй!
кра́па+	~	кра́плю, кра́пли!	ходѝ+	~ хожу́, ходи́!
дрема̀+	~	дремлю́, дремли́	колотѝ+	~ колочу́,
вёрну́+	~	верну́, верни́!		коло́тишь,
тро́ну+	~	тро́ну, тро́нь!		колоти́!
зна́й+	~	зна́ю, зна́й	сиде́+	~ сижу́, сиди́!
де́лай+	~	де́лаю, де́лай!	терпѐ+	~ терплю́, терпи́!
чита́й+	~	чита́ю, чита́й!	лежа́+	~ лежу́, лежи́!
гре́й+		~ гре́ю, гре́й!	держа̀+	~ держу́, держи́!

7.5. The Infinitive

Table 7-15. The Infinitive

Stem	Infinitive	Stem	Infinitive
жи́в+	жить	зна́й+	знать
пас́+	пасти́	де́лай+	де́лать
кла́д+	класть	чита́й+	чита́ть
пёќ+	печь	гре́й+	греть
пла́ка+	пла́кать	красне́й+	красне́ть
паха̀+	паха́ть	тре́бова+	тре́бовать
рва̀+	рвать	атакова́+	атакова́ть
кра́па+	кра́пать	кова́+	кова́ть
дрема̀+	дрема́ть	ходѝ+	ходи́ть
вёрну́+	верну́ть	сиде́+	сиде́ть
тро́ну+	тро́нуть	лежа́+	лежа́ть

Russian forms the infinitive by adding a suffix (-ть for most stems, -ти for eighteen in -с, -з, -д, -т, or -б, and -чь for fifteen in -к or -г: see 8.2.9.1 through 8.2.9.4). As in the past tense, the consonant ending -ть joins a vowel stem with no changes (пла́кать, паха́ть, рвать, кра́пать, дрема́ть, верну́ть, тро́нуть, тре́бовать, атакова́ть, кова́ть, ходи́ть, сиде́ть, лежа́ть), but stems ending in a consonant may drop it (жить, знать, де́лать, чита́ть, греть, красне́ть) or change it (класть, печь) or let it remain (пасти́). This will be dealt with systematically in Chapter 8.

The purpose of Chapter 7 has been to show how we arrive at the endings and stems. Practice in making verb forms will be supplied in Chapter 8.

7.6. Examples of Finding Stems

3rd Pl.	Minus Ending	Fem. Sg.	Minus Ending	Stem
живу́т	жив	жила́	жи	жив+
пасу́т	пас	пасла́	пас	пас+
кладу́т	клад	кла́ла	кла	клад+
пеку́т	пек	пекла́	пек	пек+
рвут	рв	рвала́	рва	рва+
пла́чут	плач	пла́кала	плака	плака+
па́шут	паш	паха́ла	паха	паха+
зна́ют	знай	зна́ла	зна	знай+
де́лают	делай	де́лала	де́ла	делай+
чита́ют	читай	чита́ла	чита	читай+
гре́ют	грей	гре́ла	гре	грей+
красне́ют	красней	красне́ла	красне	красней+
кра́плют	крапль	кра́пала	крапа	кра́па+
дре́млют	дремль	дрема́ла	дрема	дрема+
верну́т	верн	верну́ла	верну	верну+
тро́нут	трону	тро́нула	трону	трону+
тре́буют	требуй	тре́бовала	требова	требова+
атаку́ют	атакуй	атакова́ла	атакова	атакова+
кую́т	куй	кова́ла	кова	кова+
хо́дят	ход	ходи́ла	ходи	ходи+
сидя́т	сид	сиде́ла	сиде	сиде+
лежа́т	леж	лежа́ла	лежа	лежа+

Stress information will be treated in Chapter 8.

8

Verbs, Part 2

Summary and Systematic Survey

8.1. Summary and Rules for the Present, Past, Imperative, and Infinitive Forms of the Russian Verb

8.1.1. As we have seen from preceding discussions, the past tense has a single set of endings: *-л, -ла, -ло, -ли*.

The imperative has a single ending, *-и*. For the allomorph Ø, see 7.4.1.1 through 7.4.1.4.

The same is true of the infinitive, which has *-ти*, with two allomorphs, *-ть*, which appears when the *-ти* is not stressed, and *-чь*, which appears when the stem of the verb ends in *к* or *г* (see Rule 14 in 8.1.3.3 below).

8.1.2. In contrast, the present has two sets of endings (see 7.2.8), each of which is used with certain types of stems:

1.	-у	-ёшь[1]	-ёт	-ём	-ёте	-ут
2.	-у	-ишь[1]	-ит	-им	-ите	-ят[1]

The first set of endings is conventionally called those of the "first conjugation" and the second set those of the "second conjugation." We will continue this terminology.

The endings of the present tense and the imperative are *vowel* endings, whereas the endings of the past tense and infinitive are *consonant* endings. As we saw in 7.3.2, consonant endings join smoothly with vowel stems, which means that the past tense and infinitive of vowel stems will be unproblematic. From 7.2.9, we know that vowel endings join smoothly with consonant stems, so the present tense and imperative of consonant stems will be easy.

---

[1] Note that the vowel letters ё, и, and я represent softness of preceding consonant plus a vowel, not {j} plus a vowel.

Problems will arise in the present tense and imperative of vowel stems, and in the past tense and infinitive of consonant stems, when vowel plus vowel or consonant plus consonant come into contact.

8.1.2.1. Determining which verb stems go with each set of present tense endings (i.e., which verb stems are "first conjugation" and which are "second conjugation") is not difficult. Of the twenty-two verb stems cited above, only three (ходи́+, сиде́+, лежа́+) are second conjugation. If we check every Russian verb, we will find that all second conjugation stems belong to one of the three groups represented by these verbs. The groups are: 1) verbs with the suffix *-и* (not as part of the stem, as it is in the verbs пить 'drink', вить 'wind', лить 'pour', бить 'beat', шить 'sew', гнить 'rot', брить 'shave'); 2) verbs with the suffix *-е* (but not with the suffix *-ей*, such as красне́й+; note that *-е* drops in the present because of V+V truncation, whereas *-ей* just adds the endings in C+V joining, e.g. сижу́, сиди́шь, but красне́ю, красне́ешь); 3) verbs with the suffix *-а* after *ш, ж, ч, щ* but not with the suffix *-ай*, such as реша́й+ and отвеча́й+; note that *-а* drops in the present because of V+V truncation, whereas *-ай* just adds the endings in C+V joining, e.g. лежу́, лежи́шь, but отвеча́ю, отвеча́ешь.[2]

8.1.2.2. Since verbs of these three types are second conjugation, we can define first conjugation verbs very simply as those verbs which do *not* have the suffixes *-и*, *-е*, or *-а* after *ш, ж, ч, щ*.

The first conjugation thus includes all verbs with no suffix (*primary* or *non-suffixed*), plus all verbs with the suffixes *у* or *о* or *-а* not after *ш, ж, ч, щ*, plus all suffixed verbs ending in a consonant (the only consonant which occurs at the end of a suffix is *й*, as in де́лай+, чита́й+, красне́й+).

8.1.2.3. If we examine still further the three groups of second conjugation verbs, we find some interesting statistics. There are thousands of verbs with the suffix *-и*. The suffix occurs after almost all consonants, both paired and unpaired. Verbs with the suffix *-и* show all three accent patterns (fixed on the stem, fixed on the ending, and shifting) in substantial numbers. Verbs with the suffix *-и* have a wide variety of meanings.

---

[2] There are two second-conjugation verbs with a stem in *-а* not preceded by *ш, ж, ч, щ*: they are спа́+ 'sleep' (сплю, спишь) and гна́+ 'chase' (гоню́, го́нишь). There is one first-conjugation verb with a stem in *-а* preceded by *ж*: ржа́+ 'neigh' (ржу, ржёшь).

In contrast, there is a very limited number of verbs in each of the other two groups—only about forty with the suffix *-e* and about thirty with the suffix *-a* after *ш, ж, ч, щ*. The great majority of each have fixed end stress, like сиде́+ and лежа́+ (for detailed information on stress, see 8.2.2 and 8.2.3). Most of the verbs of each group show one of two meanings: 'make a noise' or 'be in a state of X'. Examples are:

галде́+ 'make a din'	бренча́+ 'jingle'
свисте́+ 'whistle'	сиде́+ 'be sitting'
храпе́+ 'snore'	лете́+ 'be flying'
шуме́+ 'make a noise'	висе́+ 'be hanging'
визжа́+ 'scream, squeal'	лежа́+ 'be lying'
пища́+ 'squeak'	молча́+ 'be silent'
звуча́+ 'sound, resound'	дрожа́+ 'be trembling'

Except for кише́+ 'swarm', the suffixes are in complementary distribution: *e* occurs only after paired consonants, *a* occurs only after unpaired consonants.

Moreover, it turns out that stems with *ш, ж, ч, щ* plus *-a* are not infrequently clearly related to other words ending in a velar consonant: визжа́+ with визг, пища́+ with писк, звуча́+ with звук, лежа́+ with лёг, легла́, молча́+ with замо́лкнуть, дрожа́+ with дро́гнуть. We have already seen one instance where velar plus *e* turns into husher plus *-a*: нове́йший but велича́йший (see 4.4.3). There are more instances in roots and derivation.

The parallels seem too strong to be attributable solely to chance. We must consider verbs in *ш, ж, ч, щ* plus *-a* as being underlying velar plus *-e*:

молке+ → молча́+	писке+ → пища́+	слыхе → слы́ша+
дроге+ → дрожа́+	леге+ → лежа́+	

We can also include here the two verbs in *я* which belong to the second conjugation: сто́йе+ → стоя́+ and бо́йе+ → боя́+-ся. All other verbs in *я* after a vowel are first conjugation: смея́+-ся ~ смеётся, ла́я+ ~ ла́ет, се́я+ ~ се́ет.

By making our representations slightly more abstract, we can then say that second conjugation verbs have the suffixes *u* or *e*, and this allows for a powerful generalization: verbs with a suffix consisting solely of a front vowel belong to the second conjugation; all other verbs belong to the first.

8.2. Conjugation Rules

8.2.1. In this section we survey the rules for stress assignment in conjugating the Russian verb in the present tense.

Rule 1: Stress is automatic in the present tense and imperative of consonant stems. Verbs ending in -*й* or -*н* have the stress on the stem, all other consonant stems have the stress on the endings in the present and imperative. Since present tense and imperative stress is automatic (other than knowing *which* syllable of the stem bears the stress in the case of verbs in *й*; consider the pairs де́лай+ versus чита́й+ and обезлю́дей+ versus красне́й+), any stress mark on the stem of a consonant stem verb refers to the pattern of stress in the past, where stress is not automatic.

Examples (also see 7.2.9):

зна́й+	~	зна́ю, зна́ешь, знал, зна́ла, зна́ло, зна́ли
ду́й+	~	ду́ю, ду́ешь, дул, ду́ла, ду́ло, ду́ли
гре́й+	~	гре́ю, гре́ешь, грел, гре́ла, гре́ло, гре́ли
чита́й+	~	чита́ю, чита́ешь, чита́л, чита́ла, чита́ло, чита́ли
отвеча́й+	~	отвеча́ю, отвеча́ешь, отвеча́л, отвеча́ла, отвеча́ло, отвеча́ли
ста́н+	~	ста́ну, ста́нешь, стал, ста́ла, ста́ло, ста́ли
де́н+	~	де́ну, де́нешь, дел, де́ла, де́ло, де́ли
пас́+	~	пасу́, пасёшь, пас, пасла́, пасло́, пасли́
грыз+	~	грызу́, грызёшь, грыз, гры́зла, гры́зло, гры́зли
плёт+	~	плету́, плетёшь, плёл, плела́, плело́, плели́
крад+	~	краду́, крадёшь, крал, кра́ла, кра́ло, кра́ли
пёк+	~	пеку́, печёшь, пёк, пекла́, пекло́, пекли́
стри́г+	~	стригу́, стрижёшь, стриг, стри́гла, стри́гло, стри́гли
жив+	~	живу́, живёшь, жил, жила́, жи́ло, жи́ли

Rule 2: Stress is automatic in the past tense of vowel stems (other than knowing *which* syllable of the stem bears the stress), since consonant endings are added to the vowel stem. Since stress in the past is

automatic,[3] any stress mark on the stem refers to the pattern of stress in the present and imperative, where stress is not automatic.

Examples:

ходи́+ ~ хожу́, хо́дишь, ходи́л, ходи́ла, ходи́ло, ходи́ли, ходи́!
сиде́+ ~ сижу́, сиди́шь, сиде́л, сиде́ла, сиде́ло, сиде́ли, сиди́!
писа̀+ ~ пишу́, пи́шешь, писа́л, писа́ла, писа́ло, писа́ли, пиши́!

Rule 3: Fixed stress on the endings is marked with the acute accent (´) over the vowel of the suffix or over the final consonant of a non-suffixed stem:

сиде́+ ~ сижу́, сиди́шь, сиди́т, сиди́те, сидя́т, сиди́!
вёз+   ~ везу́, везёшь, везёт, везём, везёте, везу́т, вёз, везла́,
        везло́, везли́, вези́, везти́

Fixed stress on the stem is marked with the acute accent over the appropriate vowel of the stem:

пла́ка+   ви́де+   тре́бова+
отве́ти+   слы́ша+

Rule 4: Shifting stress is marked with a grave accent (`) over the appropriate vowel:

ходѝ+ ~ хожу́, хо́дишь, хо́дит, хо́дим, хо́дите, хо́дят, ходи́!
жѝв+   ~ жил, жила́, жи́ло, жи́ли

Rule 5: Shifting stress in the present tense has only one pattern, in which stress is on the ending in the first person singular and on the syllable before the endings in the other five forms:

ходѝ+   ~ хожу́, хо́дишь, хо́дит, хо́дим, хо́дите, хо́дят

---

[3] For the special situation with verbs of the рва̀+ type, see the footnote to Rule 5, 7.2.11, and 8.2.7.1.

хохота̀+ ~ хохочу́, хохо́чешь, хохо́чет, хохо́чем, хохо́чете, хохо́чут

колотѝ+ ~ колочу́, коло́тишь, коло́тит, коло́тим, коло́тите, коло́тят

Since truncation is a prerequisite for stress shift, in vowel stems stress shift can only occur in the present tense.[4] See Rule 19 below. Imperative stress is in principle the same as that of the first person singular; for examples and the exceptional situation of stems whose last consonant is {j}, see 7.4.1.6 above.

Rule 6: Shifting stress in the past tense has only one pattern, in which stress is on the ending of the feminine form and on the stem or prefix in the other three forms:

жѝв+ ~ жил, жила́, жи́ло, жи́ли

на̀-чн+ ~ на́чал, начала́, на́чало, на́чали[5]

за̀-йм+ ~ за́нял, заняла́, за́няло, за́няли

Since truncation is a prerequisite for stress shift, in consonant stems stress shift can only occur in the past tense. See Rules 8 and 9 below. When the stress in the past tense shifts onto the prefix, the stem is written with the grave accent on the prefix and it is understood that the forms of the present never have the stress on the prefix:

на̀-чн+ ~ начну́, начнёшь

за̀-йм+ ~ займу́, займёшь

пѐре-жив+ ~ переживу́, переживёшь, пе́режил, пережила́, пе́режило, пе́режили

8.2.2. Additional rules apply to the past tense and the infinitive.

Rule 7: A vowel stem followed by a consonant ending joins together smoothly:

писа̀+л → писа́л   ходѝ+л → ходи́л

---

[4] Except in the case of the ten first-conjugation verbs like рва̀+ which have a non-syllabic root followed by the suffix -à and do have shifting stress in the past, e.g. рвал, рвала́, рва́ло, рва́ли; see 8.2.7.1. This applies also to the two second-conjugation verbs спа̀+ and гна̀+.

[5] For non-syllabic verbs in -н alternating with -а/я, as well as -йм/-ьм 'take', see section 8.2.9.7 below.

This rule applies to the past tense and infinitive of vowel stems.

Rule 8: A consonant stem followed by a consonant ending results in truncation of the first consonant if that consonant is *й*, *н*, or *в*:

знáй+л	→	знáл	стáн+ть	→ стать
знáй+ть	→	знать	жúв+л	→ жил
стáн+л	→	стáл	жúв+ть	→ жить

This rule applies to the past tense and infinitive of consonant stems.

Rule 9: As a result of consonant truncation stress shift *may* occur:

жúв+л, ла, ло, ли	→ жил, жилá, жúло, жúли
пúй+л, ла, ло, ли	→ пил, пилá, пúло, пúли

This rule applies to the past tense of consonant stems.

Rule 10: A consonant stem ending in *т* or *д* followed by a consonant ending beginning with *л* results in truncation of the т or д:

плёт́+у	→ плетý	вёд+л	→ вáл
плёт́+л	→ плёл	клáд+л	→ клал

This rule applies to the past tense of consonant stems.

Rule 11: A consonant stem ending in *т*, *д*, or *б* followed by a consonant ending beginning with *т* results in the change of the *т*, *д* or *б* to *с*:

плёт́+ти	→ плестú	клáд+ти	→ класть
вёд+ти	→ вестú	скрёб́+ти	→ скрестú

This applies to the infinitive of consonant stems.

Rule 12: A consonant stem ending in *с*, *з*, *к*, *г*, *х*, *п*, *б*, or *р* followed by an ending consisting *only of л* results in truncation of the *л*:

пас́+л, ла	→ пас, паслá
вёз́+л, ла	→ вёз, везлá
пёќ+л, ла	→ пёк, пеклá
стрúг+л, ла	→ стриг, стрúгла

засо́х(ну)+л, ла   → засо́х, засо́хла
осле́п(ну)+л, ла   → осле́п, осле́пла
поги́б(ну)+л, ла   → поги́б, поги́бла
тр+у   → тру,
  тр+л, ла   → тёр, тёрла

This applies to the past tense of consonant stems and stems in (ну).[6]

Rule 13: The suffix of the infinitive is -*ти*. When the -*ти* is not stressed, the *и* is reduced to Ø, leaving softness. The *и* is stressed only when the *ти* follows an end-stressed consonant stem in *с, з, т, д,* or *б.* Examples of stressed and unstressed -*ти* are:

пас́+	~ пасти́	про-ч́т+	~ проч́есть
вёз+	~ везти́	вёд+	~ вести́
грыз+	~ грызти́	клад+	~ класть
плёт+	~ плести́	скрёб+	~ скрести́

There are no stem-stressed verbs in *с* or *б*; про-ч́т+ is the only one in *т*. Verbs in *й, н, в, р,* or any vowel have only stem stress in the infinitive:

зна́й+	~ знать	т́р+	~ тере́ть
гре́й+	~ греть	писа̀+	~ писа́ть
пѝй+	~ пить	кова́+	~ кова́ть
ста́н+	~ стать	ходѝ+	~ ходи́ть
жѝв+	~ жить	сиде́+	~ сиде́ть

Rule 14: A stem ending in the velars *к* or *г* combines this consonant with the -*ти* of the infinitive to produce *ч*: пёк+ти → печь;[7] стрѝг+ти → стричь. (*х* occurs only before the "mobile" (ну): засо́х(ну)+.) For *ч* from velar plus *т*, compare English *night, nocturnal* with Russian ночь and English *daughter* with Russian дочь. For the spelling of *ь* after *ч*, see 1.3.4. This rule applies to the infinitive of consonant stems ending in a velar.

---

[6] The parentheses around the *ну* indicate that it drops in the past tense; future засо́хну, засо́хнет, imperative засо́хни!, infinitive засо́хнуть, but past засо́х, засо́хла, засо́хло, засо́хли; cf. исчезнуть ~ вчера́ они́ исче́зли.

[7] For the *e* instead of *ё*, see the discussion of verbs in a velar in 8.2.9.4.

8.2.3. The consonant mutation rules shown in Table 8-1 apply to the present tense, imperative, present active and past passive participles (see Chapter 9) and derived imperfectives (see Chapter 10).

Table 8-1. Consonant Mutations

Original	п	б	ф	в	м	к	г	х	ск
Mutated	пль	бль	фль	вль	мль	ч	ж	ш	щ
Original	т	д	ст	с	з	л	н	р	
Mutated	ч*	ж	щ	ш	ж	ль	нь	рь	

* In words of Church Slavonic origin, *т* goes to *щ* (возврати+ ~ возвращу́, возвраща́ть, возвращённый) and *д* goes to *жд*, except in the first person singular of verbs, where it always goes to *ж* (награди+ ~ награжу́, награжда́ть, награждённый). See Appendix 1.

As the chart shows, labials (*п, б, м*) and labio-dentals (*ф, в*) add a soft *ль*, while velar and dental stops and fricatives (*к, г, т, д, х, с, з*) turn into hushing sounds (*ч, ж, ш*). The resonants *л, н*, and *р* only become soft. The combinations *ск* and *ст* give *щ*, but this must be viewed as *к* and *т* going to *ч* with the preceding *с* then assimilated to the *ч*, giving *шч*, spelled *щ*. This same phenomenon of assimilation occurs in сча́стье, счита́ть, с чем, без чего́, pronounced as ща́стье, щита́ть, щем, бещево́.

8.2.4. A last set of rules is required to relate the imperative to the present tense.

Rule 15: Endings beginning with *ё, и,* or *я* soften the preceding consonant (живёт, живи́, живя́).[8] This rule applies to the present tense, imperative, and present gerund.

Rule 16: Endings beginning with *у* do not soften the preceding consonant, although that consonant may be soft by the application of another rule (живу́, живу́т, but ка́плют, дре́млют (Rule 19). This rule applies to the present tense.

Rule 17: Before endings beginning with *ё, к* goes to *ч* and *г* goes to *ж* (пеку́ ~ печёт, стригу́ ~ стрижёт). This rule applies to the present tense of consonant stems ending in a velar.

---

[8] The gerunds (verbal adverbs) are treated in Chapter 9.

Rule 18: A consonant stem followed by a vowel ending joins the two together smoothly:

жив́+у → живу́   пас́+ёт → пасёт

See 7.2.9. This rule applies to the present tense and imperative of consonant stems.

Rule 19: A vowel ending joins a vowel stem with truncation of the first vowel; consonant mutation and stress shift *may* but do not *necessarily* occur when truncation is present.

Examples:

писа̀+у   →   пишу́
писа̀+ёт   →   пи́шет
писа̀+ут   →   пи́шут (consonant mutation in all six forms and
    stress shift in all but first sg.)
сиде́+у   →   сижу́
сиде́+ишь →   сиди́шь
сиде́+ят   →   сидя́т (consonant mutation in first sg. only and no
    stress shift)
вёрну́+у   →   верну́
вёрну́+ёт →   вернёт (neither consonant mutation nor stress
    shift; {n} softens before {o} by Rule 15).

This rule applies to the present tense and imperative of vowel stems.

Note that consonant mutation normally *will* occur when the truncated vowel is {a}, {e}, {i} or {o} (but not {u}) and the second (truncating) vowel is {o} or {u} (i.e., a rounded vowel); see the examples earlier in this paragraph and also compare:

ходи́+ ~ хожу́, хо́дишь, хо́дит, хо́дим, хо́дите, хо́дят
хохота̀+ ~ хохочу́, хохо́чешь, хохо́чет, хохо́чем, хохо́чете,
   хохо́чут
колоти́+ ~ колочу́, коло́тишь, коло́тит, коло́тим, коло́тите,
   коло́тя

8.3. Systematic Inventory of Verb Types

8.3.1. Verbs in *-u*. As noted earlier (8.1.2.1), these are second conjugation verbs. They show all three stress patterns (fixed on stem, fixed on ending, and shifting), have a variety of meanings, and are numerous (over six thousand by one count). Because they are vowel stems the past and infinitive will result from straightforward addition of ending to stem (Rule 7), but the present and imperative will produce V+V truncation with the possibility of stress shift and consonant mutation (Rule 19). Since the only ending which is a rounded vowel is the *-y* of the first person sg., these verbs will have consonant mutation only in the first person sg.

Sample verbs in *-u*+:

кра́си+ 'paint'   ~ кра́шу, кра́сишь, кра́сит, кра́сим, кра́сите,
                         кра́сят, крась!, кра́сил, кра́сила, кра́сило,
                         кра́сили, кра́сить

грози́+ 'threaten' ~ грожу́, грози́шь, грози́т, грози́м, грози́те,
                         грозя́т, грози́!, грози́л, грози́ла, грози́ло,
                         грози́ли, грози́ть

люби́+ 'love'   ~ люблю́, лю́бишь, лю́бит, лю́бим, лю́бите,
                         лю́бят, люби́!, люби́л, люби́ла, люби́ло,
                         люби́ли, люби́ть

Other examples of verbs in *-u*+:

гвозди́+ 'nail'	пусти́+ 'let, release'
грози́+ 'threaten'	скали́+ 'grin, bare one's teeth'
е́зди+ 'ride'	служи́+ 'serve'
корми́+ 'feed, nourish'	труси́+ 'shake'
кра́си+ 'paint'	учи́+ 'teach; study'
кури́+ 'smoke'	ходи́+ 'go'
ла́зи+ 'climb'	эконо́ми+ 'economize'
лови́+ 'hunt; catch'	бели́+ 'whiten'
люби́+ 'love'	черни́+ 'blacken'
носи́+ 'carry'	обезле́си+ 'deforest'
пили́+ 'saw'	обнови́+ 'renew, renovate'
плати́+ 'pay'	облегчи́+ 'lighten'
посети́+ 'visit'	удво́и+ 'double'

укрепи́+ 'strengthen' утро́и+ 'triple'
усво́и+ 'assimilate'

8.3.2. Verbs in -*e*+. As noted earlier (8.1.2.1), these are also second conjugation verbs. Although they show all three stress patterns (fixed on
stem, fixed on ending, and shifting), all but a half-dozen or so have fixed
end stress (-é). The two basic meanings of this group were discussed in
8.1.2.3. These verbs are vowel stems, so the past and infinitive will result
from straightforward addition of ending to stem (Rule 7), but the present
and imperative will produce V+V truncation with the possibility of stress
shift and consonant mutation (Rule 19). Since the only ending which is
a rounded vowel is the -*y* of the first sg., these verbs will have consonant
mutation only in the first person sg.

Sample verbs in -*e*+:

сиде́+ 'sit' ~ сижу́, сиди́шь, сиди́т, сиди́м, сиди́те,
сидя́т, сиди́!, сиде́л, сиде́ла, сиде́ло,
сиде́ли, сиде́ть

терпе́+ 'bear, endure' ~ терплю́, те́рпишь, те́рпит, те́рпим,
те́рпите, те́рпят, терпи́!, терпе́л,
терпе́ла, терпе́ло, терпе́ли, терпе́ть

ви́де+ 'see' ~ ви́жу, ви́дишь, ви́дит, ви́дим,
ви́дите, ви́дят, ви́дел, ви́дела,
ви́дело, ви́дели, ви́деть (suppletive
imperative ~ смотри́!)

Verbs with fixed stem stress: ви́де+ 'see', (and its compounds
ненави́де+ 'hate', оби́де+ 'offend'), зави́се+ 'depend' (but unprefixed
висе́+ 'hang'). Verbs with shifting stress: верте́+ 'turn, twist', смотре́+
'watch, look at', терпе́+ 'bear, endure'. All others have fixed stress on
endings, like сиде́+.

Other examples of verbs in -*e*+:

галде́+ 'make a din' шуме́+ 'make a noise'
свисте́+ 'whistle' горе́+ 'be burning'
храпе́+ 'snore' лете́+ 'be flying'

висе́+ 'be hanging'   смерде́+ 'stink'
скорбе́+ 'be grieving'   бде́+ 'be watchful, be alert'

8.3.3. Verbs in *ш, ж, ч, щ* plus *-a+*. As noted earlier (8.1.2.1), these are also second conjugation verbs. Although they show all three stress patterns (fixed on stem, fixed on ending, and shifting), most have fixed end stress (-á+). The two basic meanings of this group were discussed in 8.1.2.3. Since these verbs are vowel stems, the past and infinitive will result from straightforward addition of ending to stem (Rule 7), but the present and imperative will produce V+V truncation with the possibility of stress shift and consonant mutation (Rule 19). Since however the last consonant in each of these stems is *ш, ж, ч,* or *щ,* there is no possible further mutation.

Sample verbs in *ш, ж, ч, щ* plus *-a+*:

лежа́+ 'lie'   ~ лежу́, лежи́шь, лежи́т, лежи́м, лежи́те, лежа́т,
                  лежи́!, лежа́л, лежа́ла, лежа́ло, лежа́ли,
                  лежа́ть
держа́+ 'hold' ~ держу́, де́ржишь, де́ржит, де́ржим, де́ржите,
                  де́ржат, держи́!, держа́л, держа́ла, держа́ло,
                  держа́ли, держа́ть
слы́ша+ 'hear' ~ слы́шу, слы́шишь, слы́шит, слы́шим,
                  слы́шите, слы́шат, слышь!, слы́шал,
                  слы́шала, слы́шало, слы́шали, слы́шать

Verbs with fixed stem stress: слы́ша+ 'hear'. Verbs with shifting stress: держа́+ 'hold', дыша́+ 'breathe'. All others have fixed stress on endings, like лежа́+.

Other examples of verbs in *ш, ж, ч, щ* plus *-a+*:

визжа́+ 'scream, squeal'   дрожа́+ 'be trembling'
пища́+ 'squeak'   молча́+ 'be silent'
звуча́+ 'sound, resound'   мча́+-ся 'rush, whirl along'
бренча́+ 'jingle'   треща́+ 'crack, crackle'

Here belong also стоя́+ 'stand' (← стой-е) and боя́+-ся 'be afraid, fear', as well as кише́+ 'swarm', which has *e* rather than *a* after *ш* for unclear reasons.

8.3.4. Three irregular verbs should be mentioned before we leave the second conjugation. Спа+ 'sleep' is second conjugation in spite of its infinitive in hard paired consonant plus -*a*-: сплю, спишь, спит, спим, спи́те, спят, спи́!, спал, спала́, спа́ло, спа́ли, спать. Гна+ 'chase, drive' is also second conjugation but forms its present and imperative from a suppletive stem гони́+: гоню́, го́нишь, го́нит, го́ним, го́ните, го́нят, гони́!, гнал, гнала́, гна́ло, гна́ли, гнать.

The stem ржа́+ 'neigh' is first conjugation in spite of a stem in -жа́+: ржу, ржёшь, ржёт, ржём, ржёте, ржут, ржи!, ржал, ржа́ла, ржа́ло, ржа́ли, ржать.

As mentioned earlier, past-tense stress shift in a vowel stem (спа+ and гна+) is unexpected and irregular, although most verbs of the non-syllabic root plus -*a*- type have it (See 8.2.7.1):

рва+ 'tear'	зва+ 'call', лга+ 'lie'
вра+ 'talk nonsense, lie'	(по-)пра+ 'trample; flout, defy,
дра+ 'tear, strip off, flog'	scorn'
жда+ 'wait'	рва+ 'tear, rip', тка+ 'poke,
жра+ 'gulp, eat like an animal'	weave'

The only ones with fixed past stress are сла́+ 'send', (irreg. present: шлю, шлёшь, шлёт), стла́+ 'spread' (irreg. present: стела́+: стелю́, сте́лешь, сте́лет, сте́лют), and ржа́+ 'neigh'.

8.3.5. We now turn to the first conjugation and will start with stems having the suffix -*ай*+, such as де́лай+ and чита́й+. As we saw earlier, this type will have accent fixed on some syllable of the stem (Rule 1), but never, at least in regular verbs, on the endings; thus де́лай+ and чита́й+ represent both possible accent types.

Since verbs of this group end in a consonant, the present tense and imperative are formed by straightforward addition of vowel to consonant (Rule 18): де́лай+у → де́лаю, чита́й+у → чита́ю; the loss of the ending -*u* in the imperative is treated above in 7.4.1 and 7.4.1.1.

The past and infinitive have C+C truncation, according to Rule 8 in 8.1.3.3: де́лай+л → де́лал, чита́й+л → чита́л; де́лай+ть → де́лать, чита́й+ть → чита́ть. Stress remains on the same syllable that it occupies in the stem.

Verbs in -*ай*+ are very numerous. In particular, they include all derived imperfectives; see Chapter 10. All derived imperfectives have one of three suffixes: *-ай+*, *-вай+,* or *-ывай+*. The suffixes *-ай+* and *-вай+* are always stressed; *-ывай+* never is: от-ве́ти+/от-веча́й+; раз-вѝй+/ раз-вива́й+; за-писа̀+/ за-пи́сывай+.

Sample verbs in *-ай+*:

де́лай+ 'do'	~	де́лаю, де́лаешь, де́лает, де́лаем, де́лаете, де́лают, де́лай!, де́лал, де́лала, де́лало, де́лали, де́лать
чита́й+ 'read'	~	чита́ю, чита́ешь, чита́ет, чита́ем, чита́ете, чита́ют, чита́й!, чита́л, чита́ла, чита́ло, чита́ли, чита́ть
от-веча́й+ 'answer'	~	отвеча́ю, отвеча́ешь, отвеча́ет, отвеча́ем, отвеча́ете, отвеча́ют, отвеча́й!, отвеча́л, отвеча́ла, отвеча́ло, отвеча́ли, отвеча́ть
развива́й+ 'develop'	~	развива́ю, развива́ешь, развива́ет, развива́ем, развива́ете, развива́ют, развива́й!, развива́л, развива́ла, развива́ло, развива́ли, развива́ть
запи́сывай+ 'write down, note'	~	запи́сываю, запи́сываешь, запи́сывает, запи́сываем, запи́сываете, запи́сывают, запи́сывай!, запи́сывал, запи́сывала, запи́сывало, запи́сывали, запи́сывать

Three verbs in *-ай+* (more precisely, *-вай+*) demand special attention because they drop the *-ва-* in the present tense (but not in the imperative). These three verbs are дава́й+ 'give', знава́й+ 'know', and става́й+ 'stand' (the hyphen in front of знава́й+ and става́й+ means that they only occur with prefixes; e.g. у-знава́й+ 'recognize', в(с)-става́й+ 'rise, get up'). The forms are:

дава́й+	~	даю́, даёшь, даёт, даём, даёте, даю́т, дава́й!, дава́л, дава́ла, дава́ло, дава́ли, дава́ть
у-знава́й+	~	узнаю́, узнаёшь, узнаёт, узнаём, узнаёте, узнаю́т, узнава́й!, узнава́л, узнава́ла, узнава́ло, узнава́ли, узнава́ть

в(с)-ставáй+ ~ встаю́, встаёшь, встаёт, встаём, встаёте,
            встаю́т, вставáй!, вставáл, вставáла, вставáло,
            вставáли, вставáть

8.3.6. Verbs in *-ей+* are similar in *form* to those in *-ай+*. Most of them mean 'grow/become/get something' or 'appear something', are intransitive, and have fixed stress on the *-ей+*, such as белéй+ 'show white, appear white'; глупéй+ 'grow stupid'. A small number have stress on a syllable preceding the *-ей+*; e.g. ржáвей+ 'rust, grow rusty'; за-берéменей+ 'become pregnant'; плешúвей+ 'grow bald;' and all those with the prefix *о-без-*, such as обезлéсей+ 'become deforested'. The verb грéй+ 'warm' is transitive (i.e., takes a direct object: греть воду).

Sample verbs in *-ей+*:

глупéй+	~ глупéю, глупéешь, глупéет, глупéем,
'grow stupid'	глупéете, глупéют, глупéй!, глупéл,
	глупéла, глупéло, глупéли, глупéть
ржáвей+	~ ржáвею, ржáвеешь, ржáвеет, ржáвеем,
'rust, grow rusty'	ржáвеете, ржáвеюáт, ржáвей!, ржáвел,
	ржáвела, ржáвело, ржáвели, ржáветь;
плешúвей+	~ плешúвею, плешúвеешь, плешúвеет,
'grow bald'	плешúвеем, плешúвеете, плешúвеют,
	плешúвей!, плешúвел, плешúвела,
	плешúвело, плешúвели, плешúветь;
грéй+ 'warm'	~ грéю, грéешь, грéет, грéем, грéете, грéют,
	грéй!, грéл, грéла, грéло, грéли, грéть.

Other examples of verbs in *-ей+*:

алéй+ 'show scarlet'	немéй+ 'grow dumb, numb'
белéй+ 'show/appear white'	обезлéсей+ 'get deforested'
за-берéменей+ 'get pregnant'	старéй+ 'age, become old(er)'
краснéй+ 'blush, turn red'	твердéй+ 'harden, grow hard'

8.3.7. Verbs in hard paired consonant before *-а+* include some of the most basic and common, such as плáка+ 'cry, weep' and писà+ 'write'. Since the stems end in a vowel, Rule 19 is relevant for the present tense and Rule 7 for the past. Verbs in this group either have fixed stress on the stem (like пла́ка+) or shifting stress on the suffix (like писа̀+). Consonant mutation will occur in all six forms of the present tense (before the rounded vowels *y* and *ë*), and, contrary to what we would expect, before the -*u* of the imperative.

Sample verbs in hard paired consonant before -*a*+:

пла́ка+ 'weep' ~ пла́чу, пла́чешь, пла́чет, пла́чем, пла́чете,
пла́чут, пла́чь!, пла́кал, пла́кала, пла́кало,
пла́кали, пла́кать

писа̀+ 'write' ~ пишу́, пи́шешь, пи́шет, пи́шем, пи́шете,
пи́шут, пиши́!, писа́л, писа́ла, писало,
писа́ли, писа́ть

Many verbs in this group have alternative presents in -*ай*+ instead of -*a*+, so with an infinitive of маха́ть 'wave', the presents машу́ and маха́ю both occur. The present in -*ай*+ is often colloquial or substandard, but not always.

Some other verbs in hard paired consonant before -*a*+:

бормота̀+ 'mutter'	плеска̀+ 'splash, lap'
бры́зга+ 'splash'	пляса̀+ 'dance (folk dances)'
вяза̀+ 'tie, bind'	пря́та+ 'hide'
дви́га+ 'move' (also дви́гай+)	скака̀+ 'skip, gallop'
иска̀+ 'seek'	хохота̀+ 'guffaw'
-каза̀+ 'tell; show, indicate'	чеса̀+ 'scratch; comb'
кли́ка+ 'call'	шепта̀+ 'whisper'
паха̀+ 'plow'	

8.3.7.1. Verbs with a non-syllabic root and the suffix -*a*+ have two unexpected characteristics: they do *not* mutate the final consonant in the present tense, and most of them have shifting stress in the *past* tense. Examples are:

жда̀+ 'wait' ~ жду (*not* *жжу), ждёшь, ждёт, ждём, ждёте,
ждут, жди!, ждал, ждала́, жда́ло, жда́ли,
ждать

рва̀+ 'tear'   ~ рву (*not* *рвлю), рвёшь, рвёт, рвём, рвёте, рвут,
рви!, рвал, рвала́, рва́ло, рва́ли, рвать

There are twelve verbs in this group, of which ten have shifting stress:

бра̀+ 'take'	лга̀+ 'lie'
вра̀+ 'talk nonsense, lie'	(по)-пра̀+ 'trample; flout, defy,
дра̀+ 'tear, strip off, flog'	scorn'
жда̀+ 'wait'	рва̀+ 'tear, rip'
жра̀+ 'gulp, eat like an animal'	тка̀+ 'poke, weave'
зва̀+ 'call'	

The two with fixed stress are сла́+ 'send' and стла́+ 'spread. The
verb сла́+ has unexpected mutation of *both* consonants in the present
(шлю, шлёшь, шлёт, шлём, шлёте, шлют, шли!, слал, сла́ла, сла́ло,
сла́ли, слать), whereas стла́+ mutates only the last consonant, but it in-
serts a vowel *and* has shifting stress, as if the present stem were стела̀+:
стелю́, сте́лешь, сте́лет, сте́лем, сте́лете, сте́лют, стели́!, стлал,
стла́ла, стла́ло, стла́ли, стлать.

As mentioned in 8.2.4, the stem ржа́+ 'neigh' is first conjugation in
spite of ending in -жа+: ржу, ржёшь, ржёт, and it has fixed stress in the
past: ржал, ржа́ла, ржа́ло, ржа́ли.

Three verbs in the group insert a vowel into the root in the present
and imperative: бра̀+ 'take', дра̀+ 'tear, strip off, flog', зва̀+ 'call'. Stress
in the present remains on the endings:

беру́, берёшь, берёт, берём, берёте, беру́т, бери́!, брал, брала́,
бра́ло, бра́ли, брать
деру́, дерёшь, дерёт, дерём, дерёте, деру́т, дери́!, драл, драла́,
дра́ло, дра́ли, драть
зову́, зовёшь, зовёт, зовём, зовёте, зову́т, зови́!, звал, звала́,
зва́ло, зва́ли, звать

8.3.7.2. There are several verbs in -*a*+ following {j}. They usually have
fixed stem stress (бле́я+ 'bleat', ве́я+ 'blow, waft', ла́я+ 'bark', ре́я+
'hover', се́я+ 'sow', та́я+ 'melt', чу́я+ 'feel'), but смея+-ся 'laugh'
has ending stress: смею́сь, смеёшься, смею́тся, сме́йся!, смея́лся,
смея́ться; as compared to се́ю, се́ешь, се́ют, сей!, се́ял, се́ять.

The verbs just considered have a suffix -*a*+, as opposed to боя́+-ся and стоя́+, which are second conjugation verbs with the suffix -*e*+ becoming -*a*+ after the unpaired consonant {j} (see 8.1.2.3 and 8.2.3 above).

8.3.7.3. Three verbs in -*a*+ show irregular stress in the present tense; instead of stressing the -*y* ending of the first person singular and then retracting the stress one syllable in the other five forms, they retract it in all six:

алка́+	~ а́лчу, а́лчешь, а́лчет, а́лчем, а́лчете,
'hunger for, desire'	а́лчут, алка́й!, алка́л, алка́ла,
(bookish & archaic)	алка́ло, алка́ли, алка́ть
колеба́+	~ коле́блю, коле́блешь, коле́блет,
'sway, shake, move;	коле́блем, коле́блете, коле́блют,
vacillate, waver'	коле́бли!, колеба́л, колеба́ла,
(in reflexive)	колеба́ло, колеба́ли, колеба́ть
колыха́+ 'sway, ripple'	~ колы́шу, колы́шешь, колы́шет,
	колы́шем, колы́шете, колы́шут,
	колы́шь, колыши́, колыха́й, колыха́л,
	колыха́ла, колыха́ло, колыха́ли,
	колыха́ть

8.3.7.4. A few verbs in -*a*+ do not have the expected mutation/softening in the present:

стона́+ 'groan'	~ стону́, сто́нешь, сто́нут
жа́жда+ 'thirst'	~ жа́жду, жа́ждешь, жа́ждут
for' (bookish)	
ора́+ 'yell'	~ ору́, орёшь, ору́т
соса́+ 'suck'	~ сосу́, сосёшь, сосу́т
тка́+ 'weave'	~ тку, ткёшь, ткут

Note the irregular fixed ending stress in ора́+ and соса́+.

8.3.7.5. The five verbs with the suffix -*o*+ resemble the писа́+ type very closely and seem to differ only in having -*o* instead of -*a* as the vowel of the suffix. All five have a liquid (*p* or *л*) before the suffix vowel:

борò+-ся 'fight'   ~ борю́сь, бо́решься, бо́рются, бори́сь!,
                     боро́лся, боро́лась, боро́лось, боро́лись,
                     боро́ться

коло̀+ 'prick, stab, ~ колю́сь, ко́лешь, ко́лют, коли́!, коло́л,
   thrust'   коло́ла, коло́ло, коло́ли, коло́ть

поло̀+ 'weed'   ~ полю́, по́лешь, по́лют, поли́!, поло́л,
                     поло́ла, поло́ло, поло́ли, поло́ть

поро̀+ flog, thrash; ~ порю́, по́решь, по́рют, пори́!, поро́л,
   undo, rip'   поро́ла, поро́ло, поро́ли, поро́ть

моло̀+ 'mill, grind' ~ мелю́, ме́лешь, ме́лют, мели́!, моло́л,
                     моло́ла, моло́ло, моло́ли, моло́ть[9]

8.3.7.6. Another special group of verbs with the suffix *-a+* is those which have an {ov}, spelled *ов* or *ев*, before the *-a*. These were discussed in 7.2.7 above. From the overall standpoint of verbs in *-a+*, they have two peculiarities. The first is that the *-ов-* goes to *-уй-* before a vowel ending; the second is that the stress is never shifting. If the root is stressed in the base form, then the stress remains there:

тре́бова+ 'demand, ~ тре́буешь, тре́бует, тре́буем, тре́буете,
   need, require'   тре́буют, тре́буй!, тре́бовал,
                     тре́бовала, тре́бовало, тре́бовали,
                     тре́бовать

If the suffix is stressed, then the stress transfers to the *-уй-* before any vowel ending:

атакова́+ 'attack': ~ атаку́ю, атаку́ешь, атаку́ет, атаку́ем,
                     атаку́ете, атаку́ют, атаку́й!, атакова́л,
                     атакова́ла, атакова́ло, атакова́ли,
                     атакова́ть

Both root and stem stress are very common and they are productive patterns for new verbs.

Only in the seven verbs where the ов/ев is part of the root does the stress fall on the endings of the present:

---

[9] 'Mill, grind' моло̀+ has an irreg. present stem with мел- instead of мол-.

блева́+ 'vomit'   ~ блюю́, блюёшь, блюёт, блюём, блюёте,
                       блюю́т, блюй!, блева́л, блева́ла,
                       блева́ли, блева́ть

жева́+ 'chew'   ~ жую́, жуёшь, жуёт, жуём, жуёте, жую́т,
                       жуй!, жева́л, жева́ла, жева́ло, жева́ли,
                       жева́ть

клева́+ 'peck'   ~ клюю́, клюёшь, клюёт, клюём, клюёте,
                       клюю́т, клюй!, клева́л, клева́ла,
                       клева́ло, клева́ли, клева́ть

кова́+ 'forge, hew'   ~ кую́, куёшь, куёт, куём, куёте, кую́т, куй!,
                       кова́л, кова́ла, кова́ло, кова́ли, кова́ть

плева́+ 'spit'   ~ плюю́, плюёшь, плюёт, плюём, плюёте,
                       плюю́т, плюй!, плева́л, плева́ла,
                       плева́ло, плева́ли, плева́ть

снова́+ 'warp   ~ сную́, снуёшь, снуёт, снуём, снуёте,
  textiles; scurry   сную́т, снуй!, снова́л, снова́ла, снова́ло,
  about'   снова́ли, снова́ть

сова́+ 'poke,   ~ сую́, суёшь, суёт, суём, суёте, сую́т, суй!,
  thrust, shove'   сова́л, сова́ла, сова́ло, сова́ли, сова́ть

Examples of verbs with the suffix -ова+:

адресова́+ 'address'   рисова́+ 'sketch'
ве́рова+ 'believe'   се́това+ 'lament, grieve'
диктова́+ 'dictate'   сове́това+ 'advise'
марши́рова+ 'march'   танцева́+ 'dance'
ночева́+ 'spend the night'   фехтова́+ 'fence'
пакова́+ 'pack'   целова́+ 'kiss'

8.3.8. The final group of suffixed stems is comprised of verbs with the suffixes -ну+ and (-ну+), such as толкну́+ 'shove, push' and мёрз(ну)+ 'freeze'.

Verbs with the suffix -ну+ are perfectives even without putting on a prefix and they usually mean 'do something one time'. The colloquial variant -ану+ means 'do something one time quickly and hard', e.g. толкану́+ 'give a quick hard shove'.

Verbs with the suffix (-ну+) are imperfective (unless prefixed, e.g. замёрз(ну)+, in which case they are perfective), are always intransitive, and mean 'get into a state, become X, where X is the meaning of the root:

сла́б(ну)+ 'weaken'
со́х(ну)+ 'dry up, become desiccated'

кис(ну)+ 'turn sour, ferment'
кре́п(ну)+ 'become strong, strengthen'

Verbs with the suffix (*-ну+*) always have fixed stress on the stem, and the *-ну* drops in the past tense, whether the verb is prefixed or not.

Except for вя́ну+ 'fade', the (*-ну+*) verbs always have a consonant before the (*-ну+*) suffix; thus гля́ну+ 'glance' could not be a (*-ну+*) verb. Similarly, толкну́+ could not be a (*-ну+*) verb, since the stress is on the suffix.

Examples of verbs with the suffix *(-ну+)*:

(за-)мёрз(ну)+   ~ мёрзну, мёрзнешь, мёрзнет, мёрзнем,
'get cold, freeze'   мёрзнете, мёрзнут, мёрзни!, мёрз,
                     мёрзла, мёрзло, мёрзли, мёрзнуть
сла́б(ну)+   ~ сла́бну, сла́бнешь, сла́бнет, сла́бнем,
'weaken'   сла́бнете, сла́бнут, сла́бни!, сла́б,
                     сла́бла, сла́бло, сла́бли, сла́бнуть
со́х(ну)+ 'dry up,   ~ со́хну, со́хнешь, со́хнет, со́хнем, become
desiccate'   со́хнете, со́хнут, со́хни!, сох, со́хла,
                     со́хло, со́хли, со́хнуть
кис(ну)+ 'turn sour,   ~ ки́сну, ки́снешь, ки́снет, ки́снем,
ferment'   ки́снете, ки́снут, ки́сни!, кис, ки́сла,
                     ки́сло, ки́сли, ки́снуть
кре́п(ну)+ 'get   ~ кре́пну, кре́пнешь, кре́пнет, кре́пнем,
strong, become   кре́пнете, кре́пнут, кре́пни!, кре́п,
stronger'   кре́пла, кре́пло, кре́пли, кре́пнуть

Verbs with the suffix *-ну+* may have fixed stress on the endings (толкну́+), on the stem (кри́кну+ 'shout') or in four verbs (тону́+ 'drown', тяну́+ 'pull', мину́+ 'pass, об-ману́ + 'deceive') the stress may be shifting: тону́, то́нешь, то́нет, то́нем, то́нете, то́нут, тони́!, тону́л, тону́ла, тону́ло, тону́ли, тону́ть. There is no first person form for мину́+.

Verbs in *-ну+* and (*-ну+*) do not have softening of the consonant *н* when the *y* drops, but the *н* is softened before the *ё* of endings (Rules 15, 16, and 19):

толкну́, толкну́т, but толкнёшь, толкнёт, толкнём, толкнёте
кри́кну, кри́кнут, but кри́кнешь, кри́кнет, кри́кнем, кри́кнете

Other examples of verbs with the suffix *-ну+*:

дро́гну+ 'shudder'
ду́ну+ 'blow'
за-мкну́+ 'close'
кри́кну+ 'shout'
плю́ну+ 'spit'
при/льну́+ 'stick, adhere'
резну́+ 'cut'
рискну́+ 'risk'
хвастну́+ 'boast, brag'

тону́+ 'drown' (impf.)
тяну́+ 'pull' (impf.)
мину́+ 'pass' (no 1st sg. form, impf.)
об-ману́+ 'deceive'
шепну́+ 'whisper'
толкану́+ 'give a quick hard shove'

Other examples of verbs with the suffix *(-ну)+*:

мо́к(ну)+ 'get soaked, get wet'
слеп(ну)+ 'go blind'
вя́(ну)+ 'fade'
ли́п(ну)+ 'adhere, stick'

ис-че́з(ну)+ 'disappear'
при-вы́к(ну)+ 'get accustomed'
сла́б(ну)+ 'become weak'

8.3.9. About 90 non-suffixed verb stems exist in Russian; they divide into twelve types, depending upon the final consonant and sometimes the vowel before it. Many of them are among the most frequently occurring verbs in the language.

8.3.9.1. There are three verb stems ending in *-з* and four ending in *-с*:

вёз+ 'convey, carry in a vehicle'
полз+ 'crawl'
лез+ 'climb'
гры́з+ 'gnaw'

нёс+ 'carry'
пас+ 'graze, pasture'
с-пас+ 'save, rescue'
тряс+ 'shake'

Rules 1 and 3 apply to the stress in the present and imperative; Rule 2 applies in the past tense. Rule 12 applies in the past tense and Rule 13 in the infinitive. Rules 15 and 18 apply in the present and imperative.

Sample verbs:

нёс´+: несу́, несёшь, несёт, несём, несёте, несу́т, неси́,
нёс, несла́, несло́, несли́, нести́
гры́з+: грызу́, грызёшь, грызёт, грызём, грызёте, грызу́т, грызи́!,
грыз, гры́зла, гры́зло, гры́зли, грызть

Note that the difference in stress shows up in the past tense and in-finitive.The verb лез+ has irregular stress in the present and imperative:

ле́зу, ле́зешь, ле́зет, ле́зем, ле́зете, ле́зут, лез!

The past and infinitive are regular:

лёз, ле́зла, ле́зло, ле́зли, лезть

8.3.9.2. There are three stems in -*б*. They conjugate like verbs in -*с* and -*з*, except that by Rule 11 the *б* goes to *с* in the infinitive:

грёб+ 'row': гребу́, гребёшь, гребёт, гребём, гребёте, гребу́т,
греби́!, грёб, гребла́, гребло́, гребли́, грести́

скрёб+ 'scrape' is similar

-шиб+ 'shove' has an irregular infinitive: ошиби́ться 'be mistaken'

The past active participle and past gerund use the same stem:

ошиби́вшийся, ошиби́вшись.

8.3.9.3. There are 9 stems in -*т* and 10 in -*д*. They are subject to Rule 11 in the infinitive and Rule 10 in the past tense. Rule 12 does not apply.

Inventory:

гнёт+ 'oppress' (past not used)
мёт+ 'sweep'
мят+ 'be nervous, upset, scurry about nervously (present and inf.
only, no past tense)

обрёт+ 'find' (perfective; historically prefixed; bookish)

плёт+ 'braid, weave'

раст+ 'grow'

свет+ 'grow light, dawn' (used only in neuter sg. and impersonal forms)

цвёт+ 'flower, bloom'

-чт+ 'read; count' (infinitive честь; what accent mark should be used on this stem?)

блюд+ 'observe'

брёд+ 'stroll, make one's way' вёд+ 'lead'

гряд+ 'come' (used only in present tense and present participle)

клад+ 'put, place (in a lying position)'

крад+ 'steal'

пад+ 'fall' (perfective)

пряд+ 'spin' (irreg. inf. прясть)

сед+ 'sit down (irreg. future/imperative stem and stress: сяду, сядь!)

ид+ 'go' (becomes -йд+ when prefixed; past tense formed from suppletive stem шд+: шёл, шла, шло, шли, past act. part. шёдший).

Sample verbs:

плёт+ 'braid, weave'	~	плету́, плетёшь, плетёт, плетём, плетёте, плету́т, плети́!, плёл, плела́, плело́, плели́, плести;
вёд+ 'lead'	~	веду́, ведёшь, ведёт, ведём, ведёте, веду́т, веди́!, вёл, вела́, вело́, вели́, вести́;

Compare крад+ 'steal' for accent in the past and infinitive:

краду́, крадёт, крадёшь, крадём, крадёте, краду́т, кради́!, крал, кра́ла, кра́ло, кра́ли, красть

раст+ has a present and infinitive stem раст+ and a past stem рост+:

pres.: расту́, растёшь, растёт, растём, растёте, расту́т, расти́!
pres. gerund: растя́
inf.: расти́

past tense: рос, росла́, росло́, росли́
past act. part.: ро́сший

Note the ordered application of Rules 10 and 12 in the past tense: рос́т+ adds л to make the masc., resulting in the loss of *m* by Rule 10, giving the intermediate form росл, then by Rule 12 л is dropped after *c*, giving the correct form рос. The fem., neut. and pl. forms use Rule 10, but not Rule 12.

8.3.9.4. There are seven stems in -*к* and eight in -*г*. Rule 12 applies to the past tense, Rule 14 to the infinitive, and Rules 15, 17, and 18 to the present tense. Note that *ё* changes to *e* in the stem of the infinitive.

Inventory:

влёк+ 'drag'
пёк+ 'bake'
сеќ+[10] 'chop, hack; whip'
толќ+ 'grind, pulverize'
   (irreg. masc. past толо́к, irreg. inf. толо́чь)
жг+ 'burn'
-пряѓ+ 'harness'
стриѓ+ 'shear'.

волоќ+ 'drag, draw'
-рёк+ 'say'·
берёѓ+ 'guard, protect, take care of'
-брёѓ+ (Church Slavonic form of берёѓ+)
тёк+ 'flow'
стерёѓ+ 'watch, guard'

лёѓ+ 'lie down' (future irreg. in form and stress: ля́гу, ля́жешь; imperative: ляг!)
моѓ+ (pres. irreg in stress, the only obstruent stem with shifting stress in the present: могу́, мо́жешь, мо́жет, мо́жем, мо́жете, мо́гут, imperative помоги́)

Sample verbs:

пёк+ 'bake' ~ пеку́, печёшь, печёт, печём, печёте, пеку́т, пеки́!, пёк, пекла́, пекло́, пекли́, печь
стриѓ+ 'shear' ~ стригу́, стрижёшь, стрижёт, стрижём, стрижёте, стригу́т, стриги́!, стриг, стри́гла, стри́гло, стри́гли, стричь

---

[10] Now сеќ+ for many speakers, by analogy to other verbs ending in -*к*.

Note that by proper application of the rules, even жг+ 'burn' becomes regular:

жг+ 'burn' ~ жгу, жжёшь. жжёт, жжём, жжёте, жгут, жги!,
                    жёг, жгла, жгло, жгли, жечь

The fill vowels in the masculine form of the past tense and the infinitive are determined by the fill vowel rules given in 2.2.5). Question for thought: why is no stress mark given (or needed) in the stem?

8.3.9.5. Resonant stems in -*p* comprise four verbs: м́р+ 'die' (ỳ-мр+ when prefixed), п́р+ 'go; press' (за̀-пр+ when prefixed); т́р+ 'rub'; -стр+ (only in про-ст́р+ 'stretch'). Rule 12 applies in the past tense and Rule 13 in the infinitive. Note the special form of the infinitive with -epé-, and note also the fill vowel *ё* that appears in the past tense.

Sample verbs:

ỳ-мр+   ~   умру́, умрёшь. умрёт, умрём, умрёте, умру́т, умри́!,
                    у́мер, умерла́, у́мерло, у́мерли, умере́ть
с-т́р+   ~   сотру́, сотрёшь, сотрёт, сотрём, сотрёте, сотру́т,
                    сотри́!, стёр, стёрла, стёрло, стёрли, стере́ть

8.3.9.6. There are three resonant stems in -*в*; all have shifting stress: жи́в+ 'live', плы̀в+ 'float, drift; swim', слы̀в+ 'have a reputation as, pass for'. Rules 6 and 8 apply.

Sample verb:

пѐре-жив+ 'live   ~   переживу́, переживёшь, переживёт,
   through, survive,   переживём, переживёте, переживу́т,
   experience'   переживи́!, пѐрежил, пережила́,
                               пѐрежило, пѐрежили, пережи́ть

The verb ревé+ 'roar has a present stem рев+:

реву́, ревёшь, ревёт, ревём, ревёте, реву́т

8.3.9.7. There are nine resonant stems in -*н* and two in -*м*. Both in -*м* are non-syllabic (ж́ м+ 'press, squeeze'; -ь̀ м+ 'take'). There are four non-syllabic and five syllabic stems in -*н*:

> ж́ н+ 'reap, harvest'
> м́ н+ 'rumple, crumple'
> -п́ н+ 'stretch'; -ч̀ н+ 'begin'
> де́н+ place, put' (perfective)
> ста́н+ 'become; take a standing position' (perfective)
> сты́н+ 'cool, become cold'
> -стря́н+ 'stick, get stuck'
> кле́н+ 'curse' (irreg. infinitive клясть; irreg. present tense stress: кляну́, клянёшь).

Note that when the stem is non-syllabic, -*н* and -*м* are truncated before a consonant as expected, but then the vowel -*я*- is inserted (-*а*- is used where *я* cannot be spelled).

Sample verbs:

> м́ н+　~　мну, мнёшь, мнёт, мнём, мнёте, мнут, мни!, мял,
> 　　　　　　мя́ла, мя́ло, мя́ли, мять;
> ж́ м+　~　жму, жмёшь, жмёт, жмём, жмёте, жмут, жми!, жал,
> 　　　　　　жа́ла, жа́ло, жа́ли, жать;
> де́н+　~　де́ну, де́нешь, де́нет, де́нем, де́нете, де́нут, день!,
> 　　　　　　дел, де́ла, де́ло, де́ли, деть.

The stem -ь̀ м+ 'take' shows differing forms, depending partially upon whether the prefix ends in a vowel or a consonant:

> за̀-йм+ 'occupy'　~　займу́, займёшь, займёт, займём, займёте,
> 　　　　　　　　　　займу́т, займи́!, за́нял, заняла́, за́няло,
> 　　　　　　　　　　за́няли, заня́ть
> на̀-йм+ 'take on, hire,
> 　　　　rent'
> по̀-йм+ 'understand'
> 　but

под-нм+ 'raise, lift'   ~   подниму́, подни́мешь, подни́мет,
                            подни́мем, подни́мете, подни́мут,
                            подними́!, по́днял, подняла́,
                            по́дняло, по́дняли, подня́ть
с-нь`м+ 'take off,
        remove'
о̀т-ньм+ 'take away'
    but
прѝ-йм+ 'accept'   ~   приму́, при́мешь, при́мет, при́мем,
                        при́мете, при́мут, прими́!, при́нял,
                        приняла́, при́няло, при́няли,
                        приня́ть

The stem въз-ь`м+ has the future возьму́, возьмёшь, возьми́!, but past and infinitive: взял, взяла́, взя́ло, взя́ли, взять.

The future/present tense stress of за̀-йм+, на̀-йм+, по̀-йм+, and въз-ь`м+ is automatic. Since Rule 6 says that a prefix cannot be stressed in the present/future, the vowel of the ending is the only possible one. In the case of под-нм+, с-нь`м+, and о̀т-ньм+, the stress still cannot be on the prefix, but we cannot predict which vowel, that of the root or that of the ending, will be stressed, and the shifting stress is irregular from the standpoint of the system, since shifting stress in the present tense normally occurs only in vowel-stem verbs which truncate the final vowel. If the stress in прѝ-йм+ is regarded as being on the prefix in the future (при́мешь, при́мет, при́мем, при́мете, при́мут), then Rule 6 is broken.

8.3.9.8. There are five verb stems in -ий+—three with shifting stress (вий+ 'twist, wind', лий+ 'pour', пий+ 'drink') and two with fixed (бий+ 'beat, strike', ший+ 'sew'). The sequence {-ij-} loses the {-i-} when a vowel ending is added: {vij+u → vju}. The imperative takes a fill vowel. See 7.4.1.3.

Sample verbs:

пий+ 'drink'   ~   пью, пьёшь, пьёт, пьём, пьёте, пьют, пей!, пил,
                   пила́, пи́ло, пи́ли, пить
бий+ 'beat'   ~   бью, бьёшь, бьёт, бьём, бьёте, бьют, бей!, бил,
                  би́ла, би́ло, би́ли, бить

The stem по-чи́й+ 'take rest, die' (archaic, bookish, Church Slavonic) does not drop the {-i-} and present stress is on the root: почи́ю, почи́ешь, почи́ет. The stem гни́й+ 'rot' also keeps the {-i-}, but the stress is on the endings:

гнию́, гниёшь, гнил, гнила́, гни́ло, гни́ли, гнить

This stem does not form an imperative; one can say "чтоб ты сгнил!" or загнива́й!, but not *гней! or *гний!

8.3.9.9. There are also five stems in -ый+, all with fixed stress. Before a vowel ending the ый goes to ой.

Inventory:

вы́й+ 'howl'	ны́й+ 'ache; whine, whimper,
кры́й+ 'cover'	complain'
мы́й+ 'wash'	ры́й+ 'dig'

Sample verb:

мы́й+ 'wash' ~ мо́ю, мо́ешь, мо́ет, мо́ем, мо́ете, мо́ют, мой!, мыл, мы́ла, мы́ло, мы́ли, мыть.

8.3.9.10 The stems гре́й+ 'warm, heat', ду́й+ 'blow', -у́й+ 'shoe' (only in обу́й+ 'put on footwear' and разу́й+ 'take off footwear') are regular.

8.3.9.11 Three verbs present special irregularities: бы́в+ 'be'; да́й+ 'give' (perfective); and е́д+ 'eat'.
The verb бы́в+ has a past tense with shifting stress like the other three verbs in -в+: был, была́, бы́ло, бы́ли. It has a future with irreg. stem and stress:

бу́ду, бу́дешь, бу́дет, бу́дем, бу́дете, бу́дут, будь!

The present tense forms are basically non-existent, except for the form есть, which can be used under specific conditions not only as the third person sg., but also as other forms. The use of this form is outside the scope of this book. The future meaning of буд+ argues for treating бы́в+

as a perfective verb, but usage in the past contradicts this: всю жизнь он был студентом. The clear meaning here is that he never finished being a student.

The verb дай+ has a past tense with shifting stress:

дал, дала́, да́ло, да́ли

This is of course irregular for a non-suffixed stem in -й+. It has a future with irreg. stems and endings:

дам, дашь, даст, дади́м, дади́те, даду́т, imperative дай!

The verb е́д+ has a present with an irregular stem and endings for the singular: ем, ешь, ест; and plural forms made from a stem еди́+:

еди́м, еди́те, едя́т, irreg. imperative ешь!

The past tense is regular:

ел, е́ла, е́ло, е́ли

8.3.9.12. Finally let us characterize several irregular and unproductive verb types.

The verb бежа́+ 'run' has first sg. and third pl. present from a suppletive stem бег┼:

бегу́, бегу́т (but бежи́шь, бежи́т, бежи́м, бежи́те).

The verb реве́+ has a present stem рев+:

реву́, реве́шь, реве́т, реве́м, реве́те, реву́т, реви́!

The verb ржа́+ is first conjugation in the present:

ржу, ржёшь, ржёт, ржём, ржёте, ржут.

The verb хоте́+ 'wish, want' is regular in the plural forms of the present and in the past:

хоти́м, хоти́те, хотя́т, хоте́л, хоте́ла, хоте́ло, хоте́ли, хоте́ть

But this has a stem хота+ for the three singular forms of the present:

хочу́, хо́чешь, хо́чет

The unprefixed verb does not have an imperative singular, but with a prefix it is regular: захоти́!

The verb чти́+ 'honor' has first sg. and third pl. present from a suppletive stem:

чт+: чту, чтут (but чтишь, чтит, чтим, чти́те).

The stem бре́й+ 'shave' changes the -ей to -и- before consonants:

брил, бри́ла, брить

Finally, пе́й+ 'sing' has a present which is irregular in form and stress:

пою́, поёшь, пой!

8.4. Stress on the Prefix

8.4.1. As stated above, the prefix of a Russian verb never bears the stress in the present/future form. In the past tense and some participial forms, however, the stress may be on the prefix in the masculine, neuter, and plural forms and on the suffix (-ла) in the feminine. In some verbs this prefixal stress is obligatory, in others it is optional, and in most verbs it is impossible. The details are too complicated to justify the space to describe them here. It is probably best to learn them on a verb-by-verb basis as you encounter them. As is often the case, the most common words show what is irregular from the point of view of the overall system: consider English *be, give, go, write, grow, mouse, man, child.*

The verbs which show this prefixal stress come from the groups described in Sections 8.2.9.5, 8.2.9.6, 8.2.9.7, 8.2.9.8, and 8.2.9.11, but not all verbs in those Sections show prefixal stress.

In many verbs, the prefixal stress represents an older pronunciation pattern which co-occurs with another pattern in which the masuline, neuter, and plural forms show root stress (e.g., отли́л, отлила́, отли́ло, отли́ли). The pattern with prefix stress may be the preferred variant, a supplementary variant, or of equal validity.

Forms with stress on the first syllable in the feminine forms, such as заняла, начала, and заперла, are heard often, but are definitely non-standard and should be avoided.

8.4.2. Examples of prefix stress:

умере́ть	~	у́мер, умерла́, у́мерло, у́мерли
запере́ть	~	за́пер, заперла́, за́перло, за́перли
пережи́ть	~	пе́режил, пережила́, пе́режило, пе́режили
заня́ть	~	за́нял, заняла́, за́няло, за́няли
нача́ть	~	на́чал, начала́, на́чало, на́чали
отли́ть	~	о́тлил, отлила́, о́тлило, о́тлили
прода́ть	~	про́дал, продала́, про́дало, про́дали

Exercises

I. Identifying verb types. Practice identifying and conjugating these samples:

зва̀+	рва̀+	зна́й+	лѝй+
жѝв+	гры́з+	вы́й+	атакова́+
пас́+	ка́па+	грёб+	кова́+
кла́д+	дрема̀+	де́лай+	ходи́+
пёк+	коло̀+	чита́й+	сиде́+
де́н+	вёрну́+	гре́й+	лежа́+
тр́+	тро́ну+	красне́й+	плёт́+
пла́ка+	спа̀+	тре́бова+	
паха̀+	сла́б(ну)+	стри́г+	

II. Identify and conjugate the verb stems in Appendix 2.

Participles and Gerunds

9.0. Introduction

Participles are sometimes called "verbal adjectives," since they are made from verb stems but are basically adjectives. Russian has four participles: two present and two past. One for each tense is active (the word modified *performs* the action, же́нщина, чита́ющая кни́гу; ма́льчик, сиде́вший в углу́) and one for each tense is passive (the word modified *undergoes* the action, кни́ги, раздава́емые а́вторами; кни́ги, про́данные а́вторами).

Two gerunds exist in Russian: a present (чита́я) and a past (про-) чита́в(ши). These forms are verbal adverbs: *how, when, why* did the action of the main verb occur? The English form in *-ing*, which is traditionally called a gerund, is a noun: "I like running / reading / loafing."

The two active participles do not have short forms, only long. The present passive participle has short forms, but their occurrence is very restricted. Only the past passive has regular and widely-used short forms.

Contrary to the general rule that the reflexive particle has the form *сь* after vowels and *ся* after consonants (я смею́сь, мы смеёмся, он смея́лся, она смея́лась), participles always have *ся*: смею́щаяся, смею́щегося, смею́щуюся. This is a result of the Church Slavonic (see Appendix 1) origin of both the present and past active participles (verbs with *ся* of course do not form passive participles). Gerunds have *сь*, as expected.

Perfective verbs do not form the present participles, just as they do not form the present tense. For a special case, see 9.2.1 (нераздели́мый, непобеди́мый, etc.)

9.1. The Present Active Participle

The *present active participle* is formed with the suffix *-ущ-* (first conjugation) or *-ащ-* (second conjugation). Stress and consonant mutation will be the same as for the third person plural, except that most second conjugation verbs in -*u*+ with shifting stress do *not* shift the stress back: куря́щий (кури́+ ~ они ку́рят), проходя́щий (проходи́+ ~ они прохо́дят).

Table 9-1. The Present Active Participle

Stem	Pres. Act. P.	Stem	Pres. Act. P.
жи́в+	живу́щий	зна́й+	зна́ющий
пас́+	пасу́щий	де́лай+	де́лающий
кла́д+	кладу́щий	чита́й+	чита́ющий
пёк+	пеку́щий	гре́й+	гре́ющий
пла́ка+	пла́чущий	красне́й+	красне́ющий
паха̀+	па́шущий	тре́бова+	тре́бующий
бра̀+	беру́щий	атакова́+	атаку́ющий
ка́па+	ка́плющий	кова́+	ку́ющий
дрема̀+	дре́млющий	ходи́+	ходя́щий
мёрзну+	мёрзнущий	сиде́+	сидя́щий
со́хну+	со́хнущий	лежа́+	лежа́щий

9.1.1. As mentioned above and shown in the table, stress in the present active participle is normally the same as in the form of the third pl. present. The only exception among first conjugation verbs is мог+ ~ мо́гут, могу́щий, but of course the shifting stress pattern in a non-suffixed obstruent is itself an exception. Although most second conjugation verbs in -*u*+ with shifting stress do *not* shift the stress back, there are several verbs in -*u̇*+ that do have stress shift in the present active participle. According to *Грамматика 1980*, §1626, these include:

губи́+	'destroy'	служи́+	'serve'
души́+	'strangle, stifle, smother'	суши́+	'dry'
жени́+	'marry'	тащи́+	'drag'
лепи́+	'stick, paste'	туши́+	'extinguish, stifle'
лечи́+	'heal, treat'	учи́+	'teach, learn'
лупи́+	'peel, strip; thrash'	цени́+	'value'
люби́+	'love'	черти́+	'sketch'
мочи́+	'wet; soak'	чини́+	'repair; sharpen; carry
пыли́+	'saw'		out, execute'
руби́+	'chop'		

Other second conjugation verbs (those in -*e*+ or husher plus -*a*+) with shifting stress are only five in number, as we saw above (8.2.2 and 8.2.3). They split three to two in favor of non-retraction: вертя́щий, смотря́щий, but те́рпящий; держа́щий but ды́шащий.

9.2. The Present Passive Participle

The *present passive participle* looks much like the first person plural with the adjective endings added, but there is one important difference: the stress does not shift in stems with shifting accent (люби́мый but мы лю́бим).

The present passive participle as such is made from a limited number of verbs. As stated above, it is not made from perfective verbs (but see below). It is normally made only from verbs with the suffixes -*и*+, -*ывай*+, -*ай*+, -*вай*+, -*ова*+: цени́мый, перестра́иваемый, чита́емый, узнава́емый, тре́буемый. There are a few other stems which form the present passive participle, such as коле́блемый, слы́шимый, леле́емый, ви́димый. For details, see *Грамматика 1980*, §1582–1583.

Only five obstruent stems (вёд+, вёс+, влёк+, нёс+, and пас+) form this participle in Contemporary Standard Russian (CSR), and they have -*ом*- (always stressed) as the suffix, not -*ём*- (несо́мый, влеко́мый, but мы несём, влечём). These forms in -*ом*- belong to a formal, archaic high style.

9.2.1. The form of the present passive participle from *perfective* verbs is used in one specific construction. English has affirmative and negative constructions with the suffix -*able*, and they can be made from virtually any verb: *(un)forgettable, (un)avoidable, (un)lovable, (un)resolvable,* and *(un)creebable*, where we don't know what *creeb* means, but we know that *(un)creebable* means '(not) capable of being creebed'. Russian has a corresponding construction which occurs only in the negative and normally uses the perfective form of the present passive participle: нераздели́мый 'inseparable, indivisible'; непобеди́мый 'invincible, unconquerable'; неудержи́мый 'unrestrainable'; ненаруши́мый 'unbroken, inviolable'; непереводи́мый 'untranslatable'; неосуществи́мый 'unrealized, unrealizable'; but imperfectives нетерпи́мый 'unbearable, intolerable', необита́емый 'uninhabited, uninhabitable', and неузнава́емый 'unrecognizable.'

Most words made with this construction are not in standard Russian dictionaries, just as the corresponding (un-)X-able constructions are not in English dictionaries.

9.2.2. Note the non-shifting stress in любимый, неудержимый, непереводимый, and нетерпимый. The non-shifting stress in the present passive participle, as well as in most instances of the present active participle (see 9.1.1 above) is due to the fact that both present participles (active and passive) and the past active participle are Church Slavonicisms in Russian (see Appendix 1). These three participles were lost in spoken Russian and kept in the literary language through the influence of Church Slavonic. As stated in Appendix 1, the accent in CS forms does not normally shift, except between singular and plural in nouns.

9.3. The Past Active Participle

The *past active participle* has the suffix -*ви*. The -*в* is dropped in most stems where the -*л* of the masculine past tense is dropped (see Rule 12 in Chapter 8). The suffix -*(ну+)* drops in the past active participle, but there are quite a few exceptions in which it remains, and many doublet forms, one with and the other without the -*(ну+)*: e.g. достигнувший and достигший.

Table 9-2. The Past Active Participle

Stem	Past Act. Part.	Stem	Past Act. Part.
жив+	живший	верну+	вернувший
пас+	пасший	(за-)мёрз(ну)+	(за-)мёрзший
плёт+	плётший	(вы-)сох(ну)+	(вы-)сохший
грыз+	грызший	трону+	тронувший
тр+	тёрший	знай+	знавший
жг+	жёгший	делай+	делавший
пёк+	пёкший	читай+	читавший
плака+	плакавший	грей+	гревший
паха+	пахавший	краснёй+	краснёвший
бра+	бравший	требова+	требовавший
капа+	капавший	атакова+	атаковавший
дрема+	дремавший	кова+	ковавший

Stem	Past Act. Part.
ходи́+	ходи́вший
сиде́+	сиде́вший
лежа́+	лежа́вший

As may be seen from плётший, non-suffixed verbs in *m* or *д*, , which drop the *m* or *д* before *л* in the past tense, keep the *m* or *д* before *ш* in the past active participle. Exceptions to this exception are four stem-stressed verbs in *д*, which drop the *д* and keep the *в*: кла́д+ ~ кла́вший, кра́д+ ~ кра́вший, се́д+ ~ се́вший, and па́д+, which has both па́вший and па́дший, with a difference in meaning—check it in the dictionary!

И долго буду тем любезен я народу,
Что чувства добрые я лирой пробуждал,
Что в мой жестокий век восславил я свободу,
И милость к падшим призывал.

(А.С. Пушкин)

Since the past active participle is a Church Slavonicism, a few verbs show *е́* instead of *ё*: e.g. ве́зший, пренебре́гший, забре́дший.

9.4. The Past Passive Participle

The *past passive participle* is morphologically the most complicated of the four participles. It has three suffixes: *-н*, *-ён*, and *-m*. The *-н-* of *-н* and *-ён* is doubled when making a long form: перепи́сан ~ перепи́санный; принесён ~ принесённый.

9.4.1. The suffix *-н* is used with any verb stem having *-а* as part of the suffix (i.e., for the suffixes *-а*, *-ай*, *[-вай]*, *-ова*, husher plus *-а*). If the stem stress, either shifting or fixed, is on the *-а*, then it will retract one syllable in the past passive participle in both the long and the short forms.

Although the past passive participle is made primarily from perfective stems, unprefixed stems will be used in Table 9-3 in order to save space.

Table 9-3. The Past Passive Participle

Stem	Short Form	Long Form
писа́+	пи́сан	пи́санный
пла́ка+	пла́кан	пла́канный
бра́+	бран	бра́нный
де́лай+	де́лан	де́ланный
чита́й+	чи́тан	чи́танный
держа́+	де́ржан	де́ржанный
тре́бова+	тре́бован	тре́бованный
атакова́+	атако́ван	атако́ванный
кова́+	ко́ван	ко́ванный

The stress in the long form is on the same syllable as in the short forms.

Stress can be retracted onto the last or only syllable of the prefix (a mobile vowel counts as part of the prefix) with the following stems: бра́+ (со́бранный); вра́+ (на́вранный); гна́+ (во́гнанный), дра́+ (обо́дранный), жда́+ (про́жданный), жра́+ (со́жранный), зва́+ (на́званный), лга́+, рва́+, сла́+ (ото́сланный); спа́+, стла́+ (за́стланный), тка́+ (со́тканный), знай+ (по́знанный); дай+ (перепро́данный—note that in verbs with more than one prefix, the stress goes on the last prefix). In most of these same verbs the stress can be on the ending in the fem. short form (the ending stress is sometimes archaic): пере́вран, перевра́на; про́дан, прода́на. For details, see *Грамматика 1980*, §1641.

9.4.2. The suffix *-ён* makes past passive participles from verbs with stems in *-и* or a non-suffixed obstruent. In verbs in *-и* and obstruents, if the stem has end stress, then the ppp will have stress on the *-ён* in the long form and on the endings in the short forms: при-говори́+ ~ приговорённый, приговорён, приговорена́, приговорено́, приговорены́; пере-вёд+ ~ переведённый, переведён, переведена́, переведено́, переведены́.

If the verb stem has stem stress, then the ppp will also have stem stress: воз-вы́си+ ~ возвы́шенный, возвы́шен, возвы́шена, возвы́шено, возвы́шены; у-гры́з+ ~ угры́зенный, угры́зен, угры́зена, угры́зено, угры́зены.

If a stem in *-u* has shifting stress, then the ppp will have the stress retracted onto the stem: купи́+ ~ ку́пленный, ку́плен, ку́плена, ку́плено, ку́плены.

Note that for non-suffixed obstruent stems in *-с, -з, -б, -т,* and *-д,* the stress of the past tense, the infinitive, and the ppp are interconnected; if you know the stress of one of these three sets of forms, you know the stress of the other two sets. Thus, перевёл, перевела́, перевело́, перевели́ imply: перевести́ and переведён, переведена́, переведено́, переведены́; just as переведён, переведена́, переведено́, переведены́ imply перевёл, перевела́, перевело́, перевели́ and перевести́; equally, перевести́ implies перевёл, перевела́, перевело́, перевели́ and переведён, переведена́, переведено́, переведены́. In the same way угры́зен, угры́зена, угры́зено, угры́зены imply угры́з, угры́зла, угры́зло, угры́зли, and угры́зть; also угры́з, угры́зла, угры́зло, угры́зли imply угры́зен, угры́зена, угры́зено, угры́зены and угры́зть; finally, угры́зть implies угры́з, угры́зла, угры́зло, угры́зли, and угры́зен, угры́зена, угры́зено, угры́зены.

The only exception to this generalization is found in the infinitive of stems in *-к* and *-г,* since all infinitives from velar stems end in *-чь,* but пёк, пекла́, пекло́, пекли́ still imply печён, печена́, печено́, печены́, and печён, печена́, печено́, печены́ imply пёк, пекла́, пекло́, пекли́. Similarly, стри́жен, стри́жена, стри́жено, стри́жены imply стри́г, стри́гла, стри́гло, стри́гли, and стри́г, стри́гла, стри́гло, стри́гли imply стри́жен, стри́жена, стри́жено, стри́жены.

9.4.3. All verb stem types not mentioned in 9.4.1 or 9.4.2 take the suffix *-т* to form the ppp. Since we have already discussed all verbs with the suffixes *-а, -ай, -ова,* husher plus *-а,* and *-и,* plus non-suffixed obstruents, only non-suffixed resonants and verbs suffixed with *-ей, -е, -о, -ну* remain. Most verbs in *-ей* and *-е* don't form a ppp, since they are intransitive, but гре́й+ is transitive and does form the ppp. with *-т* (прогре́тый) and про-сиде́+ does, with *-ён* (проси́женный).

Verbs with the suffixes *-о* and *-ну* use *-т.* If the stress, whether fixed or shifting, is on the suffix, then it is moved back one syllable: коло́+ 'stab, prick' ~ проко́лотый; за-верну́+ 'wrap, turn' ~ заве́рнутый; об-мана́+ 'deceive' ~ обма́нутый.

Non-suffixed resonants also use *-т,* but while fixed stress remains fixed, shifting stress shows up with the same pattern as in the past tense: fem. end stress, prefix stress in the other forms:

раз-де́н+ 'undress'	~	разде́та
раз-би́й+ 'shatter'	~	разби́та
за-кры́й+ 'close'	~	закры́та
раз-ду́й+ 'disperse, blow apart'	~	разду́та
с-т´р+ 'rub off' but	~	стёрта
пѐре-пий+ 'out-drink'	~	пе́репит, перепита́, пе́репито, пе́репиты
пѐре-жив+ 'experience, live through'	~	пе́режит, пережита́, пе́режито, пе́режиты
на̀-чн+ 'begin'	~	на́чат, начата́, на́чато, на́чаты
за̀-ньм+ 'occupy'	~	за́нят, занята́, за́нято, за́няты
за̀-пр+ 'lock'	~	за́перт, заперта́, за́перто, за́перты

Initial stress in the feminine form (на́чата, за́нята) is very common in spoken Russian, but it is not standard and should be avoided.

For yet more even messier details, see *Грамматика 1980*, §1629–31.

9.5. The Present Gerund

The *present gerund* (verbal adverb) is made with the suffix *-a*, which softens the preceding consonant:

ползя́	зна́я	чита́я	держа́
плетя́	смея́сь	де́лая	дыша́
кладя́	тре́буя	говоря́	смотря́
плывя́	атаку́я	любя́	

As can be seen from the preceding examples, stress is usually the same as that of the first person sg., but there are a few exceptions:

гляде́+	~	гляжу́, гля́дя	сиде́+	~	сижу́, си́дя
лежа́+	~	лежу́, лёжа	стоя́+	~	стою́, сто́я
молча́+	~	молчу́, мо́лча			

Some scholars argue that гля́дя, лёжа, мо́лча, си́дя, and сто́я are frozen forms that are really adverbs, and no longer present gerunds.

If the present tense has an irregular stem, it will be used for the present gerund: бра́+ ~ беру́, беря́; гна́+ ~ гоню́, гоня́; пе́й+ ~ пою́, поя́; стла́+ ~ стелю́, стеля́.

Verbs in (-)дава́й+, -знава́й+, -става́й+ keep the longer stem of the infinitive and imperative (cf. 8.2.5.1): даю́ but дава́я; создаю́ but создава́я; сознаю́ but сознава́я; устаю́ but устава́я.

9.5.3. The suffix -*a* not only softens the preceding consonant, but it also causes mutation in those first conjugation verbs with stem in consonant plus -a which form a present gerund, e.g. пла́ка+ ~ пла́ча, маха́+ ~ маша́ (and equally valid маха́я), плеска́+ ~ плеща́ (and плеска́я), and also in the few velar stems which make this form, e.g. толк+ ~ толча́, берёг+ ~ бережа́.

9.5.4. The form of the present gerund is not made or is made rarely from several types of verb stems, including velar obstruent stems (*к, г*), primary resonant stems in *р, н, м*, stems in -*ий*+ or -*ый*+, stems with non-syllabic roots (вра́+, рва́+, чт+), stems in -*о*+ or -*ну*+. First-conjugation verbs in consonant plus -*а*+, which often have an alternate stem in -*ай*+, may make the present gerund from either stem or both, or neither. Thus маха́+, alternate stem маха́й+, forms both маша́ and маха́я, whereas ма́за+ and писа́+ do not form present gerunds in Contempory Standard Russian (CSR). Sometimes the forms do occur from the verb types enumerated in this paragraph, in which case most are perceived as belonging to an archaic, formal register. Examples arc: бережа́, беря́, бия́, вия́сь, гоня́, кляня́, лия́, маша́, плеща́, толча́, тяня́. The various standard works frequently disagree about precisely which of these forms actually do exist (see the items in the *Bibliography*, especially Zaliznyak, the Орфоэпический словарь, *Грамматика 1980*, and Исаченко).

9.5.5. There is another form of the present gerund, ending in -учи (with stress always on the syllable before the -*у*), which is made from a limited number of verbs. According to *Грамматика 1980*, §1590, the following occur and belong to the conversational or substandard register: е́дучи, жале́ючи, и́дучи, игра́ючи, кра́дучись, си́дючи, уме́ючи. The verb быть has only бу́дучи, which is stylistically neutral.

9.5.6. In producing forms of present gerund from verbs in consonant plus -*a* and in a velar, the vowel {a} acts like {o}; see rule 19 in 9.1.3.4.

That is, it invokes consonant mutation, in spite of the fact that it is not a rounded vowel, e.g. толќ+ ~ толку́, толчёт, толчём, толку́т, толча́, берёѓ+ ~ берегу́, бережёт, бережём, берегу́т, бережа́, пла́ка ~ пла́чу, пла́чет, пла́чем, пла́чут, пла́ча. Interestingly, the suffix -*u* of the imperative produces the same mutation in consonant plus -*a* verbs, but not in velars:

пла́ка+	~	пла́чу, плачь!
маха̀+	~	машу́, маши́!
толќ+	~	толку́, толчёт, толчём, толку́т, толки́!
берёѓ+	~	берегу́, бережёт, бережём, берегу́т, береги́!

It should also be noted that when verbs have the mobile stress pattern in the present, only three endings bear the stress: first sg. {u}, imperative {i̦}, and present gerund {a}: ходи̇+, хожу́, ходи́!, ходя́; маха̀ ~ машу́, маши́!, маша́.

The natural question is: what do these three endings have in common that separates them from all other endings? A second, and less easily solved, question is, why does the ending of the present gerund, {a}, behave like {o̦} in velar stems? Consider these two questions in class.

9.6. The Past Gerund

The past gerund (verbal adverb) is basically formed like the past active participle (see 9.3 above), but it shows an -*u* at the end, rather than adjective endings: зна́вши, проходи́вши. In those cases where the -*в* remains and is not dropped (that is, when a vowel precedes the -*вш*-), the past gerund may have an alternate form without the -*ши*: купи́в or купи́вши, написа́в or написа́вши. For most Russians today, there is no difference in meaning between the two forms.

When the reflexive particle -сь is present, then only the longer form is acceptable: столкну́в and столкну́вши, but only столкну́вшись. If the masc. sg. past tense form has no -*л*, then only the longer form of the past gerund exists: за-влёќ+ ~ past tense он завлёк, она завлекла́, past gerund завлёкши(сь).

For details of stress in compounds of мр+ and пр+, see *Грамматика 1980*, §1644.

Table 9-4. The Past Gerund

Stem	Past Gerund
жѝв+	жи́в(ши)
пас́+	па́сши
плёт́+	плётши
гры́з+	гры́зши
тр+	тёрши
жг+	жёгши
пёќ+	пёкши
пла́ка+	пла́кав(ши)
пахà+	паха́в(ши)
брà+	бра́в(ши)
ка́па+	ка́пав(ши)
дремà+	дрема́в(ши)
вёрну́+	верну́в(ши)
(за-)мёрз(ну)+	(за-)мёрзши
(вы́-)со́х(ну)+	(вы́-)со́хши
тро́ну+	тро́нув(ши)
зна́й+	зна́в(ши)
де́лай+	де́лав(ши)
чита́й+	чита́в(ши)
гре́й+	гре́в(ши)
красне́й+	красне́в(ши)
тре́бова+	тре́бовав(ши)
атакова́+	атакова́в(ши)
кова́+	кова́в(ши)
ходѝ+	ходи́в(ши)
сиде́+	сиде́в(ши)
лежа́+	лежа́в(ши)

10

Derived Imperfectives

10.0. Introduction

Most unprefixed Russian verbs are *imperfective* in aspect:

писа̀+ 'write'	жѝв+ 'live'	коло̀+ 'stab'
де́лай+ 'do'	гры́з+ 'gnaw'	т́р+ 'rub'
говори́+ 'speak'	жг+ 'burn'	кова́+ 'forge'
держа́+ 'hold'	бра̀+ 'take'	

Verbs with the suffix *-ну* (but not *(ну)*) are perfective without a prefix:

толкну́+ 'shove'   кри́кну+ 'shout'

A few other unprefixed stems are also perfective. The list includes:

благослови́+ 'bless'	плени́+ 'capture, captivate'
бро́си+ 'throw'	прости́+ 'forgive'
встре́ти+[1] 'meet'	пусти́+ 'let, let go, release'
дай+ 'give'	реши́+ 'solve, resolve, decide'
де́н+ 'place, put'	се́д+ 'sit down'
контузи́+ 'give a concussion (to)'	снабди́+[1] 'supply, furnish'
ко́нчи+ 'end, finish'	ста́н+ 'take a standing position; become'
купи́+ 'buy'	стрели́+ 'shoot'
лёг+ 'lie down'	ступи́+ 'step, tread'
лиши́+ 'deprive'	хвати́+ 'seize; suffice'
па́д+ 'fall'	яви́+ 'manifest, show'

---

[1] Historically prefixed.

Bi-aspectual verbs have the same form for both perfective and imperfective aspects: обеща́й+ вчера он обещал (perfective), что даст мне деньги сегодня утром. Каждый день он обещает (imperfective), но денег нет.

10.1. The Effect of Prefixation on Aspect

When a prefix is added to a verb, the verb normally becomes perfective:

в-писа́+ 'inscribe'

до-писа́+ 'write up to a certain point, write additionally'

за-писа́+ 'note, write down'

ис-писа́+ 'fill or cover with writing, use up by writing'

вы́-писа́+ 'extract, copy out'

о-писа́+ 'describe'

пере-писа́+ 'rewrite, copy'

под-писа́+ 'sign, subscribe'

при-писа́+ 'ascribe'

In each of these cases the prefix not only makes the verb perfective, but it also adds a meaning. These prefixes are known as "lexical" or "semantic" prefixes. In theory at least, each Russian verb also has one prefix which only makes it perfective, without changing the meaning in any other way. This prefix is known as the "grammatical" prefix. For писа́+ the grammatical prefix is на-; на-писа́+ means the same thing as писа́+, except that it is perfective.

Sometimes a verb will have different grammatical prefixes for different meanings. In the meaning of 'hit'. the perfective of би́й+ is по-би́й+ or при-би́й+; in the meaning of 'slaughter'. it is у-би́й+; in the meaning of 'strike/ring out the time'. it is про-би́й+; in the meaning of 'shatter, smash'. it is раз-би́й+; in the meaning of 'churn" (butter) it is с-би́й+; in the meaning of 'strike' (coinage) it is вы́-бий+.[2]

10.2. Derived Imperfectives

Since пере-писа́+ does not mean the same thing as писа́+, the unprefixed form cannot serve as the imperfective to the prefixed form. In order to have an imperfective with the same lexical meaning as a lexically-prefixed verb, Russian changes the suffix: пере-пи́сывай+.

Russian has three suffixes to make *derived imperfectives*: -ыва́й+, -а́й+, and -ва́й+. The suffix -ыва́й+ never carries the stress on either syllable; the suffixes -а́й+ and -ва́й+ are always stressed: пере-писа́+

---

[2] Meanings and perfective prefixes taken from Ušakov 1934, Vol. 1, column 143.

'rewrite' ~ пере-пи́сывай+; от-ве́ти+ 'answer' ~ от-веча́й+; на-де́н+ 'put on' ~ на-дева́й+, про-говори́+ 'utter, speak' ~ про-гова́ривай+. Note that when the suffix is *-ыва́й+*, the stress always falls on the syllable immediately preceding the suffix: при-колоти́+ 'nail (to)' ~ при-кола́чивай+.

10.2.1. In verbs of the first conjugation the imperfectivizing suffixes *replace* the suffix, if any, of the perfective,[3] whereas in verbs of the second conjugation the three suffixes *are added to* the suffix of the perfective. This means that in second conjugation stems consonant mutation always occurs before the suffixes *-ыва́й+* and *-а́й+*: от-ве́ти+ 'answer' ~ от-веча́й+, спроси́+ 'ask' ~ спра́шивай+, про-сиде́+ 'sit through; serve (a sentence)' ~ проси́живай+ and it never occurs in first conjugation stems: пере-писа̀+ 'rewrite' ~ пере-пи́сывай+, пере-де́лай+ 'redo' ~ пере-де́лывай+, про-коло̀+ 'pierce' ~ про-ка́лывай+, от-толкну́+ 'push away' ~ от-та́лкивай+, про-па́д+ 'fall through, perish' ~ про-пада́й+; про-пёк+ 'bake through, bake thoroughly' ~ про-пека́й+.

10.2.2. If the last or only vowel of the root is *o*, it normally shifts to *a* before the suffix *-ыва́й+*, but not before *-а́й+*: при-говори́+ 'sentence' ~ при-гова́ривай+, про-коло̀+ 'pierce' ~ про-ка́лывай+, с-проси́+ 'ask' ~ с-пра́шивай+, от-толкну́+ 'push away' ~ от-та́лкивай+, по-мог̀+ 'help ~ по-мога́й+, о-добри́+ 'approve' ~ о-добря́й+. More precisely, if the stress in the perfective stem is on the suffix and it is thrown back onto the {o} of the root by the suffix *-ыва́й*, then the {o} will always go to {a}: от-толкну́+ ~ от-та́лкивай+, про-коло̀+ ~ про-ка́лывай+; if the stress in the perfective stem is on the {o} in the root, then it will most frequently change the {o} to {a}, but there are exceptions and doublet forms: за-рабо́тай+ 'earn' ~ за-раба́тывай+, за-ко́нчи+ 'finish' ~ за-ка́нчивай+, при-гото́ви+ 'prepare' ~ при-гота́вливай+, but раз-ро́зни+ 'break a set' ~ раз-ро́знивай+, у-за-ко́ни+ 'legalize' ~ у-за-ко́нивай+, у-полномо́чи+ 'authorize, give authority' ~ у-полномо́чивай+. From о-спо́ри+ 'dispute' both о-спо́ривай+ and о-спа́ривай+ occur.

If the {o} is part of the suffix {ova}, then the {o} does not change: пере-группирова́+ 'regroup' ~ пере-группиро́вывай+, раз-межева̀+ 'mark off, delimit' ~ раз-межёвывай+. The same is true of the half-

---

[3] Except that with the suffix *-ова+*, only the *-a* is replaced: пере-адресова́+ ~ пере-адресо́вывай+.

dozen verbs in {ova} where the {o} is part of the root: при-кова́+ 'chain to' ~ при-ко́вывай+, пере-жева́+ 'masticate' ~ пере-жёвывай+.

10.3. Distribution of the Three Suffixes

10.3.1. The suffix *-ва́й+* is used by primary resonant stems in *-й* or *-н*, and the *й* or *н* drops before the consonant *в*: про-пи́й+ 'drink up, go through by drinking' ~ про-пива́й+, за-кры́й+ 'close' ~ за-крыва́й+, про-гре́й+ 'warm thoroughly' ~ про-грева́й+, за-пе́й+ 'begin to sing' ~ за-пева́й+, раз-ду́й+ 'blow in various directions' ~ раз-дува́й+, на-де́н+ 'put on' ~ на-дева́й+, за-сты́н+ 'congeal, thicken' ~ за-стыва́й+, у-би́й+ 'kill' ~ у-бива́й+.

10.3.2. The suffix *-а́й+* is used with the following five types of stems:

10.3.2.1. Non-syllabic roots, regardless of the verbal suffix (if any); these verbs insert the vowel {i} into the root. Where the preceding consonant allows a choice, *и* will be used before *н* and *p* and *ы* will be used before other consonants.

Examples:

с-т́р+ 'rub/wipe off'	~	с-тира́й+
за-ж́м+ 'squeeze'	~	за-жима́й+
за-мкну́+ 'close, lock'	~	за-мыка́й+
на̀-чн+ 'begin'	~	на-чина́й+
при-сла́+ 'send'	~	при-сыла́й+
из-бра̀+ 'select'	~	из-бира́й+
за-гну́+ 'bend (over)'	~	за-гиба́й+
про-рва̀+ 'tear through'	~	про-рыва́й+
у̀-мр+ 'die'	~	у-мира́й+
за-жг+ 'set on fire'	~	за-жига́й
за-сну́+ 'fall asleep'	~	за-сыпа́й+
при-зва̀+ 'call, summon'	~	при-зыва́й+
рас-пн́+ 'crucify'	~	рас-пина́й+
у-по-мяну́+ 'mention'	~	у-по-мина́й+

Note that the imperfective derivation rules are ordered and the rule here in 10.3.2.1 actually has to come before 10.3.1, since otherwise incorrect forms would result: if 10.3.1 were applied first, we would get *на-чвай+ instead of на-чина́й+ from на̀-чн+. Section 10.3.1 is given first for pedagogical reasons: it is the simplest to state and covers the least stems.

If the prefix has a mobile vowel before the non-syllabic form of the root, that mobile vowel will disappear before the imperfective form with a vowel in the root: от-о-зва̀+ 'call aside' ~ от-зыва́й+, раз-о-бра́+ (future раз-беру́, past раз-о-бра́л) 'take apart' раз-бира́й+, в-о-гну́+ 'bend in' ~ в-гиба́й+, раз-о-мн+ 'knead, mash' ~ раз-мина́й+.

10.3.2.2. All other non-suffixed stems (other than those in -*й* or -*н*, treated in 10.3.1 above and the non-syllabics treated in 10.3.2.1 immediately above):[4]

с-пас́+ 'save'	~	с-паса́й+
про-тёќ+ 'flow through'	~	про-тека́й+
про-гры́з+ 'gnaw through'	~	прогрыза́й+
про-па́д+ 'fall through'	~	про-пада́й+
из-об-рёт́+ 'invent'	~	из-об-рета́й+

10.3.2.3. The majority of *factitive* verbs:

у-сложни́+ 'complicate'	~	у-сложня́й+
о-добри́+ 'approve'	~	о-добря́й+
о-чи́сти+ 'cleanse'	~	о-чища́й+
об-нови́+ 'renew, renovate'	~	об-новля́й+
окружи́+ 'surround'	~	окружа́й+
от-дали́+ 'remove, distance'	~	от-даля́й+
по-ясни́+ 'elucidate'	~	по-ясня́й+
под-тверди́+ 'confirm'	~	под-твержда́й+
про-светли́+ 'illuminate'	~	про-светля́й+
у-дешеви́+ 'devalue, cheapen'	~	у-дешевля́й+

Factitive verbs have the suffix -*и* and mean "make the object X" where X is the meaning of the adjective or noun from which the factitive

---

[4] Question for thought: which suffix do verbs in *в* use? (E.g., про-жи́в+ ~ про-жива́й+) What factors might infuence how you decide to state it?

verb is derived. English factitive verbs often have the suffix *-en*; бели+ 'whiten', сократи+ 'shorten', ослаби+ 'weaken'.

10.3.2.4. Sample verbs in *-u* which are Church Slavonic:[5]

со-общи+ 'inform, communicate'	~	со-обща́й+
из-лучи́+ 'radiate'	~	из-луча́й+
воз-врати́+ 'return'	~	воз-враща́й+
за-гради́+ 'block, obstruct'	~	за-гражда́й+

A good pair are Russian от-вороти+ 'turn away' vs. Church Slavonic от-врати+ 'repel'. The R verb has a literal meaning; the ChSl one is figurative. The future forms are отворочу́, отворо́тишь ~ отвращу́, отврати́шь, with R. -оро- in the root, ч in the first person sg., and shifting stress, vs. ChSl -ра-, щ and fixed stress. The past passive participles are отворо́ченный and отвращённый. The R form has от-вора́чивай+ for the derived impf. with *-ывай+*, whereas the ChSl has отвраща́й+ with the impf. suffix *-а́й+*.

10.3.2.5. All verbs with the suffix *(ну)* are Church Slavonic.

Examples:

за-мёрз(ну)+ 'freeze'	~	за-мерза́й+
ис-чéз(ну)+ 'disappear'	~	ис-чеза́й+

Note that the suffix (ну)+ is dropped, as we expect from a first conjugation verb (see 10.2.1 above), leaving a stem ending in an obstruent, so the imperfective suffix is а́й+, as we expect for an obstruent stem.

10.3.3. The suffix *-ывай+* is added to almost everything remaining, which means verbs in *-a, -ай, husher+a, -o, -e*.

Examples:

пере-писà+	~	пере-пи́сывай+
пере-дéлай+	~	пере-дéлывай+

---

[5] See Appendix 1.

за-держà+ 'detain, arrest'   ~   за-дéрживай+
про-колò+ 'pierce'   ~   про-кáлывай+
про-сидé+ 'sit through'   ~   про-сúживай+
рас-смотрè+ 'examine'   ~   рас-смáтривай+
о-смея́+ 'mock'   ~   о-смéивай+
от-стоя́+ 'defend'   ~   от-стáивай+

10.3.4. Verbs with the suffixes -*u* and (non-dropping) -*нy* may form the imperfective with either -*ывай*+ or -*ай*+, although a given stem will use the same suffix with all prefixes.

10.3.5. Verbs with a vowel plus {j} plus vowel will always form the imperfective with -*ывай*+, regardless of any other considerations. The {o} in the root always goes to /a/.

Examples:

при-свóи+ 'appropriate; confer'   ~   при-свáивай+
у-двóи+ 'double'   ~   у-двáивай+
у-спокóи+ 'calm'   ~   у-спокáивай+
  (but о-бес-по-кóи+ 'perturb' ~ exceptionally has
  о-бес-по-кóивай+, with /o/ remaining /o/)
рас-стрóи+ 'upset, disarrange   ~   рас-стрáивай+
у-до-стóи+ 'award'   ~   у-до-стáивай+
  (all are factitives, leading us to expect -*ай*+)
благо-у-стрóи+ 'set up with   ~   благо-у-стрáивай+
  conveniences, improve'
  (factitive *and* Church Slavonic,
  leading us to expect -*ай*+)

10.3.6. Consonants lost before the -*н*- of the suffixes -*нy* or (-*нy*) will reappear when the -*нy* or (-*нy*) is lost.

Examples:

за-гнý+ 'bend'   ~   за-гибáй+
у-вя́ну+ 'fade'   ~   у-вядáй+
за-снý+ 'fall asleep'   ~   за-сыпáй+
за-гляну́+ 'glance at'.   ~   за-гля́дывай+

за-тро́ну+	'touch upon'	~	за-тра́гивай+
с-ти́сну+	'squeeze together'	~	с-ти́скивай+
за-дёрну+	'pull, draw'	~	за-дёргивай+
раз-верну́+	'unwind, develop'	~	раз-вёртывай+
вз-дро́гну+	'shudder, start, flinch'	~	вздра́гивай+

10.3.7. Those few stems with the suffix *-ей+* which form derived imperfectives do so with the suffix *-ва́й+*: за-боле́й+ ~ за-болева́й+ 'fall sick'. о-бес-си́лей+ 'lose one's strength' ~ о-бес-силева́й+; у-целе́й+ 'remain intact/alive' ~ у-целева́й+. Exception: вы́-здорове́й+ 'get well' ~вы-здора́вливай+.

10.4. Iteratives

Iteratives (многокра́тные глаго́лы). Russian has a subcategory of the imperfective aspect called the *iterative*. It is used only in the past tense and infinitive and in general has the same suffix as the derived imperfective, but it has no prefix: пи́сывал, гова́ривал, бира́л, быва́л, дира́л, еда́л 'ate'. жива́л, знава́л, и́скивал, ку́ривал, ла́вливал, пева́л, пива́л, си́живал, чи́тывал. Some other common forms are: ви́дывал, е́зживал, обе́дывал (historically prefixed), слы́хивал, сыпа́л 'sleep'.

Iteratives denote an action which occurred frequently (although not necessarily at regular intervals) in the past and no longer does. It is also common in negative sentences: Кити никогда не ста́ивала в этой толпе (Толстой, *Анна Каренина*).

The number of verbs which form iteratives is slowly but steadily shrinking in CSR. Iterative forms are still extremely common in the popular language.

The stem быва́й+ is used in all forms and not just as an iterative; it also has meanings other than iterative. Вида́й+ and слыха́й+[6] can be used in the present and are losing the meaning of iterativity. They are very often used in negative sentences: Тако́го не вида́ла, не слыха́ла. New forms, ви́дывал and слы́хивал, have taken over the iterative slot. Examples of iteratives:

---

[6] If we treat слы́ша+ as слыхе+ (see 8.1.2.3), then the connection between слы́ша+, слыха́й+, and слы́хивать becomes clear: the suffix *-е+* is replaced by the suffixes *-а́й+* and *-ыва́й+*.

Я у них си́живал це́лыми часа́ми.
Я ли́чно знава́л мно́гих выдаю́щихся актёров.
Я никогда́ не еда́л таки́х я́блок.
Быва́ло, пи́сывала кро́вью
Она́ в альбо́мы не́жных дев...

Евгений Онегин

Стару́шка ей: а вот ками́н;
Здесь ба́рин си́живал оди́н,
Здесь с ним обе́дывал зимо́ю
Поко́йный Ле́нский, наш сосе́д.

Евгений Онегин

Я за́ уши его́ дира́ла, то́лько ма́ло.

Грибоедов

Мно́го пе́сен слыха́л я в родно́й стороне́.

«Дуби́нушка»

Ча́сто бира́л я с бо́ю то, что сле́довало мне по пра́ву.

«Станцио́нный смотри́тель»

10.4.1. Russian has a set of forms with the prefix по- and the iterative suffix -ывай+ (often without mutation of the consonant); the meaning is "do a little from time to time" or "do for a short time from time to time." A good example from Paustovskij is Они́ поку́ривали и поплёвывали, перекидываясь замеча́ниями... 'They took short smokes and spit from time to time, while exchanging remarks'.
Among the numerous other verbs of this type are:

погля́дывать (← гляде́+) 'look, glance'
погова́ривать (← говори́+) 'speak, say'
пока́шливать (← ка́шляй+) 'cough'
попева́ть (← пе́й+) 'sing'
попива́ть (← пи́й+) 'drink'
поба́ливай+ (←боле́+) 'hurt, ache'
покри́кивай+ (← крик-е́+ крича́+) 'shout'
почёсывай+ (← чёса̀+) 'scratch'

10.5. Irregularities

Stress is never irregular with the suffixes *-ывай+* , *-áй+* , and *-вáй+* .

10.5.1. Sometimes the suffix used is not the expected one: про-рéза+ 'cut through' ~ про-резáй+ (instead of the expected *про-рéзывай+). Another verb stem with this same irregular imperfective derivation is за-сы́па+ ~ за-сыпáй+ 'cover with powder, sprinkle'.

If a verb stem has irregular imperfective derivation with one prefix, it will have the same with all prefixes. Thus про-резáй+ implies от-резáй+, вы́-резáй+, за-резáй+, пере-резáй+, etc.

Further examples of irregular choice of suffix:

за-вéя+ 'waft'	~	завевáй+
за-сéя+ 'sew'	~	за-севáй+
разúну+ 'yawn'	~	разевáй+
растлú+ 'seduce, corrupt'	~	растлевáй+
затмú+ 'darken; overshadow'	~	затмевáй+
застря́н+ 'get stuck'	~	застревáй+
про-длú+ 'prolong'	~	про-длевáй+
от-волóк+ 'drag away'	~	отволáкивай+
вы́-крáд+ 'steal'	~	вы-крáдывай+
обúде+ 'offend'	~	обижáй+[7]

10.5.2. In some second conjugation verbs, the expected consonant mutation or softening does not occur: при-ступú+ 'approach, step up to' ~ при-ступáй+ (instead of *при-ступля́й+ or *при-стýпливай+). При-ступáй+ implies за-ступáй+, от-ступáй+, вы́-ступáй+, etc.

Further examples:

пере-брóси+ 'thow over'	~	пере-брáсывай+
про-глотú+ 'gulp down'	~	проглáтывай+

---

[7] Historically prefixed: об-вúде+ → обúде+

за-кипе́+ 'begin to boil'   ~   за-кипа́й+
вы́-купи+ 'ransom'   ~   вы-купа́й+
от-куси+ 'bite off'   ~   от-ку́сывай+
про-руби+ 'chop through'   ~   про-руба́й+
в(с)-скочи+ 'jump up'   ~   в(с)-ска́кивай+
за-хвати+ 'seize'   ~   за-хва́тывай+

10.5.3. Some factitive verbs use the suffix -ывай+ instead of -а́й+. See 10.3.5. The rule about using -ывай+ with all verbs ending in {VjV} is ordered before the rule about factitives using -а́й+, so у-двои́+ 'double' ~ у-два́ивай+ is expected.

The pairs вы́-ветри+ 'air out, ventilate' ~ вы-ве́тривай+, за-секре́ти+ 'secrete' ~ за-секре́чивай+, от-сро́чи+ 'put off, delay' ~ от-сро́чивай+, у-зако́ни+ 'legalize' ~ у-зако́нивай+ are unexpected.

There is no way to predict when a factitive will make the imperfective with -ывай+.

10.5.4. As is well-known, Russian has fourteen pairs of verbs of motion which form a special subdivision of the imperfective aspect, *determinate* vs. *indeterminate*. The pairs are:

бежа́+ 'run'   ~   бе́гай+
брёд+ 'roam,   ~   броди́+
   wander, amble'
вёд+ 'lead'   ~   води́+
вёз+ 'convey'   ~   вози́+
гна́+ 'chase, drive'   ~   гоня́й+
е́ха+ 'ride'   ~   е́зди+
ид́+ 'go'   ~   ходи́+
кати́+ 'roll'   ~   ката́й+
ле́з+ 'climb'   ~   ла́зи+
лете́+ 'fly'   ~   лета́й+
нёс+ 'carry'   ~   носи́+
плы́в+ 'float, swim'   ~   пла́вай+
полз́+ 'crawl'   ~   по́лзай+
тащи́+ 'drag, pull'   ~   таска́й+

In principle, when forming prefixed verbs, the determinate form makes the perfective (при-вёз+) and the indeterminate makes the prefixed imperfective (при-вози+). However, in eight of the fourteen pairs, there is a special imperfective stem which is used:

при-бега́й+	про-ка́тывай+	при-ползай+
раз-бреда́й+-ся	вы-леза́й+	при-та́скивай+
при-езжа́й+	вы-плыва́й+	

10.5.5. There are quite a few verbs in Russian which do not comprise an aspect pair, but occur only in one aspect. Very often this is connected with the meaning of the verb:

со-стоя́+ 'consist'	мечта́й+ 'dream'
зна́чи+ 'mean, signify'	владе́й+ 'possess'
со-держа̀+ 'contain'	беле́й+ 'show/appear white'
на-ме́ревай+-ся 'intend'	жужжа́+ 'buzz, hum'
на-де́я+-ся 'hope'	греме́+ 'thunder'
зна́й+ 'know'	

These are all imperfective; очути́ться 'find oneself in a situation or location' is perfective only.

10.5.6. A large number of Russian verbs express both aspects with a single form. These are called *biaspectual* stems. They can be divided into three groups.

The most numerous group is verbs in -ова+, -изова+ -ирова+, -изирова+, most of which have borrowed stems: адресова́+ 'address'. атакова́+ 'attack'. арестова́+ 'arrest'. анализи́рова+ 'analyze'. командирова́+ 'command, be in command of'. ремонти́рова+ 'repair, renovate'. организова́+ 'organize'.

The second group is verbs borrowed from Church Slavonic, or at least belonging to the formal, elevated, bookish register of CSR: обеща́й+ 'promise'. испо́льзова+ 'use'. иссле́дова+ 'investigate, study'. со-де́йствова+ 'assist'. обсле́дова+ 'investigate'. насле́дова+ 'inherit'. со-чета́й+ 'combine, connect'.

The third, and smallest, group is verbs belonging to ordinary, neutral Russian: веле́+ 'command'. женѝ+ 'marry'. казни́+ 'execute'. крести́+ 'baptize'. мо́лви+ 'say, utter'. рани́+ 'wound'.

Although these verbs may be used with the meaning of either aspect, Russian often fits them into the prevalent pattern of aspect pairs, either by prefixation to make an unambiguously perfective form (с-организова́+, про-анализи́рова+, от-ремонти́рова+, по-жени́+, по-обеща́й+, про-мо́лви+), or, if the verb ends in *stressed* ова́+, by suffixation to make an unambiguously imperfective form (аресто́вывай+, организо́вывай+).

One biaspectual verb, роди́+ 'bear, give birth'. orthoepically differentiates aspect only in the fem. past tense: perfective родила́, imperfective роди́ла. The masc., neut., and plural forms роди́л, роди́ло, роди́ли are the same for both aspects.

10.6. Imperfective Verbs Derived from Unprefixed Perfectives

Imperfectives may also be formed from unprefixed perfectives (cf. 10.0). The principles are in general the same as for imperfectives from prefixed perfectives:

благослови́+ 'bless'	~	благословля́й+
да́й+ 'give'	~	дава́й+
де́н+ 'place, put'	~	дева́й+
ко́нчи+ 'end, finish'.	~	конча́й+
лиши́+ 'deprive'	~	лиша́й+
плени́+ 'captivate; capture'	~	пленя́й+
прости́+ 'forgive'	~	проща́й+
реши́+ 'decide, resolve'	~	реша́й+
стрели́+ 'shoot'	~	стреля́й+
яви́+ 'manifest, show'	~	явля́й+.

Several pairs show irregularities:

бро́си+ 'throw'	~	броса́й+
купи́+ 'buy'	~	по-купа́й+
лёг+ 'lie down'	~	ложи́+-ся
па́д+ 'fall'	~	па́дай+
пусти́+ 'let, release'	~	пуска́й+
се́д+ 'sit down'	~	сади́+-ся
ста́н+ 'take a standing position; become'	~	станови́+-ся
ступи́+ 'step'	~	ступа́й+
хвати́+ 'seize'	~	хвата́й+

10.7. Examples of Different Stems for the Two Aspects

по-вёр(т)ну́+ ~ по-вора́чивай+ 'turn'
раз-о-гна́+ ~ раз-гоня́й+ 'disperse'
от-дохну́+ ~ от-дыха́й+ 'rest'
по-ложи́+ ~ кла́д+ 'lay, put'
до-ложи́+ ~ до-кла́дывай+ 'report'
вы́-ну+ ~ вы-нима́й+ 'take out'
за-со́х(ну)+ ~ за-сыха́й+ 'dry up'
вы́-су́ну+ ~ вы-со́вывай+ 'shove out'
от-тря́с´+ ~ от-тря́хивай+ 'shake off'

Exercises

I. Form derived imperfectives:

про-игра́й+ 'lose'   на-де́н+ 'dress'
на-ма́за+ 'smear on'   за-пи́й+ 'take to drink'
рас-печа́тай+ 'unseal'   под-ры́й+ 'undermine'
пере-страхова́+ 'reinsure'   о-сты́н+ 'grow cool'
про-смотрѐ+ 'look through'   о-кисли́+ 'oxidize'
раз-о-рва̀+ 'tear apart'   при-гласи́+ 'invite'
за-плёт+ 'braid'   раз-ве́я+ 'blow apart, scatter'
про-т́р+ 'rub through'

II. Use the verbs in Appendix 2, starting with number 70, to form de-
    rived imperfectives. Assume that all are regular. Where two forms
    are possible, give both.

Appendix 1
Church Slavonic in Russian

11.1. Church Slavonic Vocabulary

It is well-known that in English we frequently have two or more ways of saying the same thing, but those near equivalents frequently have different stylistic values. For example, it is quite normal to say "the Smiths served beef and pork for dinner." It is not normal to say "the Smiths served cow and pig for dinner." A bill might request that you "please remit the indicated amount" but it would be unlikely to say: "pay up" or "fork over." A lecturer in a physiology class can talk about "the production of urine and feces by the human body" but probably would not keep his or her job very long if s/he used the Anglo-Saxon "four-letter words" for the same substances.

English uses words of foreign origin to achieve a higher stylistic level or a more abstract meaning. The native English words usually belong to a coarser level or have a more concrete meaning: "beef" and "pork" can be elegant dishes to serve in the best of company; "cow" and "pig" are animals that live in the mud outside (but "chicken" serves for both meat and animal). The more abstract word "transfer" does not usually mean "carried from one place to another" in the literal sense that "carry across" does. We can say "Jones was transferred from the Chicago to the Boston office," but not "Jones was carried across from the Chicago to the Boston office."

For English the principal sources of abstract, elevated, polite, or scientific vocabulary are French, Latin, and Greek. All three of these languages are genetically related to English at differing distances. Russian also uses a related language as a source of the same types of vocabulary. This language is *Church Slavonic*, which is more closely related to Russian than French, Latin, and Greek are to English. For Russia, Ukraine, Bulgaria, Serbia, and other countries belonging to Orthodox Christianity, *Church Slavonic* was and is the language of religion. It was also the main language of literature from the late ninth century through the end of the Middle Ages.

Russian had two major periods of influence from Church Slavic: the first was immediately after 988, when Russia was baptized, and the second was the end of the 14th century, when many monks and other religious and intellectual figures fled from the Turks, who were conquering the Balkans. Many Church Slavonicisms relate to the sounds of the words; see sections 11.1.1 to 11.1.10 below. Others relate to the constituents of words: see 11.1.11 to 11.1.13. Many Church Slavonicisms are simply different words.

11.1.1. ChSl medial (within the morpheme) -*ра/ре/ла/ле*- corresponding to Russ -*оро/ере/оло/оло*-

хранѝть 'preserve' ~ хоронѝть 'bury'
возвратѝть 'return' ~ воро́та 'gates'
развратѝть/ развраща́ть 'debauch, corrupt' ~ развороти́ть/
    развора́чивать 'smash up, knock to pieces'
страна́ 'country' ~ сторона́ 'side' ~ страни́ца 'page'
градострои́тель 'city planner' ~ го́род 'city'
граждани́н 'citizen' ~ горожа́нин 'city dweller'

безбре́жный 'boundless' ~ бе́рег 'bank, shore'
бре́мя 'burden' ~ обремени́ть 'burden'
предсказа́ть 'foretell' председа́тель 'chairperson' (Cf. German –
    Vorsitzender) ~ перед 'before'
среда́ 'Wednesday' сре́дний 'middle; average' ~ середи́на 'middle'

глава́ 'chief, head; chapter' ~ голова́ 'head'
гла́сный 'vocal; vowel' согла́сие 'agreement' ~ го́лос 'voice'
власть 'power, rule' ~ во́лость 'administrative division in tsarist
    Russia'

отвле́чь 'distract' ~ отволо́чь 'drag away'
млекопита́ющие 'mammals' мле́чный путь 'Milky Way' ~ молоко́
    'milk' моло́чный кокте́йль 'milk shake'
плен 'captivity' ~ поло́н 'captivity' (archaic & popular)

11.1.2. ChSl morpheme-initial *pa*- corresponding to Russ *po*-:

во́зраст 'age' ~ рост 'height' водоро́сль aquatic plant'
ра́вные права́ 'equal rights' ~ ро́вное по́ле 'level/flat field'

11.1.3. ChSl -*щ*- from *m*, corresponding to Russ -*ч*-:

возврати́+ 'return' ~ возвращу́, возвраща́й, возвращённый
мощь 'power' ~ мочь 'physical might'
всенощна́я слу́жба 'vespers and matins' ~ ночна́я пого́да 'night
    weather'
летя́щая лету́чая[1] мышь 'bat in flight'
стоя́щий 'standing' ~ в стоя́чем положе́нии 'upright position'

11.1.4. ChSl -*жд*- from *д*, corresponding to Russ -*ж*-:

вождь 'leader' ~ води́ть 'lead
неве́жда 'ignoramus' ~ неве́жа 'boor, lout'
граждани́н 'citizen' ~ горожа́нин 'city dweller'
прохлади́ть 'cool off/down' ~ прохолоди́ть 'cool down seeds'
награди́+ 'reward, award', награжу́, награжда́й, награждённый.

In the first sg of ChSl verbs *д* always goes to *ж*; in the derived imperfective and the past passive participle it goes to *жд*.

11.1.5. ChSl initial *e*-, corresponding to Russ o-:

еди́нство 'unity' ~ одино́чество 'loneliness'

11.1.6. ChSl non-initial -*e*-, corresponding to Russ -*ё*-:

не́бо 'heaven' ~ нёбо 'palate'
паде́ж 'case' (cf. Latin *cāsus*, < *cadere* ' to fall, German *der erste
    Fall* 'nominative, the first case' ~ падёж 'a cattle disease'
уче́бник 'textbook' ~ плата за учёбу 'tuition'
предме́т 'object' ~ помёт 'litter, brood; dung, excrement'
приле́жный 'diligent' ~ лёжа 'lying down' (gerund)
житие́ 'hagiographical life, *vita*', ~ житьё 'lousy life'

---

[1] The forms with -*ч*- denote inherent capabilities or characteristics; the forms with -*щ*- are participles (verbal forms).

11.1.7. ChSl -*o*-/-*e*- in place of "weak"[2] -ъ-/-ь-:

вообрази́ть 'imagine, conceive of'
вопро́с 'question'
воплоще́ние 'incarnation'
возбуди́ть 'arouse' (cf. пробуди́ть 'awaken')
восста́ть 'rise up, rebel' ~ встать 'get up'
восхо́д 'rising of the sun' ~ всхо́ды 'shoots, tendrils' (of plants)
сове́т 'council; counsel, advice'
соотве́тствие 'correspondence'
собо́р 'cathedral' ~ сбор 'gathering'
содержа́ть 'contain' ~ сдержа́ть 'restrain, hold back'

11.1.8. ChSl -*u*- for R -ь- before another vowel letter:

житие́ 'hagiographical life, *vita*," ~ житьё 'lousy life'
бра́тия 'brethren' (monks) ~ бра́тья 'brothers'
пече́ние 'baking' ~ пече́нье 'cookies, baked goods'
воскресе́ние 'resurrection' ~воскресе́нье 'Sunday'

11.1.9. Unstressed nom. sg. masc. adj. ending spelled -ый instead of -*ой*. Consider the following stanza by Pushkin:

Exegi monumentum

Я памятник себе воздвиг нерукотв<u>о</u>рный;
К нему не зарастёт народная тропа;
Вознёсся выше он главою непок<u>о</u>рной
Александрийского столпа.

He rhymes the nom.-acc. sg. masc. -ый with the fem. instr. sg. -*ой* because the real Russian ending of the nom. sg. masc. was {oj}, pronounced [oj] when stressed and [əj] when unstressed, but written -ой only when stressed. The spelling pronunciation [ɨj] has been gaining ground and is now the most common one.

---

[2] The presence of a vowel is unexpected.

11.1.10. Less mobile stress: no retraction in nouns, no shifting stress in verbs.

сторона́, сто́рону, сто́роны, сторо́н, сторона́м
but страна́, страну́, стра́ны, стран, стра́нам
отвороти́+, отворочу́, отворо́тишь
but отврати́+, отвращу́, отврати́шь

11.1.11. ChSl suffix *-ствие* vs. R *-ство*:

ца́рствие ему́ небе́сное ≅ 'may God rest his soul'

11.1.12. ChSl prefix *из-* vs. R *вы-*:

исписа́ть 'use up/cover with writing' вы́писать 'copy out, extract'
износи́ть 'wear out' выноси́ть 'carry out'
изда́ть 'publish' вы́дать 'give out/away'

11.1.13. Imperfective with suffix *-ай*:

возврати́+ 'return' возвраща́й+
отврати́+ 'turn aside, avert, ward off, repel' отвраща́й+
развраща́й+ 'debauch, corrupt' развора́чивай+ 'smash up, knock
    to pieces'
награди́+ 'reward' награжда́й+

11.1.14. Normally a word will show all ChSl features or all R. See 10.3.2.4. A good pair are Russian от-вороти́+ 'turn away' vs. Church Slavonic от-врати́+ 'repel.' The R verb has a literal meaning; the ChSl one is figurative. The future forms are отворочу́, отворо́тишь ~ отвращу́, отврати́шь, with R. *-оро-* in the root, *ч* in the 1st person sg., and shifting stress, vs. ChSl *-ра-*, *щ* and fixed stress. The past passive participles are отворо́ченный and отвращённый. The Russ has от-вора́чивай+ for the derived impf. with *-ывай+*, whereas the ChSl has отвраща́й+ with the impf. suffix *-а́й+*.

11.2. Materials for Analysis

11.2.1. Read the first of the following poems by A. S. Pushkin (1799–1837) and reflect on the questions provided.

a) Why does Pushkin use глас instead of голос in stanza 3, line 4? Is he shouting so loudly that the Decembrists in Siberia can hear him, or is his "voice" a figurative one?

b) Try to find at least two more ChSl elements in this poem. You may need an etymological dictionary (see Appendix 3).

[Послание в Сибирь]

Во глубине сибирских руд
Храните гордое терпенье,
Не пропадет ваш скорбный труд
И дум высокое стремленье.
Несчастью верная сестра,
Надежда в мрачном подземелье
Разбудит бодрость и веселье,
Придёт желанная пора:
Любовь и дружество до вас
Дойдут сквозь мрачные затворы,
Как в ваши каторжные норы
Доходит мой свободный глас.
Оковы тяжкие падут,
Темницы рухнут—и свобода
Вас примет радостно у входа,
И братья меч вам отдадут.

1826

11.2.2. Consider the form, meaning, and stylistic level of the underlined words. You will need a good dictionary (see Appendix 3) or help from a teacher.

Exegi monumentum

Я памятник себе <u>воздвиг</u> нерукотворный;
К нему не зарастёт народная тропа;
<u>Вознёсся</u> выше он <u>главою</u> непокорной
Александрийского столпа.
Нет! весь я не умру: душа в заветной лире
Мой <u>прах</u> переживёт и тленья убежит—
И славен буду я, <u>доколь</u> в подлунном мире
Жив будет хоть один <u>пиит</u>.
Слух обо мне пройдёт по всей Руси великой,
И назовёт меня <u>всяк</u> <u>сущий</u> в ней язык:
И гордый внук славян, и финн, и ныне дикой
Тунгуз, и друг степей калмык.
И долго буду тем любезен я народу,
Что чувства добрые я лирой <u>пробуждал,</u>
Что в мой <u>жестокий</u> век <u>восславил</u> я свободу
И милость к <u>падшим</u> призывал.
Веленью Божию, О Муза, будь послушна;
Обиды не страшась, не требуя венца,
Хвалу и клевету приемли <u>равнодушно,</u>
И не оспоривай глупца.

1836

11.2.3. Analyze everything in «Пророк», which is saturated with Church Slavonic elements.

Пророк

Духовной жаждою томим,
В пустыне мрачной я влачился,—
И шестикрылый серафим
На перепутье мне явился.
Перстами легкими, как сон,
Моих зениц коснулся он:
Отверзлись вещие зеницы,
Как у испуганной орлицы.
Моих ушей коснулся он,—
И их наполнил шум и звон:
И внял я неба содроганье,
И горний ангелов полет,
И гад морских подводный ход,
И дольней лозы прозябанье.
И он к устам моим приник,
И вырвал грешный мой язык,
И празднословный и лукавый,
И жало мудрыя змеи
В уста замершие мои
Вложил десницею кровавой.
И он мне грудь рассек мечом
И сердце трепетное вынул,
И угль, пылающий огнем,
Во грудь отверстую водвинул.
Как труп в пустыне я лежал,
И бога глас ко мне воззвал:
«Восстань, пророк, и виждь, и внемли,
Исполнись волею моей
И, обходя моря и земли,
Глаголом жги сердца людей».

1826

Appendix 2
Verb Stems for Practice

Some of these stems are real verbs, most are invented. Assume that all
follow the rules.

1. ди́в+	25. чоди́+	49. тры́зга+
2. ла́н+	26. грезà+	50. сли́ка+
3. ла́лай+	27. мите́+	51. обесчу́бей+
4. тас́+	28. лешà+	52. бале́й+
5. гла́д+	29. гдà+	53. голò+
6. болз́+	30. фрà+	54. гоготà+
7. лёќ+	31. ргà+	55. десà+
8. гара́й+	32. земе́й+	56. роптà+
9. бла́ка+	33. лвà+	57. бле́я+
10. рахà+	34. броя́+	58. ве́я+
11. лвà+	35. змея́+	59. ралцевà+
12. бра́па+	36. ди́й+	60. вектовà+
13. гремà+	37. жи́й+	61. человà+
14. лёрну́+	38. уле́й+	62. сёт́+
15. бро́ну+	39. бре́за+	63. голкну́+
16. сла́й+	40. отсе́ти+	64. вёрз(ну)+
17. бе́лай+	41. зда́н+	65. блесану́+
18. вита́й+	42. кокотà+	66. слàз(ну)+
19. тре́й+	43. болоти́+	67. зо́б(ну)+
20. б́р+	44. нà-пн+	68. тры́й+
21. прасне́й+	45. пèре-дыв+	69. ру́ну+
22. сре́брова+	46. кра́ди+	70. от-мгну́+
23. азрабовà+	47. грозди́+	71. за-броѓ+
24. довà+	48. слюби́+	72. за-бар-ну́+

73. под-бё+
74. до-брей+
75. за̀-вий+
76. пѐре-вра+
77. из-врати́+
78. за-вы́й+
79. за-вя́рай+
80. от-глы́б+
81. от-глыз′+
82. за-гогота̀+
83. про-горо̀+
84. го́рх(ну)+
85. про-графи́+
86. про-дви́га+
87. об-двугну́+
88. пере-дей+
89. на-де́й+
90. на-де́н+
91. от-де́я+
92. под-дла́н+
93. при-до́г+
94. за-ди́ну+
95. раз-до́д+
96. по-до́я+
97. за̀-др+
98. о̀б-дра+
99. дробе́+
100. дря́х(ну)+
101. под-ду+
102. пѐѐре-жра+
103. про-зе́я+
104. до-зы́б+
105. из-зя́б(ну)+

106. из-зя́ну+
107. на-зя́рай+
108. с-клева́+
109. под-кра́д+
110. под-крёва́+
111. об-ков-а́+
112. под-коло̀+
113. за-ко+
114. за-котну́+
115. до-крей+
116. ото-лва̀+
117. при-лга̀+
118. от-лёт+
119. на-лёж-а́+
120. про̀-лий+
121. в-лобова́+
122. под-ло́га+
123. до-лоха̀+
124. под-лу́жа+
125. про-лупи́+
126. у-лы́з+
127. на-мела́й+
128. при-меси́+
129. за-мё+
130. воз-му́жа+
131. про-мчну́+
132. под-мы́й+
133. в-мяса̀+
134. у-мяхова́+
135. об-ноли́+
136. про-паха̀+
137. до̀-плыв+
138. от-пляса̀+

139. за̀-пн+
140. до-поло̀+
141. под-пру́н+
142. за-ра́з+
143. за-рва̀+
144. из-ризе́+
145. на-ря́ха+
146. сглоба́й+
147. под-сё+
148. за-сержа́+
149. под-сё+
150. про̀-сий+
151. про-сла́ви+
152. за-сла́д+
153. со-сли́в+
154. рас-сло́й+
155. про̀-слыв+
156. за-собова́+
157. под-со́х(ну)+
158. при-стелёг+
159. за-стерёг+
160. рас-стоса̀+
161. об-т′р+
162. об-у́й+
163. раз-у́н+
164. от-хохота̀+
165. от-цо́ну+
166. у-ча́х(ну)+
167. на-ч′т+
168. за-ю́хай+
169. отъ-яща́й+

Appendix 3
Bibliography

13.1. Bilingual Dictionaries

Falla, P. S., ed.: *The Oxford English-Russian Dictionary*. Oxford: OUP, 1984. Intended for the use of native speakers of English. Third edition, 2000, joined with Wheeler.

Folomkina, S. K. *English-Russian Learner's Dictionary of Combinations* Англо-русский учебный словарь сочетаемости. 1088 p. 1995.

Galperin, I. R., ed.: *New English-Russian Dictionary*. 2 volumes. Moscow: Sovetskaja Ėncyklopedija, 1972, plus a later supplement volume. Intended for the use of native speakers of Russian. Russian words are stressed, to help English speakers. In 4th edition (1988) the supplement is about 130 pages but is not integrated with the rest of the dictionary. Any changes in the body of the dictionary itself in this edition are not apparent.

Howlett, Colin, ed. *The Oxford Russian Dictionary Russian-English/ English-Russian*. Presented as revised by Howlett and based upon the Wheeler/Unbegaun and Falla dictionaries, it seems to have less words (and definitely less pages). Oxford, OUP, 1993. 1340 p.

Katzner, Kenneth. *English-Russian Russian-English Dictionary*. New York: John Wiley, 1984. Has some colloquialisms and gives American spellings, but otherwise less useful. Second, expanded edition, 1994. Also CD-ROM version, 1999.

Macura, P. *Elsevier's Russian-English Dictionary*. Four volumes. Amsterdam: Elsevier, 1990. Has the largest number of words of any Russian-English dictionary, but a great many of them are in technical fields. Useful as a place of last resort to look things up, but very expensive for individual purchase. For items which are in Wheeler and/or Smirnitsky, not really significantly more useful. New edition as: *New Great Russian-English Dictionary Three Volumes, include about 300 000 lexical units*/Новый большой русско-английский словарь в трех томах, ed. P. N. Macurov (sic!), M. S. Muller and V. Yu. Petrov. Moscow: Lingvistika, 1997, 3208 p. Issued in a printing of only 3050 copies. Type is small (7 point!!!) and layout is tough on the eye.

Marder, S. *A Supplementary Russian-English Dictionary*. Columbus: Slavica, 1992 (corrected reprint 1994, new edition 2007). Has about 29,000 terms which don't occur in Wheeler or Smirnitsky or which don't occur with the meaning given in Marder. Designed as an addition to Wheeler. Contains a lot of slang, recent additions to the language, drug terminology, political terms of *perestrojka* and *glasnost'*, the obscene vocabulary, and many other interesting items. Essential for any serious student of Russian.

Mednikova, E. M. (listed for Vol. 1 only) and Yu. D. Apresyan, eds. *New English-Russian Dictionary* Новый большой англо-русский словарь. 3 vols. Moscow: Russky Yazyk Publishers, 1993–94. A revision and expansion of Galperin's dictionary. The biggest and most useful English- Russian dictionary currently available.

Müller, V. K. *English-Russian Dictionary*. Moscow: various editions; reprinted by Dutton in USA. Intended for native speakers of Russian. Apparently completely new edition 1994.

Smirnitsky, A. I., ed. *Russian-English Dictionary*, Moscow, various editions. Also reprinted in USA by Dutton. No grammatical information; Intended for the use of native speakers of Russian.

Smith, R. E. F. *A Russian-English Social Science Dictionary*. Revised ed. Birmingham: Institute for Advanced Research in the Humanities, 1990. The standard dictionary in these fields. Very useful.

Wheeler, Marcus. *The Oxford Russian-English Dictionary, Second Edition*. General Editor B. O. Unbegaun., Oxford: Oxford University Press, 1984, 930 p. The best Russian-English dictionary. Gives stresses and grammatical information. Stronger on cultural items than Smirnitsky, but not as good for political and technical terms. Intended for the use of native speakers of English. Third edition, abridged!, 2000, joined with Falla E-R.

Zalucky, Henry K. *Compressed Russian: Russian-English Dictionary of Acronyms, Semiacronyms and Other Abbreviations Used in Contemporary Standard Russian (with their pronunciation and explicit correlates in Russian, and equivalents in English).* Amsterdam: Elsevier, 1991. Has about 40,000 entries and 920 pages. Useful, but definitely an item to use in the library.

Ермолович, Д.И. and Т.М. Красавина. *Новый большой русско-английский словарь.* Москва: Русский язык медиа, 2004. Claims 110,000 words and phrases. Stress shown for citation form, but no other stress information and no grammatical information other than noun gender. Number of words is indeed commendably high. A very good dictionary.

Панова, И. И., ed. *Большой русско-английский словарь. Russian-English Dictionary.* Minsk: Kharvest, 2003. For Russian-speaking users. No stress or grammatical information. Has geographical, mythological, and historical appendices. Printing only 5100 copies. A quick check of Panova against Wheeler 1984 shows that each has material absent from the other. I continue to use Ermolovich and Wheeler 1984 as my first sources of information.

13.2. Monolingual Dictionaries

Brown, Nicholas J., *Russian Learners' Dictionary: 10,000 words in Frequency Order*, Routledge, London and NY, 1996.

Gribble, Charles E. *A Short Dictionary of 18th-Century Russian/ Словарик русского языка 18-го века.* Columbus, Ohio: Slavica: 1976. Based upon the same differential principle as Lunt's dictionary and designed to bridge the gap between it and the dictionaries which start from the 19th century, it also covers a lot of material in just over 100 pages. Includes personal and place names, material from Classical mythology used in 18th-century literature, etc. A full dictionary of 18th-century Russian is appearing in Russia in parts, but as of 2012 it is still many years from completion.

Lönngren, Lennart, ed., *A frequency dictionary of Modern Russian.* Studia Slavica Uppsaliensia, 32, Uppsala, 1993. Both Lönngren and Brown give references to earlier frequency dictionaries.

Lunt, Horace G. *Concise Dictionary of Old Russian (11th–17th Centuries)*. Munich: Fink Verlag, 1970. In spite of the English title, this is a Russian-Russian *differential* dictionary. That is, it lists only those words which no longer exist in modern Russian (allowing for the appropriate sound changes). Because the vast majority of words, which are still used in modern Russian without change of meaning, are excluded, it manages to cover a great deal in less than 100 pages.

Большой академический словарь русского языка в 20 томах. Ed. by A.S. Gerd, L.I. Balaxonova, L.E. Kruglikova et al. Moscow-St. Petersburg: Nauka, 2004–. Nineteen volumes have appeared as of late 2012. This is a replacement for the Gorbačevič dictionary, which was to replace the 17-volume dictionary. The 19th volume only goes as far as пресс, so the set will have to comprise significantly more than the originally announced twenty volumes.

Лексические трудности русского языка. Словарь-справочник. Около 13 000 слов. М.: Русский язык, 1999.

Словарь современного русского литературного языка. 17 volumes. Moscow-Leningrad: AN SSSR, Institut russkogo jazyka, 1948–1965 (first volume was published twice, in 1948 and 1950). This dictionary, (the "Big Academy Dictionary"), which is supposed to cover the total vocabulary of the written language from Pushkin to the present day, falls far short of its goal, but does have more words than any other Russian dictionary and may be used as a last resort. It is based upon approximately the same principles as Ušakov and Barxudarov, but has more words and more examples (often with no more benefit, however, since the difference seems to be in quantity, rather than quality or careful choice). It excludes many colloquial words, any which were used only as occasional archaisms in the 19th and 20th centuries, certain rarer words used by only one or two writers, and many neologisms by such writers as Mayakovskiy which did not become a real part of the vocabulary of the literary language (Ušakov includes many of these items). All special and technical words with restricted usage and all words restricted to folklore and folk poetry are also excluded. It is in general a very unsatisfactory dictionary.

Словарь современного русского литературного языка. Издание второе, переработанное и дополненное. Gl. red. K. S. Gorbačevič.

Moscow: Russkij Jazyk, 1991–. A revision of the preceding item. Planned for 20 volumes, of which only 7 seem to have appeared.

Толковый словарь русского языка конца XX века. Языковые изменения. Gl. red. G. N. Skljarevskaja. St. Peterburg: Folio-Press, 1998. Primarily covers words which have entered or left the language or changed meanings from 1985–1997. Extremely interesting reading. Did not use Marder dictionary. Has a listing (incomplete) of other Russian dictionaries on page 35. Lots of interesting citations. Refuses to recognize some current usage, such as бизнес-школа, офис-менеджер.

Аванесов, Р. И., ред. *Орфоэпический словарь русского языка: Произношение, ударение, грамматические формы.* М.: Русский язык, 1989. Contains about 65,000 words. Has articles on pronunciation and grammatical forms. A must for serious students. Tells the correct way of pronouncing the words, including accents, and gives grammatical forms where there could be any doubt.

Бархударов, С.Г. ред., *Словарь русского языка в 4-х тт.* Moscow, 1957–1961. Known as the "Small Academy Dictionary." See below for newer edition. Full grammatical and stress information. In general arranged like Ožegov, with two major differences: one is that derived words are listed in alphabetical order, and the other is that aspect pairs for verbs are in general not given, so there is no way of knowing which prefix(es) an imperfective verb might take to make it perfective. This is the biggest single defect of the dictionary, and one that is rectified in the second edition. Abundant quotations are given to show usage and meaning, although they are often poorly chosen and do little to clarify meaning and usage.

Виноградов, В. В., ред.: *Словарь языка Пушкина в четырех томах с приложением.* Moscow, 1956–61. This is a complete dictionary of every word written by Pushkin and published in the large Academy edition of his works in 20th century. It tells where and how many times each word appears, and it gives definitions for many of the less common words. The citations make it possible to compare Pushkin's use of a word and establish more exactly what the word may have meant for him and what emotional overtones it may have had. This dictionary is also extremely useful for reading other poets of the first half of the nineteenth century, insofar as their vocabulary coincides with that of Pushkin, since special poetic meanings which a word may have had at that time will often be listed here. For the most complete listing of all of Pushkin's vocabulary in full context, but without definitions, see J. Thomas Shaw: *Pushkin A Concordance to the Poetry*, 2 volumes, Columbus, Ohio: Slavica, 1985.

Даль, В.И. *Толковый словарь живого великорусского языка*, 4-е исправленное и значительно дополненное издание. 4 volumes, St. Petersburg and Moscow, 1912–1914. This dictionary is an indispensable tool for anyone reading folklore, literary works with dialect words, pre-19th-century literature, and is valuable for literature of the 19th and 20th centuries. It includes many words which appear in none of the other dictionaries. The first and second editions were prepared by Dal' himself, but after his death the publisher entrusted the preparation of a third edition to Professor Jan Baudouin de Courtenay, in St. Petersburg, who completely redid the dictionary, adding many more words (the number of new words is placed by one study at 40,000, making the dictionary half again as large as the second edition, which had 80,000) and improving the definitions of those already in the dictionary. All the material added by Baudouin de Courtenay is placed in brackets to separate it from the portion belonging to Dal'. The 4th edition is a stereotype edition from the 3rd, and was reprinted in Tokyo in 1934, Paris in 1954, Moscow in the 1990s. The worst defect of the original dictionary was that Dal' was a violent linguistic nationalist, and did his best to substitute "Russian" terms for all foreign borrowings, even where the borrowing had become a firm part of the language and no native Russian equivalent existed. This led to the invention of a host of ridiculous terms by Dal', which never were used in the language and merely clutter up the dictionary. This problem does not, however, affect the most valuable part of the dictionary to any great degree, since that part is those words which do not appear in other dictionaries—words denoting typically Russian objects, everyday vocabulary, dialect words, and words common in folklore and folk poetry. Dal' was also not a trained lexicographer, but Baudouin de Courtenay managed to make considerable improvements on Dal''s original effort. Although the 3rd (and 4th) editions are obviously much better, the second edition was reprinted several times in the Soviet Union (1935, 1955, and more than once since then). The apparent reason for reprinting a vastly inferior edition is that Baudouin de Courteney added the entire obscene vocabulary (with definitions in Latin only) along with the other 40,000 words, and the official strong puritanism of the USSR caused the rejection of the 3rd and 4th editions, although the offending words could presumably have been simply blotted out when the photographic plates were being prepared for the reprint. The second edition and its reprints should be avoided if possible, since the 3rd and 4th editions are far better and much more useful, and, most important, far more reliable.

Евгеньева, А.П. ред. *Словарь русского языка в четырех томах.* Издание второе, исправленное и дополненное. Moscow: "Russkij Jazyk," 1981–1984. A reworking of Barxudarov, with new words added, corrections made, and aspect pairs indicated. An important work for any serious student of Russian.

Ефремова, Т. *Новый словарь русского языка. Толково-словообразовательный.* 250 000 лексических единиц. 2 тома. М.: Русский язык, 2000.

Ефремова, Т.Ф. *Современный толковый словарь русского языка в трёх томах.* AST; Astrel'. 2006. 3298pp. No grammatical or stress information except nom. sg. or infinitive.

Кузнецов, С.А. *Большой толковый словарь русского языка.* St. Petersburg: Norint, 1998. A candidate to replace Ožegov. I find it much more useful. It has a much larger number of entries (130,000), and gives words excluded from dictionaries during Soviet times (jargon, curse words, etc.). Prepared by the Russian Academy of Sciences on the basis of the same *kartoteka* (collection of materials written on file cards) as the Barxudarov and Evgen'eva dictionaries and the 17-volume dictionary (and its second edition, in progress).

Кузнецов, С. А. *Русский глагол. Формообразовательный словарь-справочник.* СПб.: Норинт, 2000. An extremely useful listing of all the forms which actually occur for virtually every verb of interest in Russian.

Лопатин, В.В., ред. *Русский орфографический словарь,* 2-е изд. Москва: РАН, 2005.

Мокиенко, Б. и Т. Никинтина. *Большой словарь русского жаргона.* СПб.: Норинт, 2000.

Мокиенко, Б. и Т. Никинтина. *Словарь русской брани*. СПб.: Норинт, 2003. A serious dictionary.

Ожегов, С.И. *Словарь русского языка*. Moscow: various editions. This is the standard Russian-Russian dictionary used by educated Russians in the USSR. It has about the same number of words as Smirnitsky, although sometimes a given word will be in one of these two dictionaries and not in the other, so it pays to check both. Ожегов has full information on grammatical forms, stress, and cases governed by verbs. It also gives imperfective/ perfective verb pairs and sample phrases (often not very useful) using the words. In cases where the imperfective is formed from a semantically prefixed perfective by suffixation, they are both entered under the perfective form. Nouns derived from verbs are usually listed under the verb entry, at the end. Adjectives derived from nouns and diminutives of nouns are usually listed under the corresponding noun entry. Revised and significantly augmented, published under title Толковый словарь русского языка, by Н. Ю. Шведова, Москва: "Азъ," 1992. Number of entries increased by about half to 72,500. Second edition with some corrections, Moscow, 1994.

Рогожникова, Р. П., ред. *Редкие слова в произведениях авторов XIX века*. Москва: Русские словари, 1997.

Рогожникова, Р. П., ред.: *Сводный словарь современной русской лексики в 2 тт*. Moscow: Russkij jazyk, 1991. Contains a listing of about 170,000 words from 14 of the most popular dictionaries, such as Ušakov, Ožegov, Barxudarov, Evgen'eva, etc. Lists only the words and indicates in which of the dictionaries they occur. Can be very useful if you have a word that you don't know and don't find in Smirnitsky or Wheeler, since instead of trying each dictionary in turn, you can look here, find out where it is given, and look there immediately.

Ушаков, Д.Н., ред. *Толковый словарь русского языка в 4-х тт*. Moscow, 1934–1940. (The first volume was put out twice, once in 1934 and once in 1935). Reprinted Ann Arbor 1948, Tokyo at least once after WWII, by Slavica in 1974 (four volumes in three covers) and in Russia ca. 1998. It is similar to the Barxudarov dictionary, although it is better about aspect pairs and some other information. It also contains an excellent sketch of rules for Russian grammar, which in effect serves as a small but very good reference grammar. The Ušakov dictionary also contains some words occurring in literature which are not to be found in other dictionaries, and should thus always be checked if a word is not located elsewhere. It is particularly useful for reading Russian literature of the 19th century, the Silver Age, and the 1920s. Less quotations than Barxudarov, but in most cases this is no loss.

Фёдоров, А. И. *Фразеологический словарь русского литературного языка в двух томах.* Moscow: Citadel', 1997. This dictionary, with more than 12,000 entries, seems to be the most complete one available to date.

Шведова, Н.Ю. *Толковый словарь...* see Ожегов.

13.3. Grammars

Borras, F. M. and R. F. Christian. *Russian Syntax: Aspects of Modern Russian Syntax and Vocabulary*, Second Edition. Oxford: Oxford University Press, 1971. This book is a companion to Unbegaun's grammar in many ways and is also to be recommended very highly. It is not an academic theoretical discussion of syntax, but rather a collection of very practical answers to basic and intermediate level questions. Contains some very good sections on near-synonyms in Russian.

Isačenko, A. V. *Die russische Sprache der Gegenwart*, Teil 1, *Formenlehre. Halle (Saale)* [East Germany], 1962. This is a somewhat condensed version of the book in Russian listed above. It is written for the German-speaking student, and thus contains a lot of useful comparisons for the English-speaking student, since the structure of English is much closer to German than to Slovak.

Offord, Derek. *Modern Russian: An Advanced Grammar Course.* London: Bristol Classical Press, 1993. Very useful.

Swan, Oscar E. *Russian Sounds and Inflections.* Bloomington, IN: Slavica, 2011. A very useful book with a large amount of valuable information, but not as easy to read as one might wish.

Timberlake, Alan. *A Reference Grammar of Russian.* Cambridge: Cambridge UP. 2004. ISBN: 0521772923. Essential reading for advanced students.

Unbegaun, Boris O. *Russian Grammar.* Oxford: Oxford University Press, 1957. The first really reliable reference grammar of Russian in English, and in some ways still the best. It is very well done by a person who was both an outstanding scholar and a first-rate pedagogue. Too short to answer some questions, but still worth reading cover to cover. Some of his stresses and forms are not in strict agreement with the postwar literary norm, but the differences are very minor. Out of print.

Wade, Terence. *A Comprehensive Russian Grammar.* Blackwell: Oxford (UK) and Cambridge (USA), 1992; second edition, 2000, revised and expanded. Be sure to get the paperback edition, which is far cheaper than the hardcover edition. While one has to be glad for what this book gives us, one has to be sad about the defects in it. The declensions, for example, are treated in a depressingly old-fashioned way, with no indication in many instances of what is regular and/or frequent and what is irregular and/or rare. See, for example, page 86 of the second edition, where море is treated as the normal soft neuter and поле is listed as another example, although in fact these and горе (sg. only) are the only examples of a soft paired consonant at the end of a neuter noun in the entire language (all others have an unpaired consonant). The genitive plural of this type is given as *-ей*, but in fact море and поле are the only two with gen. pl. in *-ей* (горе does not have a genitive plural from this stem); the normal genitive plural is in zero, which Wade treats as an exception. The Bibliography is depressingly Anglo-centric: it does not list the Smirnitsky, Marder, or Macura dictionaries; among English-language journals it lists the *British Journal of Russian Studies* and omits the American *Russian Language Journal* and *Slavic and East European Journal.* The general bibliography of books on the language lists only two books published in North America (one of which is a reprint of a Soviet book; the other is by an Australian author) as opposed to a multitude of British books.

Виноградов, В. В., ред.: *Грамматика русского языка.* Moscow: 1960. This is the large so-called "Academy Grammar," which is to be used as a last resort. It is in two volumes. The first volume is phonology and morphology. The second, which consists of two parts bound separately, is syntax. The 1960 edition is a reprint, with minor corrections, of the first edition which appeared in 1953. It was written by a team of scholars, each of whom did a specific part. This means that some parts are much weaker than others. The whole work is above all a mass of lists and facts, many of which are not digested or organized into a coherent structure. The long lists occurring in some sections can sometimes be quite helpful, and the whole book is loaded with miscellaneous facts which are to be found almost nowhere else. Using the work is complicated by the fact that the book has no index, and everything must be hunted down from the elaborate table of contents in the front, which is no easy task.

Зализняк, А. А. *Граммматический словарь русского языка.* Москва: Русский язык, 1977 and reprints. Gives full inflectional and stress information for approximately 100,000 words, accompanied by an extremely comprehensive 142-page introduction. The words are arranged in reverse alphabetical order (i. e., like a rhyming dictionary), so all the words which share a given suffix are easy to find. Does a good job of indicating which forms actually occur. This book is, along with Shvedova 1980 and Avanesov 1989, the final authority for most questions.

Исаченко, А.В. *Грамматический строй русского языка* Морфология. Volume I, 2nd edition. Bratislava, 1965. Volume II, Bratislava, 1960. Reprint: Издание 2-е. М. Языки славянской культуры. 2003. 880pp. 5-94457-147-0. Серия: Классики отечественной филологии. The second edition of Volume I differs only slightly from the first edition, chiefly in the introduction, where the first edition (published in 1954) contained the obligatory discussion of the contributions of J. V. Stalin to the field of linguistics. Volume I covers nouns, adjectives, and related categories; Volume II covers the verb. This is in many ways the best book on the structure of modern Russian ever written. It is intended for advanced students and teachers. Frequent comparisons and contrasts to Slovak are made, but an English speaker can simply ignore these parts.

Шведова, Н. Ю., гл. ред. *Русская грамматика.* 2 volumes, Moscow, 1980, reprinted 1982. The latest "Academy Grammar," this one is the most usable of the three, in my opinion. It has a very detailed table of contents and indices, although they are still not complete. It contains an enormous amount of useful information which is fairly well organized. More normative than descriptive, it is a good guide for non-Russian learners.

Шведова, Н. Ю., отв. ред. *Грамматика современного русского литературного языка.* Moscow: 1970. A one-volume new "Academy Grammar," which is more linguistically oriented, but still often easier to use than the 1960 version. This one does have a subject index, but lacks a word index, which is also needed.

13.4. Other Reference Works

Cubberley, Paul. *Handbook of Russian Affixes.* Columbus, OH: Slavica, 1994. Very good.

Cubberley, Paul. *Russian. A Linguistic Introduction.* Cambridge: Cambridge University Press, 2002. Very good.

Gribble, Charles E. *Russian Root List with a sketch of Russian word formation, second edition.* Columbus, OH: Slavica, 1982.

Offord, Derek. *Using Russian: A Guide to Contemporary Usage.* Cambridge: Cambridge Univ. Press, 1996. An enormous amount of helpful information in many areas: grammar, vocabulary, usage, stylistics, etc. Second edition, 2005.

Schaller, Helmut Wilhelm. *Bibliographie der Bibliographien zur slavischen Sprachwissenschaft.* Frankfurt aM/Bern: Verlag Peter D. Lang, 1980. (Symbolae Slavicae, Band 15.)

Schaller, Helmut Wilhelm. *Bibliographie zur russischen Sprache.* Frankfurt aM/Bern: Verlag Peter D. Lang, 1980. (Symbolae Slavicae, Band 8). No annotations, just a bare listing of 2,719 items, but still useful.

Townsend, Charles E. *Russian Word Formation.* New York: McGraw-Hill, 1968 (corrected reprint, Columbus, OH: Slavica, 1975 and 1980). The only modern and linguistically sophisticated full treatment in English of this important topic. A must for serious students of Russian.

Vasmer, Max. *Russisches etymologisches Wörterbuch*, 3 volumes. Heidelberg: Carl Winter, 1953–1958. By far the best etymological dictionary of Russian. Published in Russian translation as М. Фасмер: Этимологический словарь русского языка, translated by О. N.

Trubačev, Moscow, 1964–1973, and reprinted later. The Russian version eliminates all the obscene words and adds a significant amount of useful additional material.

Vilgelminina, A. A. *The Russian Verb Aspect and Voice.* Moscow: Foreign Languages Publishing House, 1963. A practical but very helpful discussion. Also published in Russian as *Русский глагол виды и залоги.*

Wade, Terence. *Using Russian Synonyms.* Cambridge: CUP, 2003.

Аванесов, Р.И. *Русское литературное произношение.* Издание четвертое, переработанное и дополненное. Москва: "Просвещение," 1968. The standard work.

Панов, М. В. *Русская фонетика.* Москва: "Просвещение," 1967. A good companion to Avanesov's works.

Федянина, Н.А. *Ударение в современном русском языке.* Москва: Русский язык, 1976, second, revised edition, М. 1982. Intended for both foreigners and Russians, this book has good lists of words belonging to given stress patterns.